P9-CJR-218

MODERNIZATION AND REVOLUTION IN MEXICO: A COMPARATIVE APPROACH

UNU Series on Social Transformation: 2

Major social transformations took place in non-European societies, such as those of Japan, China, Russia, and Mexico, during the last century. The UNU Project on Comparative Studies of Social Transformation explores the interactions between different social, economic, political, cultural, and international environmental factors at work in these transformations and attempts to generate a new and synthetic conceptualization of such interrelationships. *Modernization and Revolution in Mexico*, the outcome of a UNU international conference held in 1985, is a comparative study, from a global perspective, of the diverse dimensions of the period of revolution and modernization in Mexico. The third volume of the Series on Social Transformation, now under preparation, will deal with the Russian Revolution. Volume 1, *Meiji Ishin: Restoration and Revolution*, was published by the UNU in 1985.

Acknowledgement is due to Susan B. Kapilian for translation of all papers originally presented in Spanish.

The United Nations University is an organ of the United Nations established by the General Assembly in 1972 to be an international community of scholars engaged in research, advanced training, and the dissemination of knowledge related to the pressing global problems of human survival, development, and welfare. Its activities focus mainly on peace and conflict resolution, development in a changing world, and science and technology in relation to human welfare. The University operates through a worldwide network of research and post-graduate training centres, with its planning and co-ordinating headquarters in Tokyo, Japan.

MODERNIZATION AND REVOLUTION IN MEXICO: A COMPARATIVE APPROACH

Edited by Omar Martínez Legorreta

THE UNITED NATIONS UNIVERSITY

The United Nations University
Toho Seimei Building, 15-1 Shibuya 2-chome, Shibuya-ku, Tokyo 150, Japan
Tel.: (03) 499-2811 Telex: J25442 Cable: UNATUNIV TOKYO

Typeset by Asco Trade Typesetting Limited, Hong Kong
Printed by Permanent Typesetting and Printing Co., Ltd., Hong Kong

HSDB-46/UNUP-706
ISBN 92-808-0706-4
United Nations Sales No. E.89.III.A.5
03500 C

CONTENTS

PREFACE

The United Nations University (UNU), which is located in Tokyo, Japan, held a conference on Development in the Non-Western World in Tokyo in March 1982. At the conference, discussions centred around the theoretical framework of social, economic, and political development geared towards modernization in non-Western societies. In view of the success of this meeting and the interest awakened by it, the United Nations University drew up a new project in order to study the social effects of modernization in four non-Western societies.

The four cases chosen for this study were: Japan, China, Russia, and Mexico. In order to consider the case of Japan, the UNU convened a conference on the Meiji Restoration, which took place in Tokyo in October 1983. The papers presented at that conference have been published as the first in a series of four volumes (one on each of the above-mentioned countries) edited by Dr. Michio Nagai, Advisor to the Rector of the United Nations University.

After the conference on Japan, the decision was made to organize a conference on Mexico in conjunction with El Colegio de México. Entitled "The Modernization Process in Mexico (1867–1940): Social Transformations," this was held in Mexico City in March 1985, and gave rise to the papers contained in the present volume.

Traditionally, modernization in Mexico is deemed to begin in 1867, with the Restoration of the Republic, after the French Intervention and Maximilian of Hapsburg's ephemeral reign; its first phase is considered to end in 1910, the year in which the Mexican Revolution began. Once the armed strife had been concluded, around 1921, the second phase of the modernization period began, and ended around 1940.

With the support of the United Nations University, specialists on the four countries being studied were invited to participate in the conference on Mexico. As can be expected, Mexican scholars assumed the responsibility for papers giving a historical overview of their country, as well as for some of the comparative studies. The Colombian participants worked along similar lines. Most of the participants from Japan, China, and the Soviet Union were brought into contact with Mexican history for the first time, but that did not prevent them from making valuable contributions of a comparative nature, based on their knowledge both of their own nation's history and of that of the other three countries under review. The positive response and enthusiastic participation of the specialists from other countries, for the most part historians, also played a part in the papers and discussions included in this volume.

In order to study the modernization process in Mexico, it was deemed necessary to effect a historical revision. The Mexican specialists who participated were: Moisés González Navarro, who studied social transformation in Mexico during this period; Fernando Rosenzweig, whose paper dealt with the industrialization process and foreign investment; Lorenzo Meyer, who discussed the political modernization of Mexico during the period under study; Berta Ulloa, with a paper on international relations and conflicts over the nation's sovereignty in what she terms the "continuing crisis"; and Luis González, who offered a summary of the cultural changes that took place at this time, thus rounding out the historical review of Mexico.

The comparative studies between Mexico and other countries included here have been conceived within a broad framework. Tanaka's chapter analyses the social transformation processes from the viewpoint of the underclass. This analysis is followed by a more regional analysis by Romero Castilla on the impact of social transformations in Mexico and Japan on their neighbours. Lopez Villafañe compares and contrasts the transformation processes of Mexico and China from the viewpoint of a Mexican political scientist. Shao and Chen provide a contrast to Lopez Villafañe by treating the same issue from a Chinese scholarly perspective.

It is worth while to consider the reasons for including the Mexican case among "non-Western societies" in this UNU series of studies on the social transformation process. In effect, Mexico's social make-up in the era in which its modernization process commenced, as well as the range and depth of its Westernization at the close of a long colonial period lasting for three centuries, did not make it – in any respect – a typical Western country. The ethnic and cultural *mestizaje*, or mixture, in Mexico had special features which presented a distinct response to stimuli from within the country and from abroad. That is why the comparative history of the Mexican case vis-à-vis Japan, China, and Russia is of such interest to the series.

The revolutionary processes in these four countries and their subsequent bearing on the transformation of their respective states, on the class structures and dominant ideologies, make for a comparative study of great value, since these are processes that have clearly transcended their own pasts, leaving behind other countries in similar circumstances.

The Mexican Revolution, which some have called "the first social revolution of the twentieth century," was the result of Mexico's drive for modernization; in a similar way to that of Meiji in Japan and to those of Russia and China, the Mexican Revolution was responsible for the emergence of models and ideas that have international significance. It provided the necessary political force to transform the country into an industrialized nation that has reached a higher level of development than other post-colonial nations, with a degree of social eqilibrium and political stability that other Latin American countries do not enjoy. This is why a comparative study of the Mexican Revolution and other revolutions of the same period is important: the Meiji Restoration in Japan in 1868, the nationalist revolution in China in 1911, the socialist revolution in China in 1949, the socialist revolution in Russia in 1917, and the Mexican Revolution are all processes which, in their national dimension – and perhaps in their international dimension as well – have yet to be concluded: they are part and parcel of the dynamics of modernization.

At the present time, when significant social transformations are taking place in various countries, it is essential to be aware of the historical processes illustrated by the four countries selected for the UNU project – for by becoming familiar with them, we may better understand what is happening today.

Omar Martínez Legorreta
El Colegio Mexiquense
Toluca, Mexico

THE SOCIAL TRANSFORMATION OF MEXICO (1867–1940)

Moisés González Navarro
El Colegio de México, Mexico City, Mexico

Introduction

The period from 1821 to 1867 is usually characterized by several dichotomies: monarchy *v.* republic; federation *v.* centralism; democracy *v.* oligarchy; middle class *v.* clergy, military, and hacienda owners. In the end, these dichotomies are definitively separated: on the one hand, there is the constellation: federal, liberal, democratic, bourgeois, and pro-Yankee republic; on the other, monarchy, centralism, conservatism, and Europeanizing oligarchy. After Maximilian's defeat in 1867, Mexico emerged as a liberal country, capitalism developed freely, and US and European imperialism struggled for dominance.

1

Native and Agrarian Rebellions

This period of barely 75 years witnessed the fall of the hacienda, the basic unit of the colonial agricultural system, from its zenith to political extinction, as a result of the Mexican Revolution. What in fact happened was that the agricultural society was eclipsed by the new industrial society. There was a continual series of peasant revolts throughout the nineteenth century all over Mexico, some of which fall into the period we are considering – the revolt of Manuel Lozada, for example. This cacique from Nayarit, a rebel canton of

Paper presented at the Conference on the Modernization Process in Mexico (1867–1940): The Social Transformations, co-sponsored by the United Nations University and El Colegio de México, Mexico City, 19–21 March 1985.

the State of Jalisco, had maintained the independence of that region with the frequent assistance of foreign smugglers from the port of San Blas. But Lozada was also the leader of one of the most important Indian revolts in the nineteenth century; he was on the point of taking the city of Guadalajara in 1873, but was defeated by Ramón Corona. Like other caciques, he was classed as a bandit by the ruling classes, but he also defended the Indians' lands, as can be seen from Article 5 of the Treaty of Pochotitlán (24 January 1862), in which the liberal Governor Pedro Ogazán promised to defend the Indians against neighbouring haciendas with respect to land tenure. Although Lozada remained to a considerable extent politically independent in the struggle between liberals and conservatives, he inclined more to the conservative cause; in fact, in his peace plan, drawn up as he advanced on Guadalajara in 1873, he stated that he was fighting to defend Mexico from the enemies of religion and humanity.[1] Santiago Sierra proposed that the rebellion should be combated by dispersing the Indians from Alica, because this would make them lose any feelings of solidarity and provide agriculture with the labour that was needed in other regions.[2] It was unnecessary to follow this advice on that occasion because the revolt was defeated, perhaps because it found no support outside the area it controlled.

But a policy like that proposed by Sierra was followed in the war with the Yaquis. At the beginning of this century some 8,000 Indians, together with their families, were sent from Sonora to Yucatán, which weakened the resistance of the Yaquis in Sonora and provided labour for the hemp manufacturers.[3] This deportation was justified with arguments that are reminiscent of those used by Yucatán when the defeated Mayas were sold to Cuba in the middle of the nineteenth century.

The Mayas themselves took refuge in the east of the Yucatán peninsula when they were defeated in 1853, and remained there under the protection of Realize until they were finally conquered in 1904.

These were not, of course, the only Indian revolts, but they were the most important because they had a century-long tradition behind them. Among other rebellions, it is worth remembering that of Colonel Alberto Santa Fe in 1878, which had the peculiarity of having attempted an alliance between the town of San Mateo Tepetitlán and the Tlalnepantla factory workers. The following year, several towns in Guanajuato and Queretaro proclaimed a socialist plan, both to combat the haciendas and to fight against the protection of foreign industry. Once victorious, they planned to elect a municipal government and an agricultural congress to return to the Indians the lands that had been taken from them. Municipal aspirations can also be seen in the Huasteca revolt of 1881; the following year there was great insistence on the struggle against the Spanish conquest and on de-amortization, because the haciendas had turned the labourers into slaves. In 1884 several tenants of a hacienda in San Luis Potosí refused to pay the owner, appealing to the agricultural law of a priest called Zavala, and soon afterwards some 400 individuals rebelled in the same state, demanding the division of property. Indians in other towns in the state also divided up some estates, although they were eventually suppressed.[4]

The Apogee of the Hacienda

The government attempted to solve the underpopulation problem by encouraging foreign immigration. The Reform removed the obstacle of religious intolerance, which was thought to be the greatest stumbling-block to achieving this objective. The results, however, were not what had been expected, since foreigners did not flock to Mexico, as they did to the United States and Argentina, in the desired numbers.

There were three major laws governing this matter. That of 1875 authorized the setting up of commissions to demarcate, measure, and value colonizable land, with the idea of facilitating colonization. Eight years later, President Manuel González authorized the demarcation of uncultivated land by companies, who would be compensated by being granted one third of the land surveyed. The squandering of this uncultivated land was given legal sanction in the law of 1894, which removed the limit of 2,500 hectares and the obligation to colonize and cultivate the land declared. Between 1867 and 1910 40 million hectares, one-fifth of the national territory, were given away, often to the detriment of small property owners, especially in the case of the Indians' communal land, for which proper titles did not always exist. To alleviate this situation, the federal government passed a law in 1896 favouring the poor labourers; its purpose was to stop Indians from losing land declared uncultivated simply because they had no titles to it. Ten years later, the government of Chihuahua attempted something similar with the law for civilizing the Tarahumara race. In both cases it was stated that this "state socialism" left liberalism intact and was the only way to make the "minors" happy.

This, of course, did not solve the problem, because the hacienda was the main support and beneficiary of the system. In fact, the situation worsened, in spite of the efforts of the Catholic congresses that began in 1903 (with the sanction of the *Rerum novarum*), since these placed more emphasis on the humanization of rural labour and on the fight against alcoholism and living in sin. The most that was done was to request help in cases of accidents at work and illness, a "sufficient" salary, a maximum working day of 7 to 9 hours, a plot of land for the use of labourers, an increase in partnerships, the setting up of agricultural credit funds, etc. Although in October 1910 large estates were criticized as being unjust and uneconomical, in general these congresses were better at diagnosing than at effecting cures, which was only to be expected, since they were the work of the owners of large estates, urged on with difficulty by a few laymen and members of the clergy who had daring ideas for their time and class; as a result, they scarcely touched on the basic problem of land redistribution.[5] In part, these congresses tried to consolidate the hacienda; the one held in 1904, for example, stressed the need to link the haciendas by telephone, with the aim, among other things, of providing immediate information about servants who had fled. The congress of 1908 became very heated when a member of the audience asked how the workers could save, when in that very same assembly it had been recognized that their salaries were totally inadequate. One of the organizers of these congresses told him that he would see the answer in ten years, and another added that it could already be seen in Tulancingo, where three mutual benefit societies had been set up. This same member added that great profit would be obtained from the "intelligent" division of large estates. A priest requested a working day of a maximum of 10 hours (the normal day was of 12), and a salary of more than 40 cents (the usual salary in the centre of the Republic ranged from 25 cents to 3.75 cents and a share in the profits).[6]

The programme of the Liberal Party, drawn up mainly by Ricardo Flores Magón, was published in the United States on 1 July 1906. Clearly formulated in this plan are many of the principles established by the revolutionary constitution 11 years later. It spoke, of course, of obliging the landowners to provide hygienic living quarters for labourers, of cancelling the latter's debts, and of preventing the abuse of share-croppers; tenants were also to be compensated for improvements made to their land. It also spoke of recovering uncultivated land to be shared out among people repatriated from the United States, of declaring them inalienable, and of providing credit to these people through an agricultural bank.

Soon afterwards, Andrés Molina Enríquez published *The Great Problems of the Nation* (*Los grandes problemas nacionales*), in which he pointed out that as a result of the lack of a middle class among the landowners, the social structure was so disproportionate that Indian day-labourers had started to leave the haciendas.

At the end of the first decade of this century, the opposition to Porfirio Díaz came from within the dominant class itself, from several northern landowners, from many members of the middle classes and, of course, from the proletarized peasants and a growing number of workers.

Industrialization and the Class Struggle

The incipient industrial revolution worsened the already bad conditions of work in the factories. Working days of from 12 to 15 hours were, of course, common. The increasing industrialization also adversely affected work by women (especially seamstresses and women workers in the cigarette factories) and children (even in the textile industry). The Penal Code for the Federal District in 1871 laid down a punishment of from 8 days to 3 months imprisonment and a fine of from 25 to 500 pesos for anyone who tried to raise or lower salaries by means of physical or moral violence. In spite of the fact that this punishment was copied and even made more severe by several states, strikes were frequent, especially during the dictatorship of Don Porfirio Díaz, when there were at least 250, half of which were in the Federal District, followed by Veracruz, Puebla, etc. The cause of half the strikes was a reduction in wages, then, in decreasing order of importance, physical abuse, the excessively long working day, etc. The greatest number of strikes was in the textile industry (75); there were also 60 on the railways and 35 in the cigarette industry. That is to say, the strikes occurred in the most dynamic economic activities where the workers earned the highest wages, which is perhaps why they were more class-conscious.

The economy of this period is characterized by a predominance of foreign capital. To achieve this level of investment it was necessary for Porfirio Díaz to solve the old problem of the foreign public debt, which he addressed with the law of June 1885. These measures were followed by others, such as the mining law of June 1892, which permitted total rights over the subsoil, a policy directly opposed to the colonial tradition, and the law of 3 June 1893, concerning tax exemptions for anyone who established new industries. In this way, when the dictatorship came to an end, the economy depended almost totally on foreign capital, with only a few exceptions (Yucatán hemp, part of the La Laguna cotton, the Morelos sugar, and cattle-breeding in Chihuahua).[7]

Education

Like the economy, education improved noticeably under the dictatorship. In the Restored Republic obligatory education was established in four or five states, and Justo Sierra managed to have a similar federal law passed in 1887. The obligatory aspect was applied particularly to elementary school, the free aspect to primary school, and the lay aspect to all levels of official education. The lay quality of education was at the root of all the educational controversies of this period. In fact, while for the Catholics lay education was a symbol of irreligion, for the authorities it was a symbol of neutrality.

There was a clear tendency towards a reduction in the number of municipal schools; in the states they passed into the hands of the respective governments, and in the Federal District into the hands of the Ministry of Justice and Public Instruction in 1896. In the first decade of the twentieth century educational policy was activated by the naming of two undersecretaries, one for Justice and the other for Instruction. Justo Sierra occupied the latter post, and in 1905, when the section became independent, he became Minister of Instruction. In this position, he improved education by creating a Higher Council of Public Education to replace the old Board of Instruction, which by that time only had administrative duties. Another important reform was the establishment of special primary schools for the teaching of industry, commerce, agriculture, and mining. In 1902 school holidays were established, and kindergartens two years later; some of his other major achievements were the sending abroad of teachers to be trained in different fields, and the construction of buildings in accordance with the demands of hygiene and pedagogy. In 1907 a special section was established to attend to school hygiene, and it was seen that scabies, ringworm, and caries were the predominant illnesses in schoolchildren. A special school was set up the following year to take children with ringworm.

Perhaps the greatest achievement of Justo Sierra was the School Law of 1908, which for the first time recognized the prime importance of education, and considered instruction only as a means to attaining it. Teaching was divided into five years for elementary and two for higher; the former was obligatory for minors from 6 to 14. It was also required that food and clothing should be provided for those who would otherwise be unable to attend school. Amongst the achievements of his last administration, Porfirio Díaz included the inauguration of 7 large schools of higher education, 17 rural schools, and the School Law of 1908. He recognized, however, that there were still some thousands of children who did not receive elementary instruction.

To sum up, among the most important changes that occurred in primary instruction were the increasing number of government schools in the states, the tendency to balance the numbers of boys' and girls' schools, the increase in co-educational and adult schools, and the fact that the number of people attending schools grew more, proportionately, than the population as a whole; there was also a preference for preparatory and professional teaching over primary education, and in this last area urban education took priority over rural.

The National Preparatory School was established in 1868, inspired by the positivism of Auguste Comte, which earnt opposition to it from both the Catholics and the old Jacobin liberals. Both of these accused the Preparatory School of being positivistic and atheistic, and although the teachers at the school replied that positivism was a humble method that neither affirmed nor denied, the Catholic press attributed the suicides of some students there to the bad influence of the positivists.

In the capital of the republic there were also two secondary schools for women, one long-established, generally known as Las Vizcaínas, and the National Secondary School for Girls, which changed in 1889 into the Teacher Training College for Women.

In 1878 there were 59 secondary and preparatory schools – 34 private and 25 official – but by 1907 the private schools had fallen to 18 and the official ones risen to 42. Throughout the whole of the dictatorship of Porfirio Díaz the majority of secondary schools were for men. New Spain had left two main professions to free Mexico: the Church and the Law. This legacy was later augmented by the addition of the medical profession and, to a lesser extent, of engineering. In Mexico City professional teaching was carried out in schools that were independent from each other. As the nineteenth century progressed some specialities were created, such as that of nursing in 1901 and dental surgery in 1902, while in 1910 the Military Nursing School, dependent on the Practical School of Military Medicine, was established. Another institution of higher education in the capital was the Conservatoire, where music and reciting were taught; many people considered this to be a luxury in a country that had 5 million "Indians to be undonkeyfied."

The youngest of the national schools was that of Higher Studies (founded on 18 September 1910). Sierra saw it as the crowning glory of the National University, which was created on 22 September 1910, and as one of the most outstanding features of the celebrations of the centennial of independence.

In the capital there were a few private professional schools paralleling the official ones, among them the School of Jurisprudence, not to mention the old Mexico City Seminary, which had become the Papal University in 1896. In 1907 the old Palafox Seminary became the second Catholic University.

Almost all the professional institutions in the provinces imitated those in the metropolis, the major exception being, perhaps, the Jalapa Teachers' Training College, founded in 1896 and directed by two Swiss, which led to a renewal in elementary teaching throughout the country. Guadalajara had an excellent autonomous school of engineering, while several professional schools in the provinces had to close because of lack of students and funds. Law, however, was taught in almost all the states.

Technical education in the Federal District was limited to the schools of arts and crafts, for men and women, and to the school of agriculture, founded in 1856. Some states which lacked professional schools used to provide their students with grants so that they could continue their studies in the capital of the country. It is worth noting, though, that the Practical School of Mining in Pachuca seems to have fulfilled an obvious function in a country with such a deeply rooted mining tradition.

When the professional schools are taken as a whole, an increase can be seen in the number of technological and teacher training colleges, and a reduction in those that have traditionally been considered of the university type. This tendency is a clear echo of the development of the national economy.

While of the federal budget for 1877–1878 ($26,803,379) 36 per cent was allocated to war and only 3 per cent to education, of the $131,285,285 of the 1910 budget war accounted for 21 per cent, but education had risen to 7 per cent. The same phenomenon occurred in the state budgets, since of the $7,679,066 of the 1878 budget a quarter went to war, and only one tenth to education. By 1910 the proportions had reversed, since out of the $23,883,920 the amount allocated to war had decreased to 16 per cent, while education had increased to almost 25 per cent.

In 1877 an estimation was made of the number of people speaking Indian languages, and however erroneous it may be supposed to be, the absolute and relative decrease that it indicates is corroborated by the censuses. In 1877 39 per cent of the population of Mexico spoke Indian languages, and only 13 per cent in 1910. It may be that many who accounted for the increased number of Spanish speakers spoke Spanish and an Indian language, or that they were previously bilingual speakers who had forgotten their native language. The percentage of those who spoke Indian languages in the centre of the country dropped more than in the south-east, a fact which can be explained by the development of communications in the centre, which favoured the acceleration of the process of cultural mixing. The percentage of those who spoke Spanish in the country as a whole was 83, and rose in 1910 to 87.

In 1895, 14 per cent of the population of the country knew how to read and write, a figure which had risen to 20 per cent by 1910; 3 per cent only knew how to read in 1895, and 1.8 per cent in 1910. The fact that many people only knew how to read is attributed to the bad teaching methods which taught students first to read and then to write. A slightly different idea emerges from the analysis of illiteracy as such, which was 54 per cent of the population in 1900 and 50 per cent in 1910. In general, the proportion of illiterates was lower in the mestizo areas of the centre, and in the north.[8]

The population increased from 9,481,916 in 1877 to 15,160,377 in 1910, because the death rate dropped as a result of improved health measures; there was even pressure that tended to produce emigration, initially to the north, and later to the United States. Some thousands returned from the US as revolutionary soldiers.[9]

2

The Agrarian Revolution

On the eve of the revolution in 1910, the land was in the hands of the state, the large estate owners (both Mexicans and foreigners), the small estate owners, and those towns that had managed to keep their communal land. According to one of the most reliable estimates, the 200 million hectares of the country's territory were divided up as follows: 10 per cent belonged to the state, 54 per cent to the large estate owners, 20 per cent to the small estate owners, 6 per cent to the towns, and the rest was unproductive land.[10]

The Mexican Revolution was an alliance of classes, headed by the middle class; in the north, there were even some "modern" hacienda owners, although the great majority of the soldiers were peasants and, to a lesser extent, factory workers. At the beginning, the most important of these hacienda owners was Francisco I. Madero, a member of a rich family from Coahuila that was going through financial difficulties. Although in his political campaign Madero several times proposed the division of land, convinced that democracy would be more securely established on these foundations, and although he was aware of the oppression of the labourers, he continued to think that the people did not want bread but freedom, which would produce the food they needed. At the beginning of his campaign he stated that many small landowners, principally Indians, had been forcibly dispossessed of their property. He offered to return it to them and also to pay them compensation for the harm that had been done. This moderate allusion to the land problem was all that was needed to make many peasants all over the country (especially in the north and in Morelos) take up arms; the revolt in some cases resembled a *jacquerie*, a continuation of the caste wars of the nineteenth century.

Porfirio Díaz was slow to act. On 1 April 1911 he presented a bill to solve the land problem. Although the large estate owners might have committed abuses on occasions, the solution was not to take the land away from them, but to settle the disputes through legal channels. It was also necessary to activate the division of the *ejidos* and the communal lands, and to divide up the large estates, but this should be done by persuading the landowners that it would be for their own benefit. The best thing to do was to divide up the national territory, but preference should be given to those people who were most suitable, that is, those who possessed a certain capital. It was, of course, not a good idea to give away land, water, and money, because the day labourers would abandon their work with their natural farming anarchy. This plan was no more than a continuation of liberal policy, and did not question the continued existence of the hacienda.

Of course, there was no lack of truly revolutionary plans, such as that of Ricardo Flores Magón, who in May 1911 made it a condition of his alliance with the victorious Madero that the proletariat should be handed the land and the tools to work it with, a condition which, needless to say, Madero did not accept. Much less did he accept Flores Magón's manifesto of 25 November of that year, which proposed the abolition of private property and the destruction of capital, authority, and the clergy.

The slowness and timidity of Madero's land policy obliged Zapata to rebel on 28 November 1911, in Morelos. This state was the nucleus of an agricultural revolution caused by the capitalist development of the sugar mills which proletarized a large number of the region's commune members. Zapata demanded that the lands, water, and woods that had been taken from the townships and poor labourers should be returned; that they should be provided to those who needed them by expropriating them from the haciendas, after due compensation; and, finally, that the property of anyone who opposed his plan should be nationalized. Madero fought hard against his old ally, while the congressman Luis Cabrera presented a bill on 3 December 1912 which declared that the return and donation of *ejidos* to the townships was to the good of the state. The federal government would expropriate the necessary land, which would remain federal property, although the townships would have the use of it. The break between Francisco Villa and Venustiano Carranza forced this old northern landowner to pass the law of 6 January 1915, based on the idea that the Indians, owing to a lack of evolutionary development, had not adapted to the idea of individual property, so that their property had to be recognized as being communal. It was therefore necessary to return their lands to them, and in cases where this was impossible, to provide them with the land they needed to rebuild their *ejidos*.

The revolutionary ideology arose spontaneously and developed in the heat of the conflict itself. Initially the revolution was democratic, rural, and agricultural in character (the north proposed, above all, the division of the large estates, and the reconstruction of the central and southern *ejidos*); it was also nationalistic, lay, and anti-clerical (this characteristic was less prevalent in the Zapata movement). After Carranza had defeated Villa, he called a congress to establish a constitution on 14 September 1916, in which only constitutionalists (that is to say, those who were loosely in agreement with Carranza) were represented.

The 1917 Constitution

In the Constitution of 1917 education became lay only, and the different churches were forbidden to direct primary schools. Broad social guarantees were established in favour of the workers, coinciding in part with the recommendations of the Catholic congresses held in the period from 1903 to 1913; Article 27, the truly revolutionary part of this Constitution, established that the property of land and water originally corresponded to the nation, which had and continues to have the right to transfer its control to individuals, thus creating private property, which can only be expropriated for the public good and with due compensation; the substitution of *after* by *with* was a revolutionary change in comparison with Carranza's plan, or even with Zapata's. Furthermore, only Mexicans by birth or by naturalization had the right to acquire the direct control of land and water, though the state could grant it to foreigners who renounced the protection of their governments. The 6 January law was also incorporated into the Constitution. Finally, Article 130 did not recognize the churches as having legal entity, thus undermining the traditional alliance between the church and the hacienda. Intellectuals connected with the old regime and foreign investors naturally labelled this constitution as communist.

Revolutionary Institutions

The hour of triumph coincided with dissension between the revolutionaries. Of the leaders, Carranza, Zapata, Villa, and Obregón were assassinated. There was an attempt to return to the old regime in 1926 as a result of Plutarco Elías Calles' application of Article 130 of the Constitution. The bishops responded by closing the churches, which led to the *cristero* rebellion, especially important in the centre west, with the strong and direct support of many small estate owners and indirect help from large estate owners. The conflict ended when the bishops accepted declarations by the president, Emilio Portes Gil, to the effect that the government was not trying to control the church by registering priests.

After Obregón had been assassinated, President Calles declared that Mexico was for the first time faced with a lack of leaders, which meant that the country could develop from a "one-man country" into a nation based on institutions. Up until this time the revolutionary governments had promoted land reform in different ways. In fact, Carranza had stressed the recovery of the uncultivated land given away under Porfirio Díaz; Obregón had stressed the importance of the *ejido*, and Calles had followed the same course, but his main purpose had been to establish a rural middle class. In fact, during the whole period in which Calles was the power behind the presidents, with the exception of Emilio Portes Gil's government, little or no progress was made with the *ejidos*.[11]

Towards the end of 1934 there was a lot of talk of a socialist Mexico as a result of the reform to the third article of the Constitution which established socialist education. The problem was to know what socialism meant; some thought of Marxism which, naturally, would have been incompatible with the capitalism that the revolution of 1910 had institutionalized. Eventually it had to be accepted that Mexican socialism was not Marxist, and that all that was intended was to accelerate land reform and strengthen the trade union movement. In concrete terms, socialist education signified the fight against the church and the paving of the way for socialism.[12]

Marathon and a Curbing of Radicalism

During his presidential period, Lázaro Cárdenas had the help of the National Peasant League, established in 1938. It had taken three long years of organization to set it up, and the process had been a difficult one in spite of the support of the government. Previous to this project, Cárdenas had tried to unify the peasants of Michoacán when he was Governor of that state, where he had been born. The declaration of principles of the League included the following in its organization: indebted peons, share-croppers, small farmers, and other organized agricultural labourers. It stood for solidarity with the factory workers, education based on scientific socialism, the *ejido* as the cornerstone of the agricultural economy, and the division of the large estates so that they could be worked on a collective basis by organized peasants. Furthermore, preference was given to the collective *ejido* over the individual *ejido*, especially in the irrigated areas of La Laguna, the Yaqui river and North Baja California, and on the hemp plantations of Yucatán. Cárdenas supported his agricultural policies by establishing the Ejido Credit Bank in 1936, in the same way that Calles had established the Agricultural Bank ten years before. The League came into existence with almost 3 million peasants, and the leagues of agricultural communities and peasant unions formed part of it. On 29 August 1938 the Secretary General of the League, Graciano Sánchez, proposed the collective *ejido*. The League was established as part of the peasant sector of the Mexican Revolutionary Party, a new version of the National Revolutionary Party founded nine years before.

Cárdenas supported the factory workers' movement, but he did not create it as he did the peasant movement. In fact, the workers' movement had a history that went back to the nineteenth century. More recently, the Casa del Obrero Mundial (the House of the Workers of the World), founded in 1912, had had difficulties with the revolutionary regime, owing to its anarchic tendencies, and later the Regional League of Mexican Workers (founded in 1918 by Luis N. Morones) became very powerful. It reached its peak during Calles' presidential period, but as it was accused of being involved in the assassination of Obregón it was thereafter consistently persecuted.

There had been serious differences between Vicente Lombardo Toledano (a young Marxist intellectual and leader of the workers trained in the Regional League of Mexican Workers) and the National Revolutionary Party, when the second and last congress of the General League of Mexican Peasants and Workers opened on 17 February 1936 with Fernando Amilpa, another leader of the workers, as provisional president, and 1,500 delegates representing 600,000 workers. When this organization dissolved, the Confederation of Mexican Workers (CTM) was born, with Lombardo Toledano as its Secretary General. Its ultimate aim was to fight for the total abolition of capitalism, and its immediate aim was to fight for the political and economic liberation of the country: the struggle for the right to strike, to organize unions, and to fight against all religious creeds and churches and against all those who tried to place co-operativism before trade unionism and socialism. It also fought for the right of state workers to be incorporated with the rest of the salaried workers, for recognition of the international nature of the worker and peasant movement, and for direct action against the capitalists. When the CTM was founded there had been talk of calling a congress to unify the peasants, in opposition to or in parallel with the National Revolutionary Party, but Cárdenas forbade it because he had ordered the latter to unify the peasants from 9 July 1935. If the CTM competed in this effort it would only introduce fatal internal struggles within the industrial proletariat.

In January that year, 1936, during a strike at the Vidriera de Monterrey company, the bosses started to accuse Lombardo Toledano of trying to impose unlawful conditions on them. On 5 and 6 February 1936 the bosses organized a general strike in Monterrey with the support of the anarchistic General League of Mexican Workers and the Regional League of Mexican Workers, under a religious, nationalistic, and anti-communist flag. On 11 February, Cárdenas urged the bosses to recognize the need for co-operation between the government and the factors of production, and the need to create a single body of workers to end the harmful inter-union strife. He stressed the role of the government as arbiter and denied that the cause of the social agitation was the communists, who were few in number and uninfluential. Those bosses who were tired of the social strife could hand their industries over to the workers or to the government; the strike was not patriotic. The Nuevo León bosses replied to the president indirectly on 19 February, stating that communism was spreading throughout the country and that of course they were not prepared to hand over their industries either to the workers or to the government. Cárdenas answered on 14 March, saying that labour legislation was going through an inevitable experimental period, that the only motive of the bosses was to make money, and that their decision not to hand over their industries was the best proof that the latter provided them with "very considerable" profits.[13]

A few months later the Mexican Union of Electrical Workers started a strike against the Mexican Light and Motive Power Company because the company had refused to improve its workers' living conditions. The strike lasted ten days, at the end of which the company gave in to the workers' demands. This was the first victory of the CTM against a foreign company. Another victory of the CTM and Cárdenas was pay for the weekly rest period.[14]

With Cárdenas, especially in his first three years, the number of strikes rose (202 in 1934, 642 in 1935, 674 in 1936, 576 in 1937, 319 in 1938, 303 in 1939 and 357 in 1940), especially when compared with Calles' last year (27 in 1928). The increase in the number of strikers was more or less proportional (498 in 1928 and 227 in 1931, as against 14,685 in 1934, 145,212 in 1935, etc.) This was the "marathon of radicalism" that Calles denounced. Cárdenas' social work helped the country to recover from the crisis of 1929, both with the repatriation of many Mexicans from the United States and with the expansion of the internal market. In fact, the number of men out of work went down from 191,371 in 1935 to 186,904 in 1936 and to 180,128 in 1937.[15]

Cárdenas nationalized the railways on 23 June 1937, and created a workers' administration for these in mid-1938. In his report of 1 September 1938 he stated that he was satisfied that in only one month the cost of operating the system had gone down considerably. But by the end of that year the large number of railway accidents obliged him to abandon the idea of administration by the workers because the dual personality of boss-cum-worker relaxed discipline to such an extent that, on 1 September 1940, Cárdenas issued a warning to the workers about the fulfilment of their obligations. A communist leader attributes this failure not to an excess of confidence on the part of Cárdenas, but to the fact that the foreign mining companies continued to enjoy special low tariffs.[16]

In the long run, it was the expropriation of the oil industry that was of greater significance, in spite of the fact that initially it went through severe financial and labour problems similar to those of the railways. In any case, the opposition from the oil companies was so strong that from this moment on, Cárdenas' radicalism was moderated, although he pursued it verbally, since the Mexican Revolutionary Party continued to say that his plan was to prepare the people for socialism. To be exact, they spoke of establishing social security, of the progressive nationalization of heavy industry and the development of co-operativism, especially as regards consumption.[17]

Throughout the country in 1936–1937, 233 consumer co-operatives were organized. Since 1936 the need had been felt to replace the law of 1933 to stop capitalist companies from appearing to be co-operatives. On 15 February 1938 a new law was published: the consumer co-operatives continued to have very small amounts of capital, but the development of co-operatives for production was encouraged, especially in the fields of transport, fishing, the cultivation of *ixtle* fibre, and sugar production. The most important ones were created by the government itself: clothing and tool workshops and the National Graphic Workshops.[18]

Cárdenas' work in the social field was, then, an attempt to favour the workers within the capitalist system. This explains why, although he organized state workers and theoretically gave them the right to work, he did not allow them to belong to any working men's organization. Neither did he allow bank workers to enjoy the rights specified in Article 123 of the Constitution.[19]

The Rise of the Industrial Society

According to the censuses, the population diminished from 15,160,370 in 1910 to 14,334,780 in 1921. The mechanical subtraction of these two figures has led many to talk of a million dead on the field of battle as a result of the revolution. The truth is that the census of 1910 was more exact than that of 1921. It is also necessary to take into account the deaths caused by the collateral effects of the civil war, such as the pandemic of Spanish influenza, and the increase in migration to the United States. In any case, the population increased to 16,552,722 in 1930 and to 19,653,552 in 1940; that is to say, it doubled in the period 1877–1940. This increase is due, to a great extent, to the progress made in the fight against smallpox, typhus, malaria, and gastroenteritis, although heart disease and cancer started to gain ground. This progress was consolidated with the introduction of antibiotics.[20]

There was a hint of this population explosion during Cárdenas' government, but it became unmistakable after 1940; Cárdenas attributed the increase in population both to the development of health factors and to revolutionary social work.[21]

The 1930 census suppressed some data that it considered superfluous, among them the question of "race," because since Independence many Indians had ceased to be isolated and had "lost their ethnic characteristics, even their language," by mixing with others; there was, moreover, no legal trace of these racial mixtures. Above all, since 1910 the social strata no longer "obeyed ethnic categories," but were "subject to economic categories." And then there was the difficulty faced by the census-takers in determining exactly the "race" or degree of racial mixture. However, one anthropologist opposed this decision because he felt that, to a large extent, indigenous characteristics continued to exist.[22]

Other great changes in this period were the reduction in foreign investment as a result of revolutionary nationalism, and the relative reduction in the number of foreigners, except for the increase in republican Spaniards at the end of the Spanish Civil War. At about this time the official illusion of foreign colonization as the panacea for all the country's ills disappeared. Structurally speaking, the fundamental change was the transformation of the hacienda into a new type of large estate and into the *ejido*, that is to say, the change from an agricultural to an industrial society.[23]

The percentage of the population involved in industry increased from 11.3 in 1910 to 13.8 in 1940. For the same dates, the proportion involved in agriculture decreased from 71.9 to 68.3 per cent.[24] Furthermore, in 1940 the land area that was private property was 82,149,256 hectares, as against 28,922,808 belonging to *ejidos* and 6,069,359 hectares of common land.[25] The number of people on *ejidos* with land doubled from 1930 (536,883) to 1940 (1,222,859), but by this last date they had been overtaken by agricultural workers and day-labourers (1,907,199).[26]

A minimum wage was established in 1933, according to the representatives to improve the economic situation of the workers, but according to Calles to benefit the capitalists.[27]

The lay nature of society was confirmed with the defeat of the *cristeros* in 1929. One important manifestation of this was the establishment of civil marriage in 1859, and on 14 December 1874 of the separation of married partners without the bond being broken.

Venustiano Carranza decreed, on 24 December 1914, divorce by mutual and free consent providing the couple had been married for more than three years, or at any time when the causes of marital conflict were too severe to be overcome. The authorities trusted that this law would free women from their Islamic slavery and, although this was an exceptional case, it definitely constituted "one of the most satisfactory conquests of the Constitutionalist Revolution." But it was also one of the best businesses of several states.[28]

The End of the Hacienda

With the secularization of welfare, in February 1861, its facilities fell into decay.[29] In spite of the fact that at the beginning of the Porfirian period the reduction in individual charity and the increase in institutional welfare was visible,[30] some thought that the state had no obligation to be philanthropic and that its mission was limited to intervention in cases of inevitable misfortune. Soon afterwards, when the new general hospital was opened in February 1905, the government insisted that welfare was not one of its primary functions, but that since private institutions were insufficient to relieve the situation of the destitute, and in spite of the inferior status of such people, the government would apportion to welfare part of its revenue that it did not need for its primary concerns (defence of the national territory and the maintenance of order), so as to contribute to this noble work.[31] The government of Oaxaca did not want to descend into the realms of charity either, since it was the business of individuals and harmful to the destitute who, relying on begging, became idle.[32] Anyway, albeit very unwillingly, public welfare replaced church welfare and individual charity. Miguel Macedo has explained that by the beginning of the twentieth century the country had recovered from the immense upheaval that the Reform had produced in the colonial welfare institutions, to the extent that it attempted to replace private welfare with official welfare.[33]

In the 1920s, trusts started to become important in private charity, and in public welfare the government's main concern was to eradicate the idea of charity,[34] giving it the character of a social service, and stressing the right of the needy to claim assistance.[35] In this way, in some states, utopian socialism replaced charity.[36] Several politicians tried to eliminate private welfare because it was connected with religious institutions, whose disappearance was one of the strongest desires of the Reform.[37]

The first Six-Year Plan of 1934 did not devote any one section specifically to the question of assistance or charity, but outlined a vague proposal to encourage the creation of homes for the old and disabled, counselling centres for women, and campaigns against begging, because up until then these policies had been carried out in a way that was not directly connected with the revolutionary aims of the government.[38]

On 1 January 1937 Cárdenas decided to bring the socially weak into the productive process. This transformation was assured when public welfare was fused with private welfare and the independent Department of Child Care to form the Ministry of Public Assistance. This degree of importance was given to assistance not for religious reasons, nor to protect society from certain dangerous elements, but to strengthen the nation's economy with the work of the socially underprivileged. To avoid the creation of an inferiority complex, public assistance was to operate on a system of quotas.[39] The revolution accelerated the crisis of the church–hacienda structure, which had until that time been the main source of charity and welfare.

Conclusion

At the close of Lázaro Cárdenas' presidential term in 1940, Mexico, 119 years after it had gained its independence from Spain, was transformed from an agrarian country into one in the initial stages of industrialization. It had defended its sovereignty from various attempts at conquest by European countries and the United States, but its dependence upon US imperialism was consolidated, with the exception of oil, which was nationalized in 1938. Domestically, essential developments were the disappearance of haciendas and a new *modus vivendi* with the Catholic church. In 1940 there was an uneasy balance between the social groups that had initiated the 1910 Revolution: protection for unionized workers and a strengthening of the bourgeoisie. Hopes could no longer be based on foreign immigration, partly due to the start of the population explosion, to revolutionary nationalism, and to the Second World War.

Notes

1. Manuel Cambre, *La guerra de tres años* (Imp. de José M. Cabrera, Guadalajara, 1904), p. 605.
2. Moisés González Navarro, *La Confederación Nacional Campesina* (Universidad Nacional Autónoma de México, Mexico City, 1977), p. 16.
3. Moisés González Navarro, *Historia moderna de México*, vol. 4: *El Porfiriato. La vida social* (Editorial Hermes, Mexico City, 1957), pp. 258–259.
4. See note 2 above, p. 17.
5. See note 2 above, p. 19.
6. See note 3 above, p. 271.
7. González Navarro (note 2 above), pp. 19–21; Moisés González Navarro, "La era moderna," in *Historia documental de México*, vol. 2 (Universidad Nacional Autónoma de México, Mexico City, 1974), pp. 340–347.
8. See note 3 above, pp. 529–675.
9. Moisés González Navarro, *La colonización en México* (Talleres de Impresión de Estampillas y Valores, Mexico City, 1960), p. 138.
10. Moisés González Navarro, "Mexico: The Lopsided Revolution," in Claudio Veliz,

ed., *Obstacles to Change in Latin America* (Oxford University Press, London, 1965), pp. 206–207.

11. See note 2 above, pp. 20–56.
12. See note 2 above, pp. 66–68.
13. *CTM 1935–1941* (Talleres Tipográficos Modelo, Mexico City, n.d.), pp. 21–28.
14. See note 13 above, pp. 46, 104–105, 477.
15. Moisés González Navarro, *Cinco crisis mexicanas*, Jornadas 99 (El Colegio de México, Mexico City), pp. 90–92. *Anuario estadístico de los estados unidos mexicanos 1940* (Dirección General de Estadística, Mexico City, 1942), p. 431.
16. Nathaniel and Silvia Weyl, "La reconquista de México," *Problemas agrícolas e industriales de México*, vol. 7, no. 4 (1955), p. 277; *CTM* (note 13 above), pp. 275–277; *Diario de los debates de senadores*, 21 April 1978; *El Nacional*, 2 September 1938; Víctor Alba, *Las ideas sociales contemporáneas en México* (Fondo de Cultura Económica, Mexico City, 1960), pp. 253, 265, 393; *Diario de los debates de diputados*, 1 September 1940, p. 18; Valentín Campa, "El Cardenismo en la Revolución Mexicana," *Problemas agrícolas e industriales de México*, vol. 7, no. 3 (1953), p. 289.
17. See note 2 above, pp. 89–98.
18. Rosendo Rojas Coria, *Tratado de cooperativismo mexicano* (Fondo de Cultura Económica, Mexico City, 1952), p. 366; Weyl (note 16 above), p. 274; González Navarro (note 10 above), p. 226.
19. See note 2 above, pp. 89–98.
20. Moisés González Navarro, *Población y sociedad en México (1900–1970)* (Facultad de Ciencias Políticas y Sociales, Mexico City, 1974), vol. 1, pp. 297–409.
21. See note 20 above, p. 43.
22. See note 20 above, p. 39.
23. See note 20 above, vol. 2, pp. 5, 26.
24. *50 años de Revolución Mexicana en cifras* (Nacional Financiera, Mexico City, 1963), p. 29.
25. *Segundo censo agrícola ganadero de los estados unidos mexicanos 1940. Resumen general* (Dirección General de Estadística, Mexico City, 1951), p. 28.
26. See note 2 above, p. 187.
27. *Diario de los debates de diputados*, 12 September 1933, pp. 17–19; Francisco Xavier Caxiola: *El presidente Rodríguez (1932–1934)* (Editorial Cultura, Mexico City, 1938), p. 533.
28. See note 20 above, pp. 100–104.
29. Rómulo Velasco Ceballos, *Fichas bibliográficas sobre asistencia en México* (Secretaría de Asistencia Pública, Mexico City), p. 53; *Establecimientos de beneficencia apuntes sobre su origen y relación de los actos de su junta directiva coleccionados por el actual secretario en cumplimiento de lo dispuesto en la circular de 23 de enero de 1877* (Imprenta de la Escuela de Artes y Oficios, Mexico City, 1878), pp. iii, v, vii, xiii.
30. Juan de Dios Peza, *La beneficencia en México* (Imprenta de Francisco Díaz de León, Mexico City, 1881), pp. 7, 147.
31. Secretaría de Estado y del Despacho de Gobernación Beneficencia Pública, *Hospital general* México: s.p.i., 1905; s.p.
32. See note 3 above, p. 495.
33. Miguel S. Macedo, "El Municipio. Los establecimientos penales. La Asistencia Pública," *México su evolución social* (J. Ballescá, Mexico City, 1902), tome I, vol. 2, pp. 716, 720, 723.
34. *Memoria de labores del gobierno constitucional del Estado de Veracruz-Llave durante el cuatrienio 1928–1932. Texto del Informe rendido por el Ing. Adalberto Tejeda, gobernador constitucional del Estado, ante la XXXIV H. Legislatura y*

discursos de los CC. Presidentes de los Poderes Judicial y Legislativo, Lic. Luis Vega y Pavón, y Dip. Raymundo Mancisidor (Talleres Linotipográficos del Gobierno del Estado, Jalapa-Enríquez, 1932), pp. 165–168; *Informes del Gobernador del Estado C. Gral. de Div. Rodrigo M. Quevedo y del Presidente del Supremo Tribunal de Justicia. Contestaciones del Presidente del H. Congreso* (Talleres Gráficos del Gobierno, Chihuahua, 1934), p. 14.

35. *Informe presidencial y memoria del Departamento del Distrito Federal que rinde el C. Jefe del mismo Lic. Aarón Sáenz por el período administrativo comprendido entre el 1º de julio de 1933 y el 30 de junio de 1934* (Talleres Linotipográficos de la penitenciaría del Distrito Federal, Mexico City, 1934), p. 196.
36. *Informe rendido por el gobernador constitucional de Yucatán C. Dr. Alvaro Torres Díaz, ante la XXIX Legislatura el 1º de enero de 1927* (Talleres Tipográficos del Gobierno del Estado, Mérida, 1927), pp. 76–78.
37. *Memoria Beneficencia Pública 1932–1934*, pp. 10–15.
38. Secretaría Asistencia Pública, *Asistencia Social 1934–1940*, p. 15.
39. *Diario de los debates de senadores*, 21 December 1937, pp. 13–20.

FOREIGN INVESTMENTS AND THE GROWTH OF MANUFACTURES IN MEXICO (1867–1940)

Fernando Rosenzweig
Instituto Nacional de Educación para Adultos, Mexico City, Mexico

During the period with which we are concerned, manufacturing activities in Mexico underwent two stages of dynamic growth. The first of these lasted until 1910, the year which witnessed the outbreak of the Mexican Revolution. The second one began in 1920, once the new regime had been consolidated, and was interrupted only from 1929 to 1933 owing to the effects of the world economic crisis.

Actually, this was an incipient form of development, a mere beginning, a forerunner of the industrialization process that Mexico entered into around 1940, and it did not manage to produce significant changes in the structure of the economy: just as in the late 1890s, in 1935 the manufacturing sector's share in the total Gross Domestic Product was approximately 16 per cent, and the weight of this sector as a source of employment for the population remained at about 11 per cent for the whole of the intervening period (see tables 1 and 2).

The fundamental change that occurred during those years was the rise of modern factories, which came to displace wide segments of the country's traditional craft industries, and which enjoyed considerable protection from the state with regard to import substitution, especially of consumer goods.

The growth of manufacturing activities in those years reflected the major influence of internal factors that had a bearing on capital formation in that sector, and on trends in the demand for its products. Foreign investors reacted to those factors, and for this reason they made their first investments in the transformation industry, which made up barely a fraction of their total investment in the country: a little more than 4 per cent in 1910 and around 7 per cent in 1940 (the main areas invested in were mining, railways, and the generation of electricity).

Table 1. Gross Domestic Product in Mexico:
Total and manufacturing sector (in millions of pesos of 1950)

Year	Total	Manufacturing sector	
		Amount	% of total
1895	6,493	890	13.5
1900	8,250	1,360	16.5
1910	11,650	1,836	15.8
1921	11,273	1,669	14.8
1926	16,622	2,330	14.0
1931	16,016	2,296	14.3
1932	13,547	1,682	12.4
1935	17,983	2,820	15.7
1940	22,889	4,264	18.6

Source: Leopoldo Solís, *La realidad económica mexicana: retrovisión y perspectivas* (Siglo XXI, Mexico City, 1970), pp. 90–91.

Table 2. Economically active population in Mexico:
Total and manufacturing sector (in thousands of persons)

Year	Total	Manufacturing sector	
		Number	% of total
1985	4,761.9	554.6	11.6
1910	5,337.9	613.9	11.5
1921	5,883.6	534.4	10.9
1930	5,165.8	692.2	13.4
1940	5,858.1	639.6	10.9

Source: National population censuses. See Instituto Nacional de Estadística, Geografía e Informática (INEGI), *Estadísticas históricas de México* (Mexico City, 1985), vol. 1, chap. 6.

1

In 1867, the country managed to free itself from the French Intervention and both independence and republican institutions were consolidated. Thus, once the political instability that had prevailed during Mexico's first half-century as an independent nation had been overcome, its national territory came to be subject, in a real sense, to the authority of the government within a framework of legal norms formally sanctioned by a body representative of the citizenry, i.e. the Constitution of 1857. Since public peace and security and the passage of individuals and commercial goods were guaranteed, it was possible for Mexican national territory (virtually isolated from the rest of the world by protective tariffs) to begin to function as an economic sphere geared toward establishing itself within a unique market. Domestic custom-houses were abolished in 1896. The establishment of a network of railways,[1] laid out mainly with a view to bolstering exports of primary goods, allowed links to be set up between major cities, production areas, and maritime ports and border cities.

Mexico's total population had risen by a mere 30 per cent or so in the 45-year period between 1820 and 1865, that is, from 6.2 to 8.2 million inhabitants. During the following 45 years, the population increase was substantially greater in proportional terms (approximately 84 per cent), a total of 15.1 million inhabitants being reached in 1910. The annual growth rate, which was 0.8 per cent between 1846 and 1878, rose to 1.6 per cent by 1910. The tendencies experienced by the economy favoured the expansion of cities, albeit in modest fashion: the number of cities with more than 50,000 inhabitants increased from six in 1900 to seven in 1910, and the population of those cities (726,000 and 953,000 respectively) rose from 5 per cent to slightly over 6 per cent of the country's total number of inhabitants. Between 1895 and 1910, the proportion of persons who could read and write experienced a moderate yet important increase from 14 to 20 per cent of individuals older than ten years of age.

Aside from protective tariffs, manufactures were stimulated by the depreciation of the peso, which erected an additional barrier to imports, a situation which was prevalent practically without interruption until 1905, when Mexico adopted the gold standard and, along with it, a fixed parity for its currency.

The development of manufacturing was most apparent in the realm of light industries geared to producing goods for domestic consumption, among which the following were especially noteworthy: textiles (cotton and wool); shoes; food, beverages, and tobacco (especially sugar and beer); chinaware and porcelain; and wood. This period also saw the birth of the cement industry and, as of 1901, the iron and steel industry began to operate.

Many of these industrial branches sprang up exclusively as a result of the initiative and financial resources of Mexican capitalists. For example, sugar was produced mainly on large estates whose sugar-cane fields were eventually expanded in the state of Morelos and elsewhere. This expansion was financed through the owners' savings and through credit from banks, production developing on a large scale thanks to the new railway lines.

From the 1830s on, Mexico witnessed the appearance of local businessmen in its textile industry; at first they were unsure and the market for their wares was weak, but they were encouraged by a tax-exemption policy instituted by Minster of Foreign Affairs Lucas Alamán. Subsequently, in both this branch of manufacturing and others, the capital accumulated by rich businessmen living in the country found a suitable area for investment in the establishment and modernization of factories. Some of those merchants were from other countries (England, France, and Spain); their capital was amassed in Mexico. In certain branches of industrial activity (e.g. the beer and tobacco industries and, at the close of the period, the iron and steel industry), foreign capital joined hands with national capital, providing patents and technical know-how as well as financing. Few activities could be identified as the exclusive domain of foreign investors.

Foreign investment in Mexico in the year 1911 is estimated at 3.401 billion pesos (of 1911), of which a scarce 131 million – a little less than 4 per cent – was directed towards the manufacturing sector. The largest segment of that total (72 million pesos) was French and was situated in the textile, alcohol, and tobacco industries. For their part, the Germans had shown a preference for the beer, chemical, and paper industries, and US investors were participating in tanneries and flour mills.

In short, between 1867 and 1910, a period of economic development led by the boom in the export sector, Mexico experienced the onset of an industrialization process grounded on the formation of its domestic market and on the accumulation of investment capital within the country, to which were added some contributions of funds from abroad. For the export sector, foreign capital was a key factor; for manufactures, it constituted a complementary means of fostering the development of national enterprises.

Accounting for the limited growth of manufactures in Mexico before 1910 are two groups of factors, the action of which helped to determine the scenario of socio-economic crisis that arose toward the end of the Porfiriato.[2] On the one hand, the poverty of the country's masses of consumers, especially in rural areas, who were subject to a system of peonage on the haciendas, slowed down the growth of the domestic market at an early stage. On the other, the short scales of production (related to the market's weakness), and the industry's technical inefficiency (concealed by protectionism), reduced the incentives to invest in it and stripped it of any possibility of access to foreign markets.

2

Between the year 1910, which marked the outbreak of the Mexican Revolution, and 1921, when the new regime was consolidated, the country's manufacturing activities remained stagnant, vegetating amidst the adverse conditions created by the disruption of public peace and the instability of the various governments that came into power. Nevertheless, Mexico's major industries were able to stay alive, taking advantage of their existing installed capacity while making little or no new investments. The investment of foreign capital ceased altogether.

Data is not available on industrial production for the period of armed strife (1911 to 1920). The figure for 1921 indicates a lower level than that of 1910 (see table 1). The population of the country suffered a considerable setback: between those two years, the total number of inhabitants, according to census data, fell from 15.2 million to 14.3 million. The country's capital assets dwindled, especially in those states where military operations were most prolonged. In most of Mexico's national territory, communications were interrupted and it was no longer safe to travel. It is amazing that the impact of those years of conflict on the manufacturing industry was not much worse.

3

After 1921 the country was gradually restored to normality. The new Political Constitution proclaimed in 1917 included social reforms (establishing labour laws and land distribution) alongside the civil rights set down in the previous Constitution of 1857, and reaffirmed the national interest in utilizing natural resources. With the military defeat of the partisans of the old regime,[3] the new institutions were formally consolidated and, once that had been accomplished, a systemic and stable form of peace was again to reign in the nation.

The recovery of productive activities oriented toward the domestic market signalled a trend for the Mexican economy during the entire decade of the 1920s. In order to meet the people's needs, it would be necessary to regain the levels achieved prior to the period of armed conflict. The population experienced renewed growth, reaching nearly 17 million in 1930 and a little under 20 million in 1940. Moreover, the purchasing power of the working masses was favourably affected by an expansion in government spending (financed in that era by means of fiscal mechanisms of a predominantly non-inflationary nature) and by a distribution of that spending which placed greater emphasis on the objectives of social welfare and economic development. Thus, the portion of total expenditures allocated to general administration (77 per cent at the close of the Porfiriato) fell to 65 per cent during the administration of President Plutarco Elías Calles (1925–1928) and to 44 per cent during that of Lázaro Cárdenas. The portion allocated to economic development rose from 16 to 25 and 38 per cent, respectively. And insofar as social welfare was concerned, its slice of government spending rose from 7 to 10 and 18 per cent during those years.[4]

Efforts were made to build irrigation works and a national highway system, and to help support agriculture. The growth of the urban population was steady: whereas in 1910 it represented 29 per cent of the total number of inhabitants, that figure had risen to slightly under 36 per cent by 1940. The population of Mexico City reached the one-million mark in the 1930 census.

The export sector had been able to maintain its growth rate during the years of armed strife, especially in the zones of tropical agriculture near the coasts (such as the henequen-producing region in the Yucatán) and in the oil wells on the Gulf of Mexico, in response to the demand for strategic products needed by the US economy during the 1914–1918 war. In contrast, throughout the 1920s the export sector evidenced less dynamism, partly due to its reluctance to invest in accordance with the conditions set down by the new legislation enacted by the post-revolutionary government and later, during the years of crisis starting in 1929, because of the unpropitious panorama set by the world economy.

Thus, the growth of Mexican manufacturing activity which took place as of 1921 was essentially a result of the recuperating national economy's dynamics; it was also spurred on by a policy on government spending that favoured greater production and strengthened demand. As was the case at the close of the nineteenth century, foreign capital was attracted by the new opportunities that were arising and helped to enhance those opportunities. From that time on, outstanding among the new firms with foreign capital were those with US capital. In 1926 the first automobile assembly plant (Ford) was founded and in 1933 the manufacture of tyres was begun; both of these branches of industry were bolstered by the construction of highways. In 1936, the assembly of trucks (General Motors) was initiated. Other developments that occurred in industry using US capital involved the production of batteries and electrical home appliances. Later, US capital was also channelled toward the food industry. The US government estimated that by around 1940 direct investment by US citizens in Mexico totalled 358 million dollars and, of this, a mere 10 million dollars – less than 3 per cent of that figure – was in the area of manufactures. Mexico continued to be a primary exporting country, but its domestic development pattern began to pave the way for industrial investments.

As can be seen in table 1, the years of international crisis affected the growth of manufactures in Mexico, as a consequence of the general contraction of economic activity resulting from the decline in exports. The discontent in urban areas brought about by unemployment in industry and service-related fields, and the conflicts that arose in the countryside when the price of commercial crops fell, helped set the stage in Mexico for the programme of structural reforms carried out during President Lázaro Cárdenas' administration (1934–1940), the mainstay of which was land distribution and the introduction of labour legislation. These reforms, along with the public works programme and the government's policy of economic development (oriented in accordance with anti-cyclical approaches inspired by Keynes), lent firm impetus to the growth of productive activities; these soon recovered from the adverse effects of the world crisis and were to reach higher levels.

As of 1935, Mexican industry began a stage of vigorous expansion. Gradually, the idle capacity of industry was utilized more and more; the sector began to attract new investments and, soon after, foreign capital as well. Not even the expropriation of oil from US and British companies, decreed in 1938, could stop the flow of foreign investments in manufacturing. In particular, US capital found in manufacturing industries a new area for directing its resources, which in later years was to be considered preferential.

Notes

1. The number of kilometres of railways in service, which totalled approximately 1,000 in 1880, rose to some 6,000 in 1884, 11,000 in 1894, 14,000 in 1900, and 19,000 in 1910.
2. The regime of dictator Porfirio Díaz (1876, 1877–1880, and 1884–1911).
3. The Porfiriato.
4. See James W. Wilkie, *The Mexican Revolution, Expenditure and Change since 1910* (University of California Press, 1970).

Bibliography

Cosío Villegas, Daniel. *Historia moderna de México*, vol. 1: *El Porfiriato. La vida económica*. Editorial Hermes, Mexico City, 1965.

Musk, Sanford A. *Industrial Revolution in Mexico*. University of California Press, 1950.

Reynolds, Clark W. *The Mexican Economy. Twentieth-century Structure and Growth*. Yale University Press, 1970.

Sepúlveda, Bernardo, and Antonio Chumacero. *La inversión extranjera en México*. Fondo de Cultura Económica, Mexico City, 1973.

Solís, Leopoldo. *La realidad económica mexicana: retrovisión y perspectivas*. Siglo XXI, Mexico City, 1970.

Wilkie, James W. *The Mexican Revolution. Expenditure and Change since 1910*. University of California Press, 1970.

Wythe, G. *La industria latinoamericana*. Fondo de Cultura Económica, Mexico City, 1947.

THE POLITICAL MODERNIZATION OF MEXICO (1867–1940)

Lorenzo Meyer
El Colegio de México, Mexico City, Mexico

Introduction

In the realm of the social sciences, the concept of modernization has never been given a generally accepted definition. As is the case with many of our poorly defined terms, it has been necessary to resort to indicators to afford it real substance. Widely used in the 1960s, the concept itself has been the object of harsh criticism, to the extent that it has been compared to one of the several forms of evolution of national societies, i.e. the one germane to Western Europe and the United States.

Despite its limitations, the term is still useful in that it helps us to consider the major transformations of a given society from a comparative viewpoint, which could take the form – among other possibilities – of a historical comparison. Obviously, the process of change that the national societies of Western Europe underwent from the sixteenth century on constitutes one of the imperative reference points for anyone who attempts to explain macro-social change in a particular contemporary country or society. The Western European model is not the only one that can lead to modernity, and yet, undoubtedly, it is the original model.

The notion of social modernization entails – as a minimum, and of necessity – a series of transformational processes geared toward: (1) creating a productive structure capable of achieving sustained economic development

---

Paper presented at the Conference on the Modernization Process in Mexico (1867–1940): The Social Transformations, co-sponsored by the United Nations University and El Colegio de México, Mexico City, 19–21 March 1985. The author wishes to express his appreciation to the Woodrow Wilson International Center for Scholars, Washington, D.C., for the support it gave him in the preparation of this paper.

and growth, in such a way that sufficient material resources are made available to attain an improvement in the standard of living of the population as a whole, in keeping with the current technology and expectations, as well as maintaining the autonomy of the society vis-à-vis exterior forces; (2) creating – alongside the above-mentioned process – power and authority structures allowing for the formulation and implementation of national policies able to channel and co-ordinate the efforts made by the society as a whole to achieve its overall aims, one of which is material development.

Depending on the author and on the school of thought he or she represents, to these two basic processes (indispensable elements in the definition) could be added other correlated variables, such as the increasing degree of rationality and secularization, or of social mobility and political participation.[1]

From a strictly political standpoint, what we are interested in observing is the second of the above processes, involving a change in the structures and functions of power that leads to an enhancement of the system's ability to meet, with relative efficiency, the challenge of constructing a national society that is both autonomous and feasible. This increased efficiency in the utilization of social resources for the attainment of general goals can be achieved by various means, the importance and possible combinations of which will vary in accordance with the specific case in question. Thus, in certain instances the differentiation and specialization of institutions is the keystone to the process of modernizing transformation, whereas in other cases perhaps the key lies in the concentration of power in pre-existing institutions; in still others, it could be an increase in participation of the members of the system in the decision-making process. Ideally, any study of political modernization should be multi-dimensional, taking into account the reciprocal influence of the variables into which one decides to break down the phenomenon from a theoretical point of view.

Given the limitations of an essay such as this, as well as the shortcomings in knowledge regarding the topic we are analysing (the historical transformation of the Mexican political system), the approach we shall follow will emphasize the process involving the concentration of power and its effects on the efficient utilization of resources for the country's economic development. We shall also be concerned with modifications in major political structures, as well as changes in the nature of participation by the social actors in political decision-making processes. The lack of a systematic treatment of cultural variables does not mean that they are any less important, nor does it presuppose a type of causality that makes them dependent upon other changes occurring. Rather, it simply reflects the absence of monographs that would allow us to arrive at generalizations which in other fields of knowledge it is possible to draw up.

The Starting-point

Taking the year 1867 as the starting-point of the political modernization of Mexico is very arbitrary, and yet, at the same time, is even more advisable. In effect, the execution of Ferdinand Maximilian of Hapsburg in Queretaro on 19 June 1867 serves as a dramatic symbol of the defeat of the Conservative Party's political scheme, by which it purported to guide Mexico's development within the traditional framework of the monarchy. In 1867 the victorious Liberal Party, whose president and leader was Benito Juárez, was left without an enemy on the ideological front. The destruction of the Second Empire paved the way for the realization of the idea of a Mexican nation based on republican, democratic, and federal structures grounded on a liberal economy. The legal document that was to act as a framework for such a project would be the Constitution of 1857 – which had provoked a fight to the death between Liberals and Conservatives immediately following its enactment – a document that authorized the separation and balance of powers in a fashion quite similar to the American model and, in addition, all the individual freedoms befitting the most advanced brand of liberalism of the time.[2]

Unfortunately, the social and material bases for carrying out this "American-style" modernizing scheme were rather inadequate, if not totally non-existent. To begin with, Mexico's political tradition was very different from the British one: it had a heritage of three centuries of Spanish colonialism, in which there was no place for self-government in the real sense of the term. This was, rather, a paternalistic and authoritarian tradition.

In 1867 the social foundations of Mexico remained those of the indigenous population, and for that reason they were far removed from the liberal political ethos. Of the approximately 8 million inhabitants comprising Mexico's population at that time, half or perhaps more could be considered natives; that is, peasants, lacking a national awareness, who lived in small communities, partially dependent upon a subsistence economy but also supplying labour for the market economy (mainly for the haciendas and mines), who spoke a wide range of dialects and often had little or no knowledge of the Spanish language. The second group, in numerical terms, was composed of mestizos, dwellers in large towns and cities, who filled the ranks of artisans, small businessmen, bureaucrats, the army and several of the higher political posts. At the top of the pyramid were the Creoles or European mestizos, who, apart from occupying the top political and military positions, comprised the bulk of the large landowners and merchants. Finally there was a small group of foreigners who took part in directing the economy and, therefore, the life-styles of the Creoles.[3]

This social structure based on race and class had led to a significant fragmentation of Mexican society which practically all the political leaders of the era bemoaned; and yet it was extremely hard to overcome in the short term. Immigration and education were two of the solutions most stoutly advocated, but neither was really put into practice. The economy, which could have acted as a dynamic agent for social change, was in a most deplorable state. By 1860 Mexico's national income was lower (by 10 per cent) than at the turn of the century.[4] Mining, which in the past had been the dynamic sector, was still suffering from the ravages caused by the War for Independence (1810–1821), by foreign invasions, and by the constant internal strife that had preceded the triumph of the Liberals.

The victory won by Benito Juárez and the Liberal Party over the imperialists could not disguise the fact that, in 1867, Mexico's political panorama was a distressing one. From the time of Guadalupe Victoria's regime (1824–1829), the federal government had subsisted in permanent fiscal bankruptcy and in the midst of constant instability. Decades of political chaos had given way to an appreciable diffusion of power at the centre in favour of local caciques. These regional "bigwigs" had their own means of coercion and lived off the *alcabalas* (sales taxes) levied on domestic trade and other taxes that hindered the establishment of a true national market and economy.[5]

This triumph of localism and regionalism during the first half of the nineteenth century was favoured by the very geography of the country. Mexico's great mountainous barriers and deserts, and the lack of navigable rivers, fostered a retrogression to a kind of feudalization of the country, creating interests that were to resist the changes outlined in the liberal scheme.

From a cultural perspective, Mexico's social fragmentation and heterogeneity – combined with its regionalism – proved to be very significant obstacles to the creation of an effective national conscience. On the other hand, the symbols which long ago had joined the inhabitants of New Spain had since disappeared or lost their legitimacy in the eyes of the new rulers, i.e. the crown and the Catholic church. For the majority of the Mexican population in the mid-nineteenth century, the new emblems with which attempts were made to replace the old ones ("the rights of man", citizenship, democracy, the nation, etc.) simply had no meaning. Besides the Catholic faith, the basic loyalties were those felt towards the local community and the region.[6]

Economic Liberalism and Political Authoritarianism

The way in which the victors of 1867 were to solve their dilemma regarding Mexico's development was by combining economic liberalism with political authoritarianism. As one of the instigators of this process justified it at the beginning of the twentieth century, "It had been necessary to postpone political development in order to establish the material foundations upon which it could be supported."[7]

The period dominated by the figure of Benito Juárez (1867–1872) was characterized by a constant struggle between the Executive and the other branches of government. The regime of Porfirio Díaz (1876–1880 and 1884–1911) witnessed the total triumph of the presidency over the legislative and judicial branches and the victory of the federal government over the state governments, where local legislatures and judicial systems were nullified in favour of the governors. The Constitution of 1857 remained in force, but by the close of the nineteenth century it had become merely an empty shell.[8]

Juárez's fundamental task consisted of facing up to the internal divisions affecting the Liberal coalition, which on more than one occasion ended in outright rebellion. Similarly, he found it necessary to undermine the power of the army and of the big local caciques. Upon the death of Juárez, the dispute over his succession was settled in the old-fashioned way: thus in 1876, a triumphant military rebellion put General Porfirio Díaz at the head of the Mexican government.

It was during Porfirio Díaz's second term as President (1884–1888) that the bases for his dictatorship were established. At that time, the presidency came to dominate the Legislative Branch to such an extent that it did away with any possible opposition from the houses of the legislature. Once Congress had been subordinated to the will of the Executive, the Judicial Branch lost the limited autonomy it still had. After 1888, elections were held punctually and at all levels, but in no case did they serve to determine anything because, on a national level, the opposition simply disappeared, and on a local plane it was manipulated by Díaz in order to suppress the displays of independence which some governors still made. The government of the Liberals ended in a personal dictatorship which was uninterrupted.

This process involving the concentration and centralization of power, initiated by Díaz in his first presidential term, came up against its greatest obstacle in the form of the federal nature of the republic, behind which the "bigwigs" in the states had become entrenched. These men had been instrumental in the triumph of the Liberals over the Conservatives; by this time, they had added great economic power to their already established political power.[9] Gradually the central government gained definitive control, thanks to an increase in its fiscal resources and to the wise utilization of the army as an element for neutralizing the governors. And while the army decreased in numbers, its level of professionalism was enhanced.

At the beginning of the twentieth century, General Díaz's power reached its peak. Legal opposition was non-existent and the clandestine opposition had yet to be consolidated. By then efforts in favour of economic modernization had already started to bear fruit and continued without serious obstacles until the moment the Mexican Revolution commenced, in 1910. Between 1877 and 1910, Mexico's Gross Domestic Product rose by a factor of 3.2 in real terms. In certain specific branches of the economy – above all, in most modern ones – the progress made was even more remarkable. Thus, for example, the network of railways increased from 893 to 19,205 kilometres; the value of silver production jumped from slightly under 25 million pesos to over 85 million; and the production of industrial metals, such as copper and lead, was initiated. Ports were modernized, as well as the textile industry; a banking system worthy of bearing that name arose for the first time; and exports went up from 60 million pesos in 1877 to 270 million in 1910.[10]

The main basis of support and *raison d'être* of the Porfirian system was a small yet powerful oligarchy composed of landowners, which enhanced its wealth enormously in that period by acquiring lands expropriated from the church by the Liberals and lands similarly expropriated from native communities and through the transfer of public lands. According to the source used, it is estimated that by 1910 between 82 and 97 per cent of the heads of families classified as peasants owned no land at all.[11] Nevertheless, the heart of Mexico's modern economy – railways, mines, banking, electricity and oil – was in the hands of foreign capital, rather than the domestic oligarchy. It was only at the close of this period, and exclusively insofar as the railways were concerned, that national control was eventually felt. But this was accomplished by the state, using foreign loans rather than private savings.

The destruction of Porfirio Díaz's regime in May 1911 – when the old dictator resigned as President and went into exile, forced to do so because of the triumph of the revolutionary forces – was due mostly to the regime's inability to transform its structures so as to accommodate the new political actors. Indeed, the extraordinary process of economic modernization had created a middle class for which there was no place in the Porfirian political set-up; the same was true of the working class which began to spring up in the shadow of railways, mines, foundries, and textile mills. It goes without saying that peasants and small landowners were not represented in any way at all. Even within the oligarchy itself there were dissatisfied sectors, because a mere handful of favourites – especially those of the so-called group of *científicos*[12] whose leader was the Minister of the Treasury – monopolized the positions of power. The process of renewal within the various élites was conspicuous by its absence in the Porfirian dictatorship, which, in the end, was a genuine gerontocracy.

Revolution and Renovation

The Mexican Revolution of 1910 began almost entirely as a movement claiming the reinstatement of the political rights destroyed by the dictatorship. At first, demands calling for profound changes in the social structure were few in number. The leadership of this movement was essentially, although not exclusively, middle-class and even included some disaffected members of the upper class. There were not many leaders from the sectors comprising the majority, i.e. the peasantry. The regional nature of the movement was apparent from its outset, so much so that current Mexican historiography speaks not of a single revolution but of several which occurred simultaneously.[13] The initial political demands, born of the middle classes' desire to open up the system in order to share power with the landholding groups, were accompanied, not long thereafter, by the demands of the popular sectors allied to the revolutionary bourgeoisie. The political banner of the revolution can be summed up in the slogan of the Plan de San Luis of November 1910 (which is the initial document of the revolution): *Sufragio efectivo, no reelección* (effective suffrage, no re-election). However, it was not long before a group appeared taking up the cry of "land and liberty" as the motto for its struggle. The original demand posed by these agrarians was the return of the communal lands taken over by the large haciendas, but with the passage of time they would call for the destruction of the haciendas themselves and the distribution of the lands – regardless of their primary source – among the peasants who worked them. Lastly, the nascent workers' movement – independently at first, and later in conjunction with other sectors – pressed for the right of affiliation, the right to strike and, finally, a commitment on the part of its political allies to the effect that the new regime arising out of the revolution would back up all the demands made by the labour movements of the era, demands that had only been accepted in very few places: an eight-hour work-day, a minimum wage, special protection for women and children, medical services, housing, schools, etc.

The revolution came up against serious obstacles in the form of the army of the old regime at first, and of foreign powers later. In 1914, the combined forces of the different revolutionary movements achieved the total destruction of the professional army. At the same time, the international conflict of the revolution gave way to a strong anti-imperialist sentiment which harbingered greater control of foreign capital by the new state. Between 1914 and 1916 the distinct tendencies of the revolution fought one another in an attempt to gain hegemony. The victor of this fierce intra-revolutionary strife was the most moderate faction, committed to effect political changes and, to a much lesser degree, social ones. In any event, this group led by Venustiano Carranza – who owned land in the state of Coahuila and had played a minor role as a politician under Porfirio Díaz – was to adopt a new Constitution in February 1917, wherein the agrarian reform and workers' rights (enumerated very extensively) were codified, the oil deposits which were being exploited by foreign companies were nationalized, and virtually all rights for religious organizations were cut off. In addition, the new Constitution maintained the separation of powers, although it clearly gave preference to the Executive over the other two branches and it assigned the state greater responsibilities with regard to the promotion of economic development. The vision of the world held by those who forged this new constitutional framework was not liberal, and although private property continued to constitute the basis of the economy, it was no longer the sole basis for it.[14]

The Constitution of 1917, rather than reflecting the situation that actually prevailed in Mexico, was much more a plan for the future. In reality, it was a new programme designed to attain an old objective: a stable political and social order – social justice being the indispensable condition for stability – and a modern economy. This economy still appeared to be based on agriculture and the extractive industries. Very few, if any, dared to conjure up the image of a truly industrial Mexico.

When the new Constitution was put into effect, the political disintegration of the country was far from being remedied. In fact, between 1914 and 1916 a national government simply did not exist. The political system was broken up into different segments and, as in the past, the caciques dominated the regions.[15] Carranza's main task, as the first president elected in accordance with the norms established by the new Constitution, consisted of trying to put an end to the elements of rebellion and banditry which were laying the country to waste, and of ensuring that the authority of the President prevailed over that of the army. In the end, he was not completely successful in this undertaking and he lost his life to a military rebellion launched by the new revolutionary army.

The rebellion of 1920 which stripped Carranza of power was the last one to be successful in Mexico. Indeed, it laid the foundations for a period of stability which few at the time would have imagined was to be one of the longest-lasting in Latin America.

The Organization of the New Regime

The main task that fell to the government headed by General Alvaro Obregón (1920–1924) was to negotiate the surrender or elimination of the various groups of revolutionaries or reactionaries still up in arms. It had great success in this endeavour, for it secured the surrender of the agrarian revolutionaries known as *zapatistas*[16] in the south and of the remaining forces of Francisco Villa in the north; the withdrawal of the reactionary movement under the orders of General Félix Díaz, nephew of the old dictator; and the surrender of the counter-revolutionary movement led by Manuel Peláez in Tamaulipas, of peasant bands under Saturnino Cedillo in San Luis Potosí, and of many other less important groups.

To a large extent, Obregón achieved his goal by means of co-optation, legitimizing (through recognition by the central government) the power and presence of groups and caciques in the regions where they were actually influential. Thus, the central government's power was derived from its ability to negotiate with its most important generals and with the rebels who had laid down their arms. From 1923 to 1929 there were three attempts at military rebellion which were struck down by the federal government. Upon the elimination of each of them, the government gained increasing strength.

President Plutarco Elías Calles (1924–1928) found that he was strong enough to face up to the rebellion of the Catholic church, which had not resigned itself to the tremendous limitations imposed upon it by the new Constitution. Between 1926 and 1929, the central part of the country suffered the consequences of a fierce religious war which ended in 1929 only after it had become apparent that the government could not replace the Catholic ecclesiastical structure with a new national Catholic church linked to the revolutionary regime, nor could the rebels aspire to destroy the new regime.[17] From the year 1929, a kind of *modus vivendi* began to take shape between the Catholic church and the state which, to a large extent, alienated the Catholic hierarchy from the political process. In this way, the state reaffirmed the dominant position it had gradually gained since the triumph of the Liberals, in 1867.

In 1928–1929 the new political system that had been born as a result of the revolution was put to a difficult test, from which it was to emerge greatly strengthened. In 1928, contrary to the fundamental principles of the revolutionary movement, General Obregón – the great *caudillo* (commander) of the era – managed to get the Constitution amended so as to allow him to be re-elected for the 1928–1934 term of office. Nevertheless, shortly after the elections he was assassinated by a religious militant. The disappearance of the most important *caudillo* figure enabled General Calles to re-establish the principle of non-reelection before he himself left office, as well as to begin to organize a government political party in which practically all the prominent personages of the times were included. Thus, the National Revolutionary Party (PNR) became the framework within which political life in Mexico was to develop from that time on; that was how the importance of the army as an essential political instrument came to decline.[18]

From its very beginnings, the PNR became *the* dominant party, and not just "another party." Its major role would not be to win elections, since its victory was assured, in advance, through legal and illegal channels. From that moment forward, its main function consisted of instilling a stern sense of discipline in the members of the revolutionary coalition (i.e. in the "revolutionary family," as it was then called) and of transforming itself into a machine for social mobilization and propaganda during election periods.

The programme of the PNR was, in essence, to implement the most progressive articles of the Constitution of 1917. Yet, during its first years in existence, the real actions taken in that sense were rather limited, because the party's leadership became quite conservative. The party was not very democratic on an internal level: there was much imposition from above, from its leaders, especially from General Calles who, despite the fact that he was no longer President of the country, continued to be the *factotum* of Mexican politics until the middle of 1935. He personally – and not the party's conventions – determined who was to fill the presidency, governorships, and seats in the legislative houses. Without a doubt, with the demise of the last *caudillo* of the revolution – namely, General Obregón – and the founding of the PNR, there was a concentration of power, but that concentration was in the hands of a single person, rather than an institution. This was because from 1929 to 1935, Calles (who could not become president again) refused to accept formal posts within the political structure. When he did so, he was prompted by specific circumstances and only remained there for a brief time. Basically, Calles' power was informal, although it was exceedingly real.

By the end of the 1920s, it was evident that the political system of the new regime had an essential feature in common with the old one – that is, the existence of democratic forms devoid of all content. In effect, at that point it was evident to all observers that the partisan opposition had absolutely no possibility of coming to power and that the separation of powers existed only to the extent that certain governors had a force of their own – be it military or social – capable of allowing them to negotiate with the central government, rather than due to a federal set-up that was truly in force. The same thing happened with the Congress: representatives and senators only wielded power to the degree that they represented strong governors. For its part, the Judicial Branch never had an opportunity to exercise its supposed independence.

The Culmination of the Process

In 1934 the official candidate to the presidency, General Lázaro Cárdenas, was victorious over an almost non-existent opposition. It was expected that his government would continue to be dominated by the figure of Calles, but towards the middle of 1935, with the support of the army on the one hand and of the workers' organizations on the other, Cárdenas wrested informal power from Calles and embarked upon a rapid and remarkable process whereby power became concentrated in the presidency.

Once Calles had been eliminated as a political factor in the latter part of 1934, General Cárdenas placed himself at the forefront of a drive to organize the masses of peasants and urban workers. In order to achieve this goal in the countryside, Cárdenas proceeded to carry out a land reform that virtually did away with the haciendas. In his six-year term of office (from 1934 to 1940), he distributed twice as much land as all his predecessors combined, starting with Venustiano Carranza. And along with land, he handed over arms to the peasants, uniting them in the first real national agrarian organization, the National Peasant Confederation (CNC), whose leaders were unconditional supporters of the President.

Parallel to the political transformations occurring in the Mexican countryside, another similar process took place among urban labourers. In that sector there were already several federations contending for control of the workers, but as the result of an alliance forged between the President and union leaders in the heat of the conflict with Calles, the Mexican Workers' Federation (CTM) was established.

This organization sought to group together all existing unions and, at the same time, step up the process of unionization among a great mass of labourers and employees who still were not organized at all. Therefore, the CTM had the full support of the state and embarked upon a process of organization and strikes, the apogee of which was the strike of the recently established National Union of Oil Workers, culminating in the expropriation of that industry in March 1938. The strikes and joint contracts negotiated by the unions – with Cárdenas as a benevolent onlooker – resulted in a material improvement of the conditions of the organized working class in exchange for which the workers supported presidential policies, albeit with a slightly greater degree of autonomy than that enjoyed by the peasant sector.

In 1938, Cárdenas not only consolidated the nationalism of the revolution through the expropriation of the country's petroleum resources, but also modified the internal structure of the PNR so as to provide for the changes made in the organization of labourers and peasants. The official party was transformed into the Party of the Mexican Revolution (PRM), which would no longer be organized on the basis of individual affiliation but, rather, by means of its sectors. The four basic sectors were peasants, labourers, the military, and the popular sector (which was, essentially, members of the governmental bureaucracy). With this corporative structure – a product of Cárdenas' policy favouring the masses – the presidency acquired even greater power than it had enjoyed under Porfirio Díaz. Yet, unlike the old regime, this power was centred in the presidency rather than in the person of the President, as was clearly apparent in 1940, when Cárdenas left the leadership of the country in the hands of his successor, General Manuel Avila Camacho, without attempting to get himself re-elected, as Obregón had done, or trying to wield power "from behind the throne" like Calles.[19]

The elections held in 1940 were very violent. The opposition to the official party and to its populist policies (the PRM proposed to build a democracy of the workers) not only originated in the old counter-revolutionary sectors, but also in the very heart of the group in power. The right wing of the revolution abandoned the PRM and lent its support to the candidacy of General Juan

Andrew Almazán. However, both the President and the PRM overpowered their adversary using every means at their disposal, including force. The important thing is that once the elections were over, the opposing coalition simply disbanded, and once again the official party remained without a single adversary.[20] In December 1940, the new president – General Manuel Avila Camacho – ordered the military sector within the PRM to be disbanded. In order to guarantee its existence, the authoritarianism of the revolution no longer needed the army, or at least not in the way it had used it in the past; the organizations of the masses were to be its true basis of support.

By 1940, all the major components of the current political system were already in place. Unlike the old regime, which was a product of the triumph of Liberalism, the new regime that had arisen as a result of the Mexican Revolution had wide social foundations, and was willing to include in the coalition all the major social forces that economic change would fashion in the future. The concentration of power was just as appreciable as under the dictatorship of Porfirio Díaz, yet this time the centre of power was no longer personalized, but rather institutionalized in the presidency, and the holder of that office had no chance of being re-elected. Therefore the turnover, every six years, of part of the political élite was also institutionalized.

With this more diversified and institutionalized power structure, based to a greater degree on participation by the diverse sectors of society than the one that had prevailed until 1910, the country entered a stage of economic growth such as it had not experienced since the beginning of the revolution. This growth was soon to change the traditional agrarian nature of Mexican society.

Notes

1. To this effect, cf. Daniel Lerner and James Coleman, "Modernization."
2. Regarding the process of elaborating the Constitution and the spirit of its authors, see Francisco Zarco, *Historia del congresco extraordinario constituyente de 1856–1957* (Talleres de "La Ciencia Jurídica," Mexico City, 1898–1901).
3. The classical study concerning Mexican social organization in the nineteenth century is the one by Andrés Molina Enríquez: *Los grandes problemas nacionales* (Imprenta de A. Carranza e Hijos, Mexico City, 1909).
4. See John Coatsworth, "Obstacles to Economic Growth in Nineteenth-century Mexico" *American Historical Review*, vol. 83, no. 1 (1978), p. 82.
5. On this point, besides the above-mentioned work by Coatsworth, the reader may consult Ciro Cardoso et al., *México en el siglo XIX (1821 a 1910). Historia económica y de la estructura social* (Nueva Imagen, Mexico City, 1980). See also the pertinent section in Leopoldo Solís, *La realidad económica mexicana. Retrovisión y perspectivas* (Siglo XXI, Mexico City, 1970).
6. For a notion as to the average Mexican's way of life during that era, see Luis

González et al., in Daniel Cosío Villegas, ed., *Historia moderna de México. La República Restaurada. La vida social* (Editorial Hermes, Mexico City, 1957).

7. This is the conclusion reached by Justo Sierra in his work entitled *La evolución política del pueblo mexicano* (Fondo de Cultura Económica, Mexico City, 1950).
8. For a detailed account of political processes during the regimes of Benito Juárez and Porfirio Díaz, see the volumes on Mexican domestic political life in: Daniel Cosío Villegas, *Historia moderna de México* (Editorial Hermes, Mexico City, 1955, 1970, and 1972).
9. A case exemplifying this regional power can be found in the figure of Luis Terrazas, a "bigwig" in the State of Chihuahua; in this regard, see José Fuentes Mares, *Y México se refugió en el desierto: Luis Terrazas, historia y destino* (Editorial Jus, Mexico City, 1954).
10. For an account and analysis of the economy during Porfirio Díaz's regime, see Daniel Cosío Villegas, ed., *Historia moderna en México. El Porfiriato. La vida económica*, 2 vols. (Editorial Hermes, Mexico City, 1965). For these statistical figures, see El Colegio de México, *Estadísticas económicas del Porfiriato* (El Colegio de México, Mexico City, 1960).
11. See Moisés González Navarro, *Estadísticas sociales del Porfiriato, 1887–1910* (Dirección General de Estadística, Mexico City, 1956), pp. 40–41; also Jesús Silva Herzog, *El agrarismo mexicano y la reforma agraria. Exposición y crítica* (Fondo de Cultura Económica, Mexico City, 1966), p. 502.
12. Literally, the "scientists," the group of officials who surrounded President Porfirio Díaz and made up the "inner cabinet" of his government. The *científicos* were greatly influenced by the positivist philosophy of Auguste Comte and believed that Mexico could progress fastest by the use of scientific methods.
13. Some of the studies underlining most clearly the nature of leadership and its regional variations are, *inter alia*: James Cockroft, *Intellectual Precursors of the Mexican Revolution, 1900–1913* (University of Texas Press, Austin, 1968); John Womack, Jr., *Zapata and the Mexican Revolution* (Alfred A. Knopf, New York, 1968); Héctor Aguilar Camín, *La frontera nómada. Sonora y la Revolución Mexicana* (Siglo XXI, Mexico City, 1977); Romana Falcón, *Revolución y caciquismo. San Luis Potosí 1910–1938* (El Colegio de Mexico, Mexico City, 1984); and Frans Schryer, *The Rancheros of Pisaflores. The History of a Peasant Bourgeoisie in Twentieth Century Mexico* (University of Toronto Press, Toronto, 1980).
14. For a concise analysis of the forces that shaped the Constitution of 1917, as well as their importance and implications, see Charles C. Cumberland, *Mexican Revolution: The Constitutionalist Years* (University of Texas Press, Austin, 1972); also Eberhardt V. Niemeyer, *Revolution at Queretaro: The Mexican Constitutional Convention of 1916–1917* (University of Texas Press, Austin, 1974).
15. For an example of this form of rule by caciques, see Romana Falcón (note 13 above).
16. Followers of Emiliano Zapata, one of the major leaders of the Mexican Revolution.
17. On this point, see the work by Jean Meyer entitled *La cristiada*, 3 vols. (Siglo XXI, Mexico City, 1973).
18. For more on this topic, See Alejandra Lajous, *Los orígenes del partido único en México* (Universidad Nacional Autónoma de Mexico, Mexico City, 1979).
19. An analysis of the nature of Cardenism can be found in Arnaldo Córdova, *La política de masas del cardenismo* (Editorial Era, Mexico City, 1974).
20. See Albert L. Michaels, "Las elecciones de 1940," in *Historia mexicana*, vol. 21 (1971), pp. 80–134.

CONFLICT THREATENING MEXICO'S SOVEREIGNTY: THE CONTINUING CRISIS (1867–1940)

Berta Ulloa
El Colegio de México, Mexico City, Mexico

Introduction

The purpose of this paper is to present a summary of the long struggle in which Mexico was engaged with its powerful neighbour to the north from 1867 to 1940 in order to defend its sovereignty. In this struggle, Mexico's successive governments relied primarily upon legal means allied to their own tenacity and perseverance; only twice in the twentieth century did the country have to take up arms in order to meet force with force, and this was during the invasions of Mexican territory ordered by President Woodrow Wilson.

In 1867, Benito Juárez put forward the international policy he proposed to follow and which, until 1888, was observed by all the presidents who came after him. With regard to Europe, this policy was negative and passive; it prolonged Mexico's state of isolation and reinforced its dependence upon the United States, the only country with which it had official relations until 1876, when Porfirio Díaz gained power. For that reason, and because of its proximity and growing power, the United States was able to put pressure on Mexico, particularly with regard to claims for damages caused to US citizens and their investments, many of which stemmed from the treaties of Guadalupe Hidalgo and La Mesilla and the forced loans that the different factions demanded of them in civil conflicts. Mexico defended itself by diplomatic means, by the creation of mixed commissions, by appealing to international arbitration, and when it felt that the decisions were unjust, it attempted to have the cases reconsidered, sometimes successfully. One of the objectives of the United States was the annexation of Mexican lands; this it tried to carry out under the pretence of crossing the border in pursuit of Indians and cattle thieves. In order to put a stop to this, Mexico presented a draft treaty in 1877 which was signed the following year, and renewed annually on several occasions. According to the treaty, powers were granted to the presidents of both countries to authorize the reciprocal passage of troops for the purpose of pursuing wild Indians and cattle thieves; the time limit and places authorized were determined, as well as the permitted extent of entry into the other country; it was prohibited to go into populated areas or into zones in which forces were stationed. In addition, the two governments promised to punish their respective troops in the event of any abuses, and to respect the territorial rights of the other country.

On the other hand, the Liberals of 1867 had blind faith in the power of modern means of communication and transportation to ensure peace, promote the settlement of uninhabited areas, and increase prosperity, and they proposed to attract foreign capital, be it through loans or investments, with no regard for the dependence that such an action would produce. Thus, they granted special concessions with lower tax rates, effected legislative modifications, and conducted sales at ridiculously low or fictitious prices, all of which was eventually to provoke pro-nationalist and anti-Yankee sentiment. Porfirio Díaz, at the end of his regime, attempted to counterbalance this dependence upon the United States, taking measures that were not well received by the US government, such as the cancellation of permits for the US Navy in Bahía Magdalena, the reduction of the volume of water supplied from the Nazas River to the Tlahualilo Company, the creation of the company Ferrocarriles Nacionales de México (National Railways of Mexico) in which the Mexican government had a 50 per cent share of the total investment, the tax-exempt concession granted to the Englishman Pearson to find oil, and a contract to run the Tehuantepec Railroad Company. When the 1910 Revolution began, the most serious problems could be attributed to three main causes: the seditious activities of the political emigrés who influenced the inhabitants of Mexican origin in the southern US; the lack of security of Americans and their interests within Mexican borders; and the armed struggle between Mexicans near the dividing line, which gave rise to serious threats and the mobilization of US troops. These factors contributed to Porfirio Díaz's resignation and to Madero's order that the siege of Ciudad Juárez be lifted in order to avoid an armed invasion of Mexico. This threat subsisted in 1912 and 1913, promoted by Ambassador Henry Lane Wilson.

Venustiano Carranza rebelled against the usurper Victoriano Huerta in February 1913, and obtained the unconditional surrender of his regime in August 1914. It was Carranza's firm and resolute attitude in defence of Mexico's sovereignty that prevented the direction of Mexico's internal affairs from falling into the hands of the United States. Carranza also passed nationalist decrees regarding foreign properties and investments; proclaimed the Constitution of 1917, which affected foreign interests; and resisted all kinds of threats from the United States aimed at making him modify it. He also managed to get the two armed invasions that Wilson had ordered in 1914 and 1916 withdrawn from Mexican territory without any conditions or commitments on the part of Mexico, and de facto and de jure recognition for his government in 1915 and 1917, respectively. To all of the above, we must add that Carranza was very clever in his handling of the possibility of an alliance with Germany during the First World War, keeping the United States on the watch until 13 April 1917, when he declared officially that Mexico would remain neutral in the war. Almost a year later, on 1 January 1918, he put forward the doctrine which bears his name and which embodies the fundamental principles of Mexico's foreign policy: the equality of nations, mutual respect, and non-intervention. In short, when his term of government ended in 1920, an enormous nationalist force had been awakened, giving substance, for the first time, to the idea of the Mexican nation.

The presidents of Mexico who succeeded Carranza continued to face grave problems with the United States, ranging from the recognition of the government of Alvaro Obregón, which in 1920 was linked to the signing of an agreement for safeguarding the acquired rights of US citizens (affected by the Constitution of 1917), to the excessive protection of US interests, involving the constant threat of armed intervention, the blocking of markets, and economic blockades, originating with the expropriation of oil decreed by Lázaro Cárdenas in 1938. Obregón attained diplomatic recognition on 31 August 1923, after the Bucareli Agreements according to which Americans kept all rights acquired before 1917, but he obtained the said recognition without modifying the Constitution or signing a single treaty, since these agreements did not have the status of an international instrument. In addition, the texts of the claims conventions were approved. Previously, in 1922, an agreement had also been reached with the International Committee of Bankers whereby Mexico acknowledged a debt of nearly $600 million.

With Plutarco Elias Calles, the most serious problems arose from the fact that between 1925 and 1926, in accordance with the Constitution of 1917, legislation went into effect regarding hydrocarbons and the law regulating this matter, whereby it was stipulated that title deeds came to be mere concessions of the government, subject to confirmation for 50 years, and the "positive act" principle was enacted (this referred to those lands on which a "positive act" had been carried out, that is, on which some drilling or other kind of activity had demonstrated the owner's intention to extract oil prior to 1 May 1917); a term of one year was given in order not to lose those rights. The oil men refused to comply with the law and, with the support of US Ambassador Sheffield, demanded the armed invasion of Mexico. Calles found himself obliged to modify oil legislation in the sense that the perpetuity of acquired rights was acknowledged and that the rights of these companies would not be affected because they had refused to comply with the law of 1925, unless at some future time they were to fail to obey the new laws. In response, the Department of State informed the oil men that they should no longer deal with their problems through diplomatic channels, but rather take them to the Mexican courts. A new agreement on the debt was reached with the International Committee of Bankers in October 1925, and Mexico made its first payment the following year. In the period known as the "Maximato" – during which Calles continued to govern although he was no longer the President of Mexico – no further attempts were made to affect the rights acquired by the oil men and confirmatory concessions continued to be granted. Nevertheless, the level of production of hydrocarbons which had been established years before continued to drop. As a result, the Mexican government experienced a decrease in its revenues, and consequently suspended the payment of its debt to the International Committee of Bankers in 1930. Later a new agreement was negotiated, but once again in 1931 payment was postponed for another two years and, in 1932, indefinitely. Although an analysis of the claims derived from the Bucareli Agreements was begun immediately, owing to the greater number of such claims, the Commissions did not pronounce their verdicts until 1934.

During the presidential term of Lázaro Cárdenas, a new crisis with the United States began to develop; this arose from the fact that, in 1936, the Mexican Congress passed a law allowing for the expropriation of any property by reason of public utility, postponing the corresponding indemnification for up to ten years. Added to this was the strike called by the Union of Oil Workers of Mexico in May 1937, with demands for salary increments and various fringe benefits. The foreign companies refused to pay the sums requested of them. After conducting a study on the oil companies, the Mexican government determined that they should pay more than a third of the amount requested by the workers, and that their policies and actions ran counter to the national interest. The companies went to the Mexican courts, and the Mexican Supreme Court (Suprema Corte de Justicia) decided against them on 1 March 1938, giving them a time limit of seven days to comply with the orders of the Mexican authorities. The companies agreed to pay what had been stipulated, so long as the Mexican government accepted their conditions concerning future labour laws. As a result, Cárdenas decreed the expropriation of the oil companies because of their rebellious attitude in the face of the decisions reached by the judiciary of a sovereign country. Expropriation was the high point of the nationalism arising from the Mexican Revolution and was backed by the entire population. National unity was a reality.

Still pending was the solution of the problem of how to pay off the oil companies. The government resolved that this should be done in accordance with the law of 1936, and preferably with oil, but the companies rejected this decision, with the support of the United Kingdom. Insofar as the US authorities were concerned, Franklin D. Roosevelt accepted the fact that Mexico had the right to expropriate oil, but demanded immediate and suitable indemnification, and the Department of State increased its diplomatic and economic pressures on Mexico, cutting off its silver and oil markets, and refusing to provide equipment and assistance to the new government enterprise Petróleos Mexicanos. When almost all was lost, the Sinclair Oil Company broke away from the united front formed by the foreign companies, and negotiated with Cárdenas. Thus, in May 1941, when Manuel Avila Camacho had already taken office as president of the country, Mexico signed an agreement whereby it promised to pay $8.5 million in three years, part in cash and part in oil, at a price lower than the market price.

For this paper, we analysed published works dealing with Mexico's international relations and included findings obtained previously in Mexican and foreign archives, complemented by personal reflections.

A Long History of Troubled Co-existence

With the triumph of the Liberal Party headed by Benito Juárez over the Conservatives, the French Intervention, and Maximilian's empire in June 1867, the republican form of government was re-established and the seeds of modernization and nationalism sown. Between 1867 and 1911 Liberals occupied the presidency; first two civilians, Benito Juárez (1867–1872) and Sebastián Lerdo de Tejada (1872–1876), and then two army men, Porfirio Díaz (1876–1880, 1884–1911) and Manuel González (1880–1884). All of them had three basic goals: re-establish order, meaning peace, concord, law, and a systematic government organization; political liberty, freedom of work, expression, and the market-place; and continuous material progress. Political life was governed by the Constitution of 1857 and in varying degrees the country was pacified and the public treasury revitalized. The two civilian presidents tended to weaken the army, but in the end it triumphed with Porfirio Díaz and Manuel González. In the social sphere, efforts were made to attract foreign immigration, to create small landholdings, and to assure freedom of assembly and of work. In the economic sphere, railways were constructed, foreign capital was brought in, new crops and farming methods were tried out, manufacturing was developed, and Mexico managed to become an international bridge, both between Europe and the Far East and between the United States and South America. On the international level, Mexico battled continually to defend its national sovereignty in the face of United States encroachments.[1]

Juárez developed, and then made public on 8 December, 1867, the foreign policy Mexico proposed to follow; this was put into practice by his government and faithfully followed by Lerdo de Tejada, by Porfirio Díaz during his first presidential period, and by Manuel González during the first three years of his administration. In 1884 it was modified, and Díaz almost completely abandoned it in 1888, but Juárez's foreign policy survived intact the first dozen years of the Porfiriato.[2] With respect to the European powers, Juárez pointed out in 1867 that it was they who had broken off diplomatic relations with Mexico, some of them had made war on her, and the rest had not recognized the republic but rather the spurious regime of Maximilian. Mexico, continued Juárez, did not refuse to re-establish relations, but would do so only when three requirements were met: when the powers showed a sincere desire to do so, when they agreed to terminate all treaties and conventions in force before the Intervention, and when those that replaced them were negotiated on a "just and convenient" basis. This negative and passive policy, according to Daniel Cosío Villegas, prolonged Mexico's international isolation and reinforced its dependence on the United States, the only country with which Mexico maintained official relations until Porfirio Díaz took over in 1876.[3]

Problems with the United States began to develop before the republic triumphed over its enemies, for on 26 March 1867 the United States warned of the possibility of war if Mexico did not sign a treaty agreeing to pay claims for damages caused to US citizens and their interests during the French Intervention and to repay forced loans required of US citizens.[4] Mexico protected herself against this threat by signing a convention on 4 July 1868 and another in August 1869 which created the Mixed Claims Commission, to examine claims pending since the Treaty of Guadalupe Hidalgo of 2 February 1848 and the above-mentioned forced loans. The commission was composed of a member from each country and an arbiter who would intervene in the case of a deadlock. It functioned from August 1869 until 20 November 1877, with interruptions in 1871, 1873, and 1876; 2,075 claims, of which 998 were Mexican and 1,077 from the US, were examined; 167 Mexican and 186 US claims were accepted. Mexico was required to pay 4,125,662.22 pesos and only received 158,498.42 pesos. More than a third of the Mexican claims, the most important ones, derived from non-compliance with obligations incurred by the United States in Article XIV of the Treaty of Guadalupe Hidalgo; it was argued that the claims were beyond the scope of the commission's jurisdiction, or that damages had been done by private parties and not government authorities, or that Article II of the Gadsden Treaty of 1853 relieved the country of those obligations. Mexico specified that these responsibilities had been cancelled from the date of signing but had no effect on the claims pending between 1848 and 1853. The disagreement between the commissioners led to suspension of the talks in 1873 and in order that they should be resumed Lerdo de Tejada yielded, accepting both the resignation of the Mexican commissioner who had opposed the United States attitude and the US contention that it was not responsible for filibuster attacks. However, Lerdo did win one victory: claims for 320 million pesos presented by various concessionaries of the Tehuantepec Railroad were declared unacceptable.

The Mixed Claims Commission sent some cases for arbitration, but several verdicts were so unjust that Mexico later managed to have them reconsidered and payments already made were returned, as in the case of Benjamin Weil's embargoed cotton (almost 335,000 pesos) and the mining company La Abra of Sinaloa, which had stopped work because of high costs and abandoned its machinery (600,000 pesos). The most important of unjust verdicts was the Pious Fund of the Californias, which the Jesuits had set up during the colonial period in order to maintain their missions; once the secularized wealth of the clergy had been turned over to the Mexican government, it agreed to pay 6 per cent annual interest. In 1886 the diocese of Alta California claimed two-thirds of the interest that had not been paid since 1842; Mexico argued in its defence that Articles XIII, XIV, and XX of the Treaty of Guadalupe Hidalgo cancelled all US claims and debts and that the United States should have paid the interest with the money that it had retained for this purpose. Mexico also argued that the decree of 1842 concerning the 6 per cent interest had not been satisfied by the Mexican National Congress, that the province of California had ceased to exist as such when it became a bishopric, and that, as the property claimed was within Mexican territory, the case would have to be tried in Mexican courts. The arbiter was the British minister in Washington, Edward Thornton, and, in spite of the evidence, he decided that Mexico should pay 904,070.79 pesos, plus interest at 6 per cent. The legality and tenacity with which Mexico defended these three cases later led to appeals and a favourable sentence was obtained in the La Abra and Weil cases in 1889. Mexican sovereignty over the guano islands of Yucatán was recognized in 1886 and over the Isla de la Pasión in the Pacific in 1897; the Pious Fund of the Californias would have to wait until 1967.[5]

The international controversy over the territory to the south of the Bravo River, El Chamizal, which both Mexico and the United States claimed, was reviewed in three ways: diplomatically; by the International Border Commission in 1889; and by an arbitration court. El Chamizal physically and legally belonged to Mexico and was recognized as such by the United States in 1852, when the Emory-Salazar line was drawn; it continued to be Mexican when both the Treaties of Guadalupe Hidalgo and the Gadsden Purchase went into effect (1848 and 1853). However, with time the bed of the Bravo River began moving south in two ways: one was gradual, because of the slow erosion of the right bank and alluvion deposits on the left, and the other was due to flash floods that took place in 1864 and 1868, with considerable river-bed changes that made the territory of El Chamizal lie within the United States.[6] Texan authorities started exercising jurisdiction over El Chamizal from 1864 and Benito Juárez protested on 5 December 1866, but the government of the United States claimed that the dividing line between both countries was still the Bravo River. Although Mexico in 1884 accepted that the dividing line was the middle of the river bed, it specified that this should be the case only when changes in the river's course were slow and gradual, not when it overflowed its banks or when a new bed was carved out. Mexico finally had its rights recognized in 1962.

To this problem was added that of water distribution of the border Bravo and Gila rivers, which the United States was using in ways detrimental to Mexico. The repeated complaints of the Mexican government only achieved in response a suggestion from the United States that an international dam be constructed near El Paso, Texas, to be administered by the United States, in order to distribute fairly water between the two countries. In 1894 the Mexican government demanded $35 million for the unwarranted use of the water, based on a study made by lawyers Ignacio L. Vallarta and José María Mata: they argued that a state bordering a river that was higher topographically could not build installations that would affect a bordering but lower state, and that installations already begun should be destroyed and the construction of new ones prohibited. The International Border Commission decided in favour of Mexico on 25 November 1896 and recommended that a treaty be signed. However, the opposing opinion of the Attorney-General of the United States, Judson Harmon, prevailed; from 1896 on he insisted that Article VII of the Treaty of Guadalupe Hidalgo referred exclusively to the international part of the two rivers but not to their national one, so that Americans could construct irrigation systems in their own territory. Mexico was forced to sign a convention on 21 May 1906 which legalized the *fait accompli*.

Another border problem that also resulted from the Treaty of Guadalupe Hidalgo was the fact that the new dividing line was placed near the populated part of Mexico, creating new human settlements on both banks and increasing commercial exchange. In 1852 Mexico established a free tax zone for European products in Tamaulipas in order to aid that region. The United States protested that since 1868 those articles had entered their country as contraband and asked the Mexican government to abolish the free zone. Although Juárez was willing, because European goods were also contrabanded into the interior and damaged local economies, the Mexican National Congress not only refused to abolish the free zone but in 1870 had it include Coahuila, Nuevo León, and Chihuahua, which only increased international tensions.[7]

From the time of the restoration of the republic, the most serious border problems were the tribes of warring Indians that killed, destroyed, burned, and stole cattle in Sonora, Chihuahua, Nuevo León, Coahuila, and Tamaulipas. These raids also took place on the other side of the dividing line and provoked violent reactions on the part of the United States government, which wanted permission for its troops to cross the border in order to pursue and punish the thieves. Juárez's government did not accept this, but ordered a strict watch to be kept over the Mexican side and prohibited the bringing in of booty captured in the United States. The governments of the two countries named commissions to investigate the situation. Mexico's were called *pesquisadores*; one was set up in the north-east and another in the north-west, and these reported between 1872 and 1874 that Indians from the United States had stolen 200,000 head of cattle and murdered numerous people, with the help of Texas bandits and marauding Indians from the Mexican side; they found that Americans were protecting them, both officials and buyers of stolen cattle; that the US side was the one that suffered least but exaggerated its damages in order to justify possible annexations of Mexican territory. The Mexican commissions suggested that both governments safeguard the border of their respective territories, that the extradition treaty be reformed, or that cattle rustling laws be modified.

The United States government never ceased pressuring Mexico to solve the problem. The Texas legislature in 1875 named a committee to investigate lack of security along the border and turned in a report very unfavourable to Mexico. To this was added a series of attacks on the outskirts of Corpus Christi which were attributed to men from the Mexican side, thus aggravating existing tensions. The Mexican government found that the report presented by the authorities of Tampico on the Corpus Christi attack was very different and that the evidence, which Americans themselves had gathered, showed that almost all the dead were Mexicans and theirs were the ranches burned. The United States did not accept its own evidence and insisted that its forces cross the border and occupy the Mexican part of the Bravo River. The federal government of Mexico denied permission for this, but the state authorities of Chihuahua and Sonora accepted crossings when the immediate apprehension of outlaws was necessary.[8]

Relations between Mexico and the United States became more tense in 1876, both because of the seditious activities in Texas of Porfirio Díaz and his followers – Díaz was fighting the re-election of Sebastián Lerdo de Tejada, who had assumed the presidency after Juárez's death in 1872 – and because of fighting among Mexicans close to the border that caused damage on the US side. Díaz finally took Matamoros in April and in September declared null and void the contracts that were "a burden to the nation," since Lerdo had authorized a series of concessions, especially for railways, to foreigners. Díaz's declaration was a double-edged sword, for he won popular Mexican support but the enmity of the United States.

Porfirio Díaz declared himself provisional president in November 1876, and faced the first of two great crises with the United States (at the beginning and the end of his long administration). In 1876 the two great problems with Mexico's neighbour to the north were the state of unrest along the border and the discredit which Mexico had brought on itself through its internal disturbances and its incapacity to pay its debts. Díaz decided to solve both, beginning with the restoration of order and with making, in the same month of November, the first annual payment that the Mixed Claims Commission had fixed at 300,000 pesos. This amount was obtained through forced loans to merchants and industrialists, and an extraordinary tax. The United States minister in Mexico, John W. Foster, in spite of the lack of relations, made diplomatic recognition of the new government conditional on the arrangement of all pending business, especially banditry along the border; the Secretary of Foreign Affairs, Ignacio L. Vallarta, replied that a government's right to recognition could not be conditioned, and that as long as Díaz did not receive recognition, pending business would not be discussed. As far as border conditions were concerned, they did not improve, even though Díaz designated General Jerónimo Treviño chief of the armed forces in the north-east zone, which were continually reinforced. However, the US press demanded the establishment of a protectorate over Mexico.[9]

Díaz took possession of the constitutional presidency in May 1877, and was recognized by several European powers, but the United States government not only did not recognize him but on 1 June 1877 ordered General Ord to put an end to border unrest, crossing the border whenever necessary to pursue and punish guilty parties and recuperate stolen goods. This decision caused indignation in Mexico and strengthened Díaz's image as defender of national sovereignty, especially as he ordered General Treviño to meet force with force and had his minister in Washington, Ignacio L. Mariscal, present a note of protest to the State Department. This argued that Ord's orders had been given to force the Mexican government into action and to satisfy United States public opinion. It was also suggested through Foster that an agreement be signed concerning the reciprocal crossing of troops for all border problems: Indian raids, cattle rustling, the free zone, and the prohibition on foreigners owning real estate in that zone. His old insistence that foreigners be excluded from forced loans in the entire republic was repeated. Although the Secretary of Foreign Affairs, Ignacio L. Vallarta, made a counter-proposal drawn up by José María Mata concerning the reciprocal crossing of troops, he clarified the point that no treaty would be signed without previous recognition of Díaz's government.

The US press continued to stir up trouble. The *New York Times*, on 17 July 1877, clamoured for the annexation of the peninsula of Baja California and the states of Sonora, Sinaloa, Durango, Chihuahua, Coahuila, and part of Nuevo León, to the consequent indignation of the Mexican public. Under these conditions, Vallarta presented Foster with a draft for a treaty on 10 September in which authority was given to the presidents of both countries for drawing up agreements that would permit the reciprocal crossing of troops in pursuit of raiding Indians and cattle rustlers, and for determining the duration of the treaty and the designated crossing-places; 20 leagues would be the maximum distance allowed and troops could not enter population centres or cross the border if local soldiers or police were able to continue the pursuit; both governments agreed to punish abuses by their troops and respect the territorial rights of the other.[10]

The border problem would take years to resolve. In the meantime, Porfirio Díaz stimulated interest in US investors through his confidential agent in Washington, Manuel de Zamacona. This was a success, and railway and industrial businessmen managed to get the United States Congress to investigate the "Mexican Case" in committee, with the conclusion that the problems were due basically to the frankly hostile attitude of the Secretary of State towards Mexico. Consequentially the Díaz government was recognized on 9 April 1878, and Minister Phillip H. Morgan arrived on the 15th with instructions to foster good relations and protect the interests of his fellow citizens.

In spite of the recognition, the order of 1 June 1877 for crossing the border was not revoked and the US press continued to clamour for the establishment of a protectorate over Mexico. Many difficulties remained, especially the matters of forced loans that Mexicans had demanded of Americans during armed rebellions, the free zone in the north of Mexico, and unrest along the border. The first presidential term of Díaz finished without allowing the crossing of US troops.

During the presidency of Manuel González, Indian raids increased on both sides of the border. After much controversy an agreement was reached on 29 July 1882, and a treaty was signed, to be effective for one year; it was renewed in 1883 and 1884, as well as other years during the successive presidencies of Porfirio Díaz (1885, 1886, 1890, and 1899), always at the request of the United States government and with the limitations that Vallarta had imposed in the proposal of 1877. Stable relations with the United States were gradually achieved once other basic problems had been solved: when Porfirian peace became widespread and permanent, the problem of forced loans disappeared, and the free zone became smaller as US industry produced higher-quality goods at prices similar to European ones and United States railways brought them cheaply and regularly to the border. Local leaders, whose indifference or complicity had been an obstacle to the efficient and continuous pursuit of raiding Indians and cattle rustlers, fell under the watchful eye of the federal authorities; also, other local leaders arose whose interests coincided with the establishment of peace and order. The north was populated with people from the interior, accustomed to more stable employment, and communications in general improved.

Important and rapid changes were taking place in the United States. The migratory wave reached the west and left behind a stable agricultural population; Indians and cattle rustling disappeared with the spread of barbed-wire fences; ranching was now practised in a civilized manner and on a small scale; state–federal government relations improved, and Texas's immediate relations with Mexico were no longer so important.

Finally, another change affected both countries; wariness of the Colossus of the North gave way to the urgencies of economic progress and the inevitable conviction that this could only take place with foreign capital.[11]

The Liberals of 1867 had unlimited confidence in the power of modern means of communication and transport for obtaining peace, population growth, and wealth. Facing a lack of national capital, they proposed attracting foreign capital, as loans or investments, without thinking about the economic dependency this would create. The attempt failed on the restoration of the republic because the bellicose spirit of the preceding 60 years was still present, and was moreover aggravated by insecurity and unhealthy conditions, by Mexico's external debt and the fact that its foreign relations were limited to the United States only. Its investors, along with the British and the French, did not see a secure or promising environment. Concessions had started to be made during Juárez's presidency, and had increased during Lerdo de Tejada's, especially in railways; during the Porfirian period they multiplied considerably, thanks to decreased taxes, legislative modifications, concessions, fictitious or ridiculously low prices, etc. This would eventually provoke anti-Yankee and pro-nationalistic feelings.[12]

Towards the end of the Porfirian period problems with the United States were of two kinds: internal measures taken by the Mexican government and the clash over its Central American policies. As far as the first is concerned, the controversy about El Chamizal stands out; other contentious issues included the cancellation of permits given in 1877 so that the US navy could carry out military manoeuvres and install coal refuelling stations in Bahía Magdalena; the decision of the Mexican Supreme Court to decrease the volume of water of the Nazas River to the Tlahualilo Company for the irrigation of its fields; the creation of Ferrocarriles Nacionales de México (National Railroads of Mexico) in 1906, in which the Mexican government invested 230 million pesos out of a total investment of 460 million; the concession to exempt from taxes Mr. Pearson, an Englishman who was looking for petroleum deposits on national lands and had the contract to administer the Tehuantepec Railroad; and the arming of the Isthmus of Tehuantepec. Because of their differences of opinion concerning Central America, Díaz refused to cooperate with the United States in 1907 in order to guarantee peace in that region, and in 1909 he sent a ship to take into exile the President of Nicaragua, José Santos Zelaya, thrown out of office by an armed rebellion supported by the United States. None of these problems was very serious. The most severe of the entire Porfirian period began in 1910 with the seditious activities of Mexican political emigrés who disliked Díaz, for instance the Floresmagonistas and the Maderistas, with their hostile publications, contraband weapons, enlistments, and organization of expeditions. The feelings of hatred aroused infected Texan and Californian populations of Mexican origin, who threw their support behind the revolution as though Mexico were still their native country.[13]

When armed rebellion broke out, relations with the United States became tenser because of two concerns: the security of foreigners and of their investments in the interior of the country and the battles taking place among Mexicans in northern border towns. The governments of the great powers in 1910 were sure that Porfirio Díaz would wipe out the rebels with one blow, but a few months later they began to have doubts and in March 1911 they lost confidence in his regime and considered that their nationals, with their large investments in mines, railways, petroleum, plantations, etc, were in danger. The US ambassador, Henry Lane Wilson, contributed a great deal to creating this impression, and on 7 March 1911 President William H. Taft ordered the mobilization of 20,000 soldiers and sent warships to the border and to Mexican ports on the pretext of carrying out military manoeuvres and refuelling. To this situation was added the fighting taking place among Mexicans in the border towns of Agua Prieta and Ciudad Juárez, with its very serious threat of United States armed intervention; this contributed to the resignation of Porfirio Díaz and Madero's orders to end the siege of Ciudad Juárez. With the signing of treaties on 22 May tensions lessened.

During the ambiguous government of Francisco León de la Barra and the short and nationalist one of Madero (November 1911 to February 1913) the problem of seditious activities in the southern United States again presented itself. Taft's administration was more inclined to aid than impede such activities, as can be seen from the cases of Bernardo Reyes and Emilio Vázquez Gómez. Difficulties increased when between January and March 1912 there was fighting again in Ciudad Juárez and a new mobilization of US troops along the border. The situation in the interior of the country was even more alarming, because of nationalistic revolutionary measures put into effect by the government and because the armed movements of rebel groups were exaggerated by Wilson, causing great concern in the United States. The ambassador felt an ever-increasing hatred towards Madero, whom he considered incapable of restoring law and order – indispensable for the prosperity of foreign firms – and of keeping the great powers from taking initiatives belonging to the sphere of influence of the United States. Between March and April 1912 his government ordered the 9,000 Americans who resided in Mexico to leave all dangerous zones. He blamed the government and the Mexican public for acts committed against his countrymen; in August more warships were sent and in September he accused the government of negligence in its investigation into the death of 17 Americans; he also protested against the 20 centavos a barrel tax on extracted petroleum, and the decision taken against the Tlahualilo Company and other decisions against US firms. The September note was really an ultimatum, in which the United States reserved the right to take measures that it considered adequate, questioning the sovereignty of Mexico and its capacity to comply with its basic obligations.[14]

Madero's overthrow in February 1913, plotted by counter-revolutionaries

Félix Díaz and Bernardo Reyes, and helped by the treachery of Huerta and the complicity of Henry Lane Wilson, with few exceptions satisfied the diplomatic corps stationed in Mexico. During the first days of the Decena Trágica (the Tragic Ten Days), Wilson, as was his custom, exaggerated the seriousness of the situation and once more moved in troops and warships, with the ambassador expressly threatening armed intervention. Wilson contacted the counter-revolutionaries and convinced them to sign the so-called Pact of the Embassy, which put Huerta in power from February 1913 to July 1914. The usurping administration was recognized by the principal powers, but not by the United States, even at Wilson's insistence. He hoped that withholding recognition would force Mexico to accept US solutions to problems between the two countries.[15]

The problem of Huerta's recognition fell to the new US President Woodrow Wilson, who, with his "moralist" policies, condemned Madero's overthrow. This was an attitude not expected by the European powers, the ambassador, or foreign investors. The US President proposed to intervene in Mexican internal affairs, paying no attention to his ambassador and sending special agents instead. Using the most outstanding of them, John Lind, he put pressure on Huerta to resign, even trying bribery in August 1913, and, when unsuccessful, he exercised all his influence to prevent Mexico from obtaining European credit, especially British, in exchange for favourable treatment in the use of the Panama Canal and the protection of European interests in Mexico. Once European co-operation had been obtained by Mexico in spite of Wilson's efforts, the President decided on armed intervention: this took place at the port of Veracruz on 21 April 1914, without motive and without previous warning, causing a heavy toll among the population. The pretexts were two: the first was the brief detainment of the crew of the warship *Dolphin*, which disembarked without authorization in Tampico during an internal Mexican conflict, an issue that Rear-admiral Henry T. Mayo made into a *casus belli*: either the Huerta administration would publicly make amends and honour the United States flag or force would be used. The second pretext was the arrival of an arms shipment for Huerta aboard the German steamship *Ypiranga*. After the occupation of Veracruz, Wilson was trapped in a blind alley; he could not make Huerta resign and Mexico was provoked into strong feelings of resentment against the United States. Mexican public and world opinion was also adverse. In order to find a way out, a supposed arbitration took place by Argentina, Brazil and Chile, called the ABC countries; these met according to the whim of Wilson, who pushed them aside when they disagreed with him. Huerta agreed to participate in the conferences, which took place at Niagara Falls from 21 May to 30 June 1914, and in which Mexican internal affairs were discussed; almost no mention was made of the international incident and it was decided to adjourn until the Mexicans could arrange their own differences. The firm and decided attitude of Venustiano Carranza in defence of Mexico's national sovereignty prevented Wilson from running the internal affairs of the country.[16]

Huerta never had effective power over the entire country. The most important opposition group had taken up arms in defence of constitutional legality in February 1913, under the command of Venustiano Carranza, followed by the legislature of Sonora. In the south, independently of the aforementioned, the Zapatistas added their force to the anti-Huerta groups. The constitutionalists were invited to participate in the ABC conferences but did not accept because they had never recognized the right either of the mediators or of the United States to discuss the internal affairs of Mexico. The only point they were willing to negotiate was the international problem between Mexico and the United States, which arose because of the invasion of Veracruz, a situation that Carranza had energetically protested against from the beginning. The constitutionalists continued to oppose Huerta and their military victories finally forced the dictator to resign on 10 July 1914; a month later, with the treaties of Teoloyucan, his regime surrendered unconditionally. The same happened with the Americans, who finally left Veracruz on 23 November 1914, without imposing any conditions or obligations.

The revolutionary movement broke up into factions during the second half of 1914 and civil war spread all over the country; the economy entered a period of crisis, and there were famine and epidemics. The Zapatistas and the Villistas became allied in November 1914 during the Aguascalientes Convention, but each one would soon start looking after his own interests, the south and the north respectively. The Convention assembly was installed for a time in Mexico City, with three presidents who at times were in power simultaneously; Carranza fought them all and installed his administration in Veracruz. As Woodrow Wilson had not obtained satisfactory information about the existing situation, on 2 June 1915 he sent an ultimatum to local leaders; if they did not reach an agreement among themselves, the United States would take whatever means were necessary to "save" Mexico. In answer Carranza published a manifesto in which he blamed Wilson for obstructing his work, and the latter, who had promised to impose his solution to the Mexican problem, had to resort again to the ABC, now with Bolivia, Uruguay and Guatemala added, to mediate among the factions and establish a provisional government. Villa and Zapata accepted mediation but Carranza rejected it because it encroached upon the nation's sovereignty; he continued to fight until he had defeated the remaining Villista forces. The United States and the ABC countries finally recognized the de facto government of Carranza on 19 October 1915.[17]

Diplomatic recognition and its implications provoked Villa's ire, and he immediately attacked Wilson in a manifesto; to this was added the shooting of 16 American miners in Santa Isabel, Chihuahua, on 10 January 1916, and the attack on Columbus, New Mexico, on 9 March. United States forces crossed the border in pursuit of the attackers, abetted by a wave of indignation among the US government and public. Carranza ordered Villa's arrest and alerted Mexican generals along the border; he deplored the incident and suggested drawing up an accord similar to those of the nineteenth century, permitting the troops of both countries to cross the border in pursuit of bandits. He made it clear, however, that US troops could only enter Mexico if the right were reciprocal. In spite of these measures, the punitive expedition under the command of John J. Pershing entered Mexican territory on 15 March, constituting the second armed intervention in Mexico during Wilson's administration; it stayed for 10 months and was eventually more than 10,000 strong, but it never found Villa and provoked three serious clashes with the Mexican government that made relations extremely tense. This international incident resulted in the long negotiations between both governments that took place between 6 September 1916 and 6 January 1917 in New London, Atlantic City, and Philadelphia. In these the United States tried to make Pershing's withdrawal conditional on the protection of foreign lives and interests and the explicit recognition of its property rights, the formation of mixed commissions to examine pending questions, and the nullification of various Carranza decrees concerning increased taxes on mining and concessions to parties that did not begin working them immediately, the waiver of diplomatic protection in defence of foreign interests, the prohibition on drilling new oil wells, the cancelling of bank concessions for printing paper money, etc. The Mexican delegates, under US pressure, in principle accepted the demands, but Carranza refused authorization; finally the punitive expedition withdrew from Mexican territory on 5 February 1917 and the government was given de jure recognition by the United States.[18]

During the previous months, and in order to neutralize US pressure while the punitive expedition was in Mexico, Carranza manipulated with great ability a possible alliance with Germany; he tolerated its propaganda, was friendly to its minister in Mexico, and bought German weapons; his attitude towards Japan was similar. Mexico was very important in those days as the world's largest petroleum producer – especially necessary for the opposing naval fleets of Great Britain and Germany during the First World War. The latter formally proposed a defensive and offensive alliance on 17 January 1917 against the United States, providing financial support with the aim of recovering territories that the United States had seized from Mexico during the nineteenth century. Carranza kept the United States in suspense until 13 April, when he declared Mexico formally neutral, and on 1 May he took formal possession of the constitutional presidency.

From 20 November 1916 to 31 January 1917, the Constitutional Congress met at Queretaro, where it proclaimed the Magna Charta on 5 February. From then on Mexico's principal problem was the interpretation of the nationalistic aspects of the Constitution; this brought protests from foreign investors, especially oil men, who hoped for an invasion or the ceding of Mexican territory to the United States. Their best allies were Secretary of State Robert Lansing, and the ambassador in Mexico, Henry P. Fletcher. Carranza resisted all pressures and threats, and on 1 December 1918 set forth the doctrine which carries his name: that diplomacy will not be at the service of particular interests, nor will it exert undue pressure to make weak countries change unfavourable laws to suit powerful countries' interests; the fundamental principles of Mexico's foreign policy are "equality, mutual respect for institutions and laws, firm and constant determination not to intervene ever, under any pretext, in the internal affairs of other countries . . . trying all the while to obtain treatment equal to that given, that is, that national sovereignty always be considered . . . " Lansing continued in his threatening attitudes, and in 1919 expressly asked President Wilson on two occasions to declare war on Mexico, either for the safety of investments or because of the self-kidnapping of William O. Jenkins. Towards the end of the regime of Carranza, who was assassinated in May 1920, an enormous nationalistic force had been unleashed that permitted for the first time a clearer concept of what, for Mexico, it meant to be a nation.[19]

The Plan of Agua Prieta overthrew Carranza, and the triumphant group from Sonora controlled politics until 1935. Their fundamental interest was in gaining United States diplomatic recognition, and as usual the northern neighbour made this conditional on the prior arrangement of pending business, specifically an accord which would protect the rights of Americans; however, this was not accepted by Provisional President Adolfo de la Huerta. During the constitutional presidency of the real head of the group, Alvaro Obregón (1920–1924), the accord demanded by the Americans was not signed, but they did receive the required guarantees backed by concrete action: five favourable decisions by the Mexican Supreme Court overruling the petroleum decrees of Carranza in 1918. Also, Obregón courted foreign merchants and bankers. As a result, on 16 June 1922 an agreement was signed by De la Huerta and Thomas Lamont, President of the International Committee of Bankers on Mexico, in which Mexico recognized a debt of close to $600 million and agreed to an annual payment of $30 million (23 per cent of the federal government's revenue) for the first four years and $50 million thereafter. $207 million in interest was cancelled. The agreement was ratified by Obregón and by the Mexican National Congress but diplomatic recognition and the renovation of loans was not achieved. A year later, in May–August 1923, the Bucareli Conferences took place; of these the minutes are known only of the 15 formal sessions in which the following agreements were reached: the naming of a Mixed Claims Commission in order to determine the amount of US claims caused by the revolution from 1910 to 1920; and the creation of a General Mixed Claims Commission in order to examine claims that had accumulated since 1868 (the date at which the last claims convention had been signed between Mexico and the United States) and those that were not included in the special agreement. The most controversial of the points was the "official pact," an understanding about the manner in which future petroleum and agrarian legislation would apply to Americans, whose agrarian properties were in fact excluded; it was also agreed not to make Article 27 retroactive, so that it would only apply to the granting of new concessions. In the end the Americans kept all the privileges acquired before the Constitution of 1917. As a result of the conferences, on 31 August 1923 diplomatic relations were re-established, Ambassador Charles B. Warren arrived in September, and Obregón's hand was strengthened. In the opinion of Lorenzo Meyer the Bucareli Agreements had an ambiguous result: the United States clipped the wings of revolutionary nationalistic legislation, and Obregón achieved diplomatic recognition without having to change the Constitution and without signing a treaty, since the Bucareli Agreements never had the status of international instruments, among other reasons because they were not presented to the Mexican or the United States Congress for ratification, and carrying them out depended on the good will of the two countries. The only thing submitted to the Mexican National Congress were the texts of the claims conventions, and these were approved after recognition was given, first by the United States and then by the European powers, with the exception of Great Britain.[20]

During the constitutional presidency of Plutarco Elías Calles (1924–1928), petroleum production initiated during the period of his predecessor continued to decline, with the resulting loss to the government of tax revenues. Calles regulated paragraph IV of Article 27, defaulted on the annual payment of the foreign debt because of the expenses of the Delahuerta rebellion, and suspended the agreement with the bankers. This resulted in a new agreement, signed on 23 October 1925, between Alberto J. Pani and Lamont, which reduced the debt to close to $500 million, the railway part being separated and assigned to Ferrocarriles Nacionales de México (National Railroads of Mexico), and the government returning its confiscated lines. Thus, Calles was able to comply with the new agreement and made the first payment in 1926 of $107 million. In spite of everything, during 1925 and 1926 relations with the United States were very tense because President Calvin Coolidge (1925–1929), as well as his predecessor Warren G. Harding (who succeeded Wilson in 1921), decided to defend aggressively US interests abroad. Also, Mexico put into effect, in December 1925 and April 1926, hydrocarbon legislation and its corresponding regulations, which stipulated that property titles previous to 1917 would become government concessions subject to confirmation for 50 years; it also enacted the "positive act" principle, which referred to those lands on which a "positive act" had been carried out, that is, on which some drilling or other kind of activity had demonstrated the owner's intentions to extract oil prior to 1 May 1917. A year was given in which to comply with this. With United States government support and the approval of Great Britain and Holland, the oil men refused to comply, and speculation arose not only about the breaking of diplomatic relations with Mexico but also about armed intervention, which was demanded by US ambassador James R. Sheffield because, according to him, Calles was serving the Bolsheviks, had confiscated or invalidated rights, and supported the Liberal Party of Nicaragua against the United States marines, who were supporting Adolfo Díaz. So in February 1927 US troops were once more mobilized towards the border, though this time it was not crossed because the predominantly Democratic Congress opposed another armed intervention in Latin America to protect petroleum and banana interests. The International Committee of Bankers on Mexico, particularly John Pierpont Morgan, also opposed armed intervention because Mexico would then fall behind on its payments, which were being made punctually by Calles. Coolidge began to negotiate; towards the middle of 1927 he changed his policies towards Mexico and the new ambassador Dwight W. Morrow was given instructions to avoid a conflict. Morrow gave relations a new face because he was neither arrogant nor racist; he showed due respect for a sovereign nation with a valuable culture, considered that the revolution had ended and that its radicalism was a thing of the past, and thought that he could convince Calles and other authorities that the best way to carry out modernization was by combining Mexico's interests with those of the United Stats. Morrow's achievements were notable; in November 1927 petroleum legislation was changed, thanks to a decision by the Mexican Supreme Court concerning non-retroactivity; in December Articles 14 and 15 of the 1925 law were modified to the effect that government concessions recognized perpetually acquired rights and that the rights of industries that had refused to comply with the 1925 law would not be affected, unless in the future they did not observe new regulations. On the other hand, the State Department informed the oil men that they could no longer deal with their problems through diplomatic channels, but would have to do so before Mexican courts.[21]

As far as Mexico's political stability was concerned, Morrow's negotiations also were successful, both as a mediator between Provisional President Emilio Portes Gil and Archbishop Leopoldo Ruiz y Flores during the Cristera rebellion, and as an intercessor with the United States government, enabling Mexico to smother the revolt of Gonzalo Escobar against Calles. Morrow's only problem in the end was that he could not arrange Mexico's external debt, because internal rebellions created many expenses for the government and the progressive decrease in petroleum production diminished revenues, so that Mexico had to suspend payments agreed upon between Pani and Lamont. In July 1930 another agreement was signed with the International Commission of Bankers on Mexico, called the Montes de Oca-Lamont, by which Mexico recognized a debt of a little over $250 million, plus back interest, and agreed to pay $12.5 million annually in the beginning and $15 million thereafter. Mexico made an immediate payment of $5 million against interest, but in January 1931 had to postpone the following payment for two years, and then in 1932 indefinitely, as did many other countries as a consequence of the Great Depression of 1929.

Between 1928 and 1935 Mexico had a system of dual power, exercised by Calles as the "Jefe Máximo," and four presidents chosen and directed by him: Emilio Portes Gil, Pascual Ortiz Rubio, Abelardo Rodríguez, and Lázaro Cárdenas in his first months. The fact that Calles continued to run the country guaranteed the United States the continuance of agreements with the Mexican government, so that from 1928 rights previously acquired by the oil industry were not affected and oil leases subject to government confirmation continued to be issued. Also, the study of claims derived from the Bucareli Agreements was immediately begun, but because of their large number, the decisions took several years. The Special Commission for damages to US citizens examined 3,176 claims worth $42,300,132. In 1930 a total sum was agreed upon that included European claims and in April 1934 it was decided that Mexico would pay 2.64 per cent of the total, almost $5.5 million, and with this the problem was practically solved. The General Claims Commission began its meetings towards the end of 1924; it received 3,617 claims, of which 2,822 were American, worth $389,170,870, and 795 Mexican, worth $245,158,395. As 1935 approached, Mexico had acquired a greater sense of identity; it had weakened its economic and cultural ties with Europe and reaffirmed them with the United States. Railways, petroleum, electrical energy, and other industries remained in foreign hands.

The government of Lázaro Cárdenas (1934–1940) was subject to less hostility from the United States, as Franklin D. Roosevelt had become president in 1933, and with his Good Neighbor policy (initiated under his predecessor Herbert Hoover, 1929–1933) began to unify Latin America in the face of German and Italian expansionism in Europe and Japanese expansion in Asia. In order to achieve unification, the United States had to promise to respect the principle of non-intervention at the International Conferences of American States in 1933–1936, with the result that it had to evacuate its marines from Nicaragua and Haiti between 1933 and 1934. The US ambassador in Mexico was Josephus J. Daniels, that Secretary of the Navy who in 1914 had ordered the occupation of Veracruz, and was now a fervent believer in the Interamerican Alliance and the Good Neighbor policy. Like Morrow, Daniels maintained close personal relations with well-placed Mexican authorities and in the beginning accepted many of the measures taken by Cárdenas for the expropriation of rural landholdings and support for workers' organizations; later he tried to modify this postion when rural expropriations without their corresponding indemnification were involved. The greatest crisis in relations with the United States began in 1936 when the Mexican National Congress approved a law that permitted expropriations for the public good of any kind of property and postponement of payment for up to ten years. The Syndicate of Oil Workers of the Mexican Republic negotiated its first collective bargaining contract, asking for a salary rise and benefits of 65 million pesos a year. The companies only offered 14 million, a strike broke out in May 1937, and a study done by the government showed that the companies could afford 26 million and that their policies and activities were contrary to national interests. The oil industry took its case to court in Mexico, arguing that it could not pay 26 million nor allow almost all office staff to belong to the union. Finally the Mexican Supreme Court decided against the companies on 1 March 1938, and gave them seven days to comply. Cárdenas, the companies and the governments of the United States, Great Britain, and Holland negotiated and the companies finally agreed to pay the 26 million, but only if the Mexican government would accept certain conditions concerning future labour policies. Thus pressured, Cárdenas expropriated the foreign firms because of their rebellious attitude towards the decisions of the Judicial Branch of a sovereign country. With the oil expropriation, nationalism born of the Mexican Revolution reached a peak and enjoyed the support of the Mexican public. National unity had become a reality.

The international problems created by the expropriation were partially solved by offering to indemnify the companies in accordance with the law of 1936. However, Mexico wanted to pay with petroleum, which the companies refused. They were backed by Great Britain, with whom Mexico broke off relations. In the United States case, Daniels advised moderation; Secretary of State Cordell Hull tried to have the properties returned to the companies; Roosevelt accepted Mexico's right to expropriate but demanded immediate and adequate compensation. Finally the State Department increased its diplomatic and economic pressure on Mexico, closing its silver and petroleum markets and denying the equipment and technical assistance that Petróleos Mexicanos, the new government petroleum industry, needed. When all seemed lost, the Sinclair Oil Company broke with the united front presented by the others and negotiated with Cárdenas, so that in May 1941, with Manuel Ávila Camacho now as president, Mexico signed an agreement which obliged it to pay $815 million in three years, part in cash and part in petroleum, at a price lower than the market one.[22]

The expropriation, according to Lorenzo Meyer, was the touchstone of Mexican economic independence. In 1920 direct US investment came to more than a billion dollars and in 1940 it was only 300 million. Quantitatively and qualitatively the presence of foreign capital had become less influential in Mexico, and what is more important, the image Mexicans had of themselves became much more positive and confident.

Conclusion

The period from 1867 to 1940 was characterized by a constant struggle on the part of Mexico to defend its sovereignty, which was continuously threatened by the United States by means of different types of pressures, ranging from making diplomatic recognition conditional on the prior settlement of its claims, to repeated mobilizations of troops and warships to the US–Mexican border and to Mexican ports, to two armed invasions of Mexican territory, one in 1914 and the other in 1916. Additional forms of pressure included ultimata, commercial and economic blocks, and President Woodrow Wilson's "moralist" policy, by means of which (aside from the above-mentioned pressures) he attempted to conduct the internal affairs of Mexico, involving various Latin American countries on two different occasions.

The most constant threats in this period of Mexican history were a result of the damages caused to Americans and their interests, both in times of war and in times of peace. Insofar as the former were concerned, their claims began during the era of the French Intervention and lasted until the subsequent civil wars. With regard to claims made in times of peace, their protests were unceasing, since they believed that their interests were affected by the measures taken by the Mexican authorities, among which were nationalist decrees and legislative modifications, the Constitution of 1917, and the expropriation of oil in 1938. To all of the above must be added the conflicts that arose in the Mexican-US border zone, such as raids by wild Indians and cattle rustlers, filibuster attacks, a series of seditious activities carried out by political exiles, skirmishes between Mexicans in the vicinity of the dividing line, and some raids on US villages. We should also take into account the intention of the United States to set up a protectorate in Mexico or to annex part of Mexican territory, be it El Chamizal, the Baja California peninsula, Sonora, Sinaloa, Durango, Chihuahua, Coahuila, Nuevo León or the oil region, as well as to usufruct to its advantage the waters of the Bravo and Gila rivers. Another point of conflict was the clash between Mexican and US policies on Central America.

Two US ambassadors were especially hostile to Mexico, Henry Lane Wilson and James R. Sheffield; the former, owing to the repeated requests he made between 1912 and 1913 for his government to order an armed intervention in Mexico, his complicity in the coup d'état against President Madero, and the Embassy Pact of 1913; the latter, owing to his insistence on encouraging and even demanding armed intervention between 1925 and 1926, claiming that President Calles was at the service of the Bolsheviks, that he had confiscated acquired rights, and that he supported the Liberal Party of Nicaragua in opposition to the United States.

Secretary of State Robert R. Lansing was also decidedly unfavourable towards Mexico, since as of the proclamation of the Constitution of 1917, foreign investors – mainly the oil men – protested and sought to have the United States invade or isolate Mexican territory, always with the support of Lansing. In 1919, he asked his government on two different occasions to declare war on Mexico, once to safeguard foreign investments and once because of the self-kidnapping of the US consular agent in Puebla, William O. Jenkins, who acted as he did to demonstrate the unsafe conditions under which his fellow US citizens were living in Mexico.

Two US presidents, Woodrow Wilson and Calvin Coolidge, also had very unfortunate attitudes toward Mexico. Wilson, with his "moralist" policy, constantly attempted to intervene in Mexico's internal affairs from 1913 until 1917, when he ceased to do so in a direct fashion because the First World War absorbed all his attention. During the first two years of his administration, he exerted every possible type of pressure upon Victoriano Huerta to resign as president. For example, he prevented him from obtaining credit in Great Britain in exchange for favourable treatment for that country in the Panama Canal and protection for her citizens and interests in Mexico. In June 1915 he sent an ultimatum to the three main revolutionary leaders in Mexico to the effect that unless they settled their differences he (Wilson) would decide on the way to "save Mexico." Moreover, his forces occupied part of Mexico's territory for 17 months because of incidents that could have been settled through diplomatic channels. The first invasion was ordered in April 1914, when, without any prior warning or declaration of war, US troops occupied the port of Veracruz, causing fatalities and damage to property, and remained there for seven months. The second invasion was carried out in March 1916 when, once again without prior warning or declaration of war, US troops crossed the border in pursuit of Francisco Villa, causing death and damage, and remained in the State of Chihuahua for ten months. After each of these invasions of Mexican territory, Wilson involved several Latin American countries in a series of conferences for the supposed purpose of mediation geared toward solving the international problem, but the mediators always acted in accordance with Wilson's whims. They never addressed the problem of solving the international conflict but instead became involved in Mexico's internal affairs, pressing for the appointment of a provisional government or president to the liking of President Wilson, in addition to promoting the US government's traditional aims: the protection of the lives and interests of foreigners and the explicit recognition of their property rights; the creation of mixed commissions for pending business; the annulment of various decrees issued by Venustiano Carranza regarding a rise in taxes on mining and the withdrawal of government concessions to those who did not begin work immediately, the renunciation by foreigners of diplomatic protection in defence of their interests, the prohibition against drilling new oil wells, the cancellation of the concession granted to banks to print currency, etc. Carranza did not accept any condition or make any commitment in order to ensure that the US would withdraw its troops from Mexico, but rather on the two occasions in question demanded withdrawal regardless of any possible conditions; not only did he manage to achieve this in November 1914 and February 1917, but his government also received de facto recognition on 19 October 1915 and de jure recognition on 5 February 1917.

When Carranza died in May 1920, Woodrow Wilson was still President of the United States, and his administration made diplomatic recognition of the Mexican government – which was now in the hands of the rebels who had assumed power – conditional on the signing of an agreement that would safeguard the acquired rights of US citizens. In response, Alvaro Obregón's government signed an agreement in mid-1922 with Thomas Lamont, President of the International Committee of Bankers, wherein Mexico acknowledged a debt of some $600 million, pledging to make four annual payments of $30 million each and to cover the rest in annual payments of $50 million. In spite of this, Obregón's government was not recognized. The following year, the Bucareli Conferences were held and it was agreed to name two mixed commissions: one to determine the total sum of US claims resulting from the 1910–1920 revolution, and the other to assess claims accumulated since 1868 that were not part of a special agreement. The most controversial issue discussed at those conferences was the understanding regarding the manner in which Mexico was to apply its oil and agrarian legislation to US citizens in the future; owing to the fact that US citizens managed to preserve all rights acquired before 1917, diplomatic relations were resumed on 31 August 1923. Thus, the United States discouraged Mexican nationalist revolutionary legislation and Obregón obtained recognition without modifying the Constitution and without signing any treaty, since the Bucareli Agreements never had the status of an international instrument, among other reasons because they were not presented either to the Mexican Congress or to the US Congress for ratification. The only thing that was submitted to the Mexican Congress was the texts of the claims conventions, and these were not approved until after recognition.

In the United States, Warren G. Harding and Calvin Coolidge took office as presidents after Wilson, in 1921 and 1925 respectively. Both were faithful supporters of US citizens and their interests abroad. The most serious problems with Mexico arose between 1925 and 1927, since at that time Mexican legislation on hydrocarbons and the law regulating this matter were passed, by means of which title deeds existing prior to 1917 became government concessions, subject to confirmation for 50 years; also, the "positive act" principle was enacted, and a one-year time limit was established to avoid the loss of those rights. Because of pressures exerted by foreign companies on the United States government, there was speculation about a break in diplomatic relations and another armed intervention in Mexico. However, in the end, the latter did not occur because the United States Congress was opposed to continuing to take bellicose measures to defend oil and banana companies in Latin America.

The oil crisis, which marked the close of the period under review in this paper, had its beginnings in 1936 when the Mexican Congress approved a law for expropriating any property by reason of public utility, postponing the corresponding indemnization payment for up to ten years. Discontent among the foreign companies was heightened because the Union of Oil Workers of Mexico demanded salary increments and fringe benefits for a total of 65 million pesos. The companies were only willing to pay 14 million pesos, and a strike broke out in May 1937. The Mexican government reached the conclusion that the aforementioned companies could pay 26 million pesos, and that their policies and actions ran counter to the national interest. On 1 March 1938 the Mexican Supreme Court decided against them, but the companies refused to abide by their decision, conditioning the payment of the 26 million pesos to the Mexican government's acceptance of their stipulations for future labour laws. President Lázaro Cárdenas ordered the expropriation of the oil companies on 18 March 1938, and this act was the high point of the nationalism produced by the Mexican Revolution.

Notes

1. Luis González, "El liberalismo triunfante," in *Historia general de México* (El Colegio de México, Mexico City, 1986).
2. See note 1 above.
3. Daniel Cosío Villegas, *Historia moderna de México. El porfiriato. Vida política exterior*, part 2 (Editorial Hermes, Mexico City, 1963), p. xxxii.
4. See note 3 above.
5. Josefina Vázquez and Lorenzo Meyer, *México frente a los Estados Unidos, un ensayo histórico, 1776–1980* (El Colegio de México, Mexico City, 1982).
6. Antonio Gómez Robledo, *México y el arbitraje internacional. El Fondo Piadoso de las Californias. La isla de la Pasión* (Editorial Porrúa, Mexico City, 1965); César Sepúlveda, *Dos reclamaciones internacionales fraudulentas contra México (Los casos de Weil y de La Abra, 1868–1902)* (Secretaría de Relaciones Exteriores, Mexico City, 1965).
7. See note 5 above.
8. See note 5 above.
9. See note 5 above.
10. See note 5 above.
11. See note 5 above.
12. See note 1 above.
13. Cosío Villegas (note 3 above); Berta Ulloa, *La revolución intervenida. Relaciones diplomáticas entre México y Estados Unidos, 1910–1914* (El Colegio de México, Mexico City, 1976), p. xii.
14. Ulloa (note 13 above).
15. Ulloa (note 3 above).
16. Ulloa (note 13 above).

17. Berta Ulloa, *La revolución escindida* and *La encrucijada de 1915* (El Colegio de México, Mexico City, 1981).
18. Berta Ulloa, *La constitución de 1917* (El Colegio de México, Mexico City, 1983).
19. Berta Ulloa, "La lucha armada, 1911–1920," in *Historia general de México* (El Colegio de México, Mexico City, 1986); Ulloa (note 18 above).
20. See note 5 above.
21. See note 5 above.
22. See note 5 above.

THE CULTURAL MODERNIZATION OF MEXICO (1857–1958)

Luis González
El Colegio de Michoacán, Zamora, Michoacán, Mexico

The Four Phases of Modernization

The process by which Mexico broke away from the form of society and the values bequeathed by the encounter between the Spaniards and the natives during the seventeenth century can be divided into four phases: the Enlightenment, Independence, the Liberal Reform, and the Mexican Revolution. None of these four phases of a modernization process whereby the doctrines and practices of the neo-Spanish world were abandoned, and the principles and customs deemed to be modern by French and American society were adopted, was the work of the majority. Without a doubt, the so-called modernization of Mexico was achieved – with very few exceptions – by a social group that has been assigned the labels of "proprietary class," "oligarchy," "people of order and progress," "aristocracy," or, according to the epoch, the enlightened, the insurgents, the liberals, or the revolutionaries.

The class that called itself "enlightened" during the second half of the eighteenth century, "insurgent" in the course of the first half of the nineteenth century, "liberal" and "progressive" in the second part of that same century, and "revolutionary" during this century has, in general, been distinguished by its sympathy with "modern" ways of living and has allowed itself to be guided by tightly knit groups of intellectuals or select minorities emerging from ecclesiastical seminaries or the universities.

Dominating the ruling minorities of the first phase of our modernization process, i.e. the Enlightenment, were the groups that were formed during that period in seminaries (to a greater extent) and in the university (to a

Paper presented at the Conference on the Modernization Process in Mexico (1867–1940): The Social Transformations, co-sponsored by the United Nations University and El Colegio de México, Mexico City, 19–21 March 1985.

lesser extent). As is well known, in the case of the first ruling minority of Mexico's modern era, intellectual leadership fell to a handful of Jesuits who were expelled from the country in 1767. Another group, almost all of whom were clergymen and former students of the Jesuits, carried on the renovation initiated by their teachers, declaring themselves to be supporters of modern experimental science and disseminating the results of their investigations in periodical publications they themselves founded. The intellectual fruits of the bellwethers of modernization in its initial phase were made public in short-lived journals such as *Mercurio volante, Gaceta de literatura* and *Asuntos varios sobre ciencias y artes útiles*.

Neither of these movements had a major effect upon the vast majority of the population. The only things that were to influence the masses – firmly established as they were within economic, political and cultural patterns dating from the encounter between the Spaniards and the natives – were the frivolities of the "enlightened": amusements such as pool and billiards, the consumption of *chinguirito* (inferior quality rum) and other distilled and intoxicating beverages, indecent dances, and so forth. Apart from this, the Mexican people still demonstrated a contempt for this world and an attachment to the Catholic liturgy, to miracles, to the tortuous style of Baroque art, and to the will of the powerful; on the other hand, they showed an aversion to modernizers who preached the merits of a hygienic way of life, good health, neo-classical art, secular morals, laws, ironclad reasoning, and experimental science.

The second phase of our modernization came to involve the masses to a greater degree, and was popularized in the cities. This was a period in which those making a contribution were part of an enlightened minority of individuals born between 1748 and 1764, who cursed the tyranny of Spain and were taken in by the appeal of the French Revolution, the rebellion of the British colonies to the north and the making of the United States of America. The generation of Father Hidalgo (although he himself was the only one to take up arms against the Empire) opposed not so much the cultural values conveyed by tradition as the political status of their country, i.e. Mexico's dependence. As is well-known, the desire to change the political situation spread and led to the rebellion of 1810, commonly referred to as "Hidalgo's Revolution"; this was later followed by "Morelos' Revolution," the work of a different minority.

The principal caudillos of the insurgent movement were born between 1765 and 1780. Many of them were clergymen devoted to modernity, introduced by the Jesuits. They attempted to transfer civic loyalty owed to the King to the realm of their motherland and to replace the royal will with legal obligations and juridical norms arising from collegiate bodies, i.e. congresses elected by popular vote.

Both the insurgent generation and the one responsible for consummating our independence strove to instil in the populace love and loyalty for the nation and observance of the law. The authorities who took the place of the Spaniards not only fought amongst themselves, but also went about the business of legislating juridical norms and of demanding respect for them. Within the congresses, they drafted and promulgated a considerable number of constitutions and other laws. The main pastime of the Mexican moralists during the second stage of the modernization process consisted of drawing up political constitutions and revolutionary programmes. Although extensive use was made of buffer tactics (i.e. war), that half-century was fundamentally legalistic. Then what the common people term "buffer tactics" were employed for the purpose of imposing what the minority called "laws."

At any rate, my intention is not to expound upon the half-century of Enlightenment – the last century of colonial rule – nor on the half-century of our struggle for independence – the first one Mexico experienced as an independent nation. Instead, I shall refer to the century encompassing the two latter phases of Mexico's modernization process, during which time it was no longer priests or clergymen who led the struggle, but, rather, an anti-clerical or outrightly irreligious element. The ruling minorities of the liberal phase showed signs of a weakened religious sentiment and of a will to fight against traditional religion. The jurists who designed the Reform – authors of our Magna Charta of 1857 and of laws stipulating the disentailment of the property of the clergy, the establishment of (civil) registrars' offices, religious tolerance, the separation of church and state, and the secularization of cemeteries – drew up laws that put a close to the era of Enlightenment and armed strife and, around the year 1860, led the way for the culture of liberalism.

Liberal Culture

Liberal culture was the achievement of a small fraction of the élite, which had triumphed in the Ayutla and Three Years' revolutions, and was supported openly by the government of the United States and indirectly by the French monarchy through an intervention; a fraction which, claiming to be allied with the Conservatives, was in fact friend to the Liberals. This new stage took place between 1856 and 1910, covering half a century. The political leaders of Mexico during that period were Benito Juárez and Porfirio Díaz. The period was one of unrest for the first third of the time and of peace for the remainder. In the course of those (more than 50) years, the Mexican population nearly doubled. In addition, the majority of the 200 regions comprising the country's territory were linked to the capital by means of railways and telegraph; a policy of centralization was adopted; new land was put under cultivation and a small-scale industrial revolution was launched. The governments claimed to be republican, federal, and elected by popular vote.

Political organization became stable, vigorous, and even less democratic towards the end of the period, during the Porfiriato.

As in the first half of the nineteenth century, throughout the second half politics was the main concern of the minorities governing the life of the nation. The leading figures who assembled around Juárez, the associates of Porfirio Díaz, the *científicos* of the heyday of the Porfiriato and even the "modernists" were, with few exceptions, politicians (presidents, congressmen, ministers, ambassadors, etc.) who complacently made armchair decisions concerning foreign relations; conflicts between church and state; disputes among different state jurisdictions, workers and capitalists, and peasants and landowners; punishments; jail sentences and other such matters reserved to the government in a liberal milieu. Many of those leaders wrote about politics and laws, publishing copious books on power and ways of wielding it, as well as numerous reflections for newspapers and other periodicals on the rulers and political principles of the day. They were not very concerned with economics, but showed great interest in the arts of government. This half-century we are referring to was one with a good deal of politics and very little management.

Be that as it may, the tremendous preoccupation with politics evidenced by the dominant group in each of the 15-year periods between 1855 and 1911 was not shared by the great majority of the Mexican people. At no time during the 50 years of Liberal rule did the people participate in elections or other democratic rituals. Here democracy (even under Benito Juárez) was government by the élite and for the élite. The concerns of the common people in terms of participation were of more of a social nature than a political one. Craftsmen and labourers did not seem to aspire to changes in structure but appeared to be interested in gathering together in mutual benefit societies and in wielding the weapon available to them, i.e. strikes. The majority of the populace, located in rural areas, was even less revolutionary. It seldom went beyond defending the property of the villages threatened by the disentailment law promulgated by the leaders of Liberalism.

In the realm of culture, in the series of values commonly described by words such as pleasure, well-being, aesthetic taste, morality, philosophy, and religion, modernization did not penetrate the soul of the people either. At the top of the social pyramid the influence of the French could be perceived, especially where the pleasures of the senses were concerned. The masculine members of the élite were fond of the *tandas* of light theatre (a single showing in a series of continuous performances), and of the few inches of skin shown by young, brazen dancing girls who pirouetted and swayed around the stage. Another favourite pastime of these males was reading pornography. The young wanted to pattern their lives after Baudelaire's dissolvent doctrines; thus they enthusiastically gave themselves up to the enjoyment of sex, alcohol and drugs in bars and brothels. Amongst the chic, it was a point of pride to be Gallic in terms of food, women, dress, and drink. The great masses, and especially the people in villages and rural settlements, remained unaware, or almost so, of pleasures other than those to be had by drinking *aguardiente*.

Although a concern for health and for human life was no longer a novelty among the élite during the *paz porfiriana*, what was new was the secularization of this branch of culture. The cities of the dead ceased to be sacred burial grounds and were turned into cemeteries and graveyards administered by the civil government. Modern medicine, which satisfied the desire of the rich and powerful to remain healthy, abandoned the realm of spiritual assistance. Religious orders gave way, at least partially, to orders of non-religious nurses and doctors, hospitals, hospices, and insane asylums. Another new development was that sports, such as horseback riding, baseball, football, and basketball, were played increasingly. Moreover, in the elegant country houses of the upper and middle classes, proper bathrooms became the rule. For the first time one could observe the spectacle of a bourgeoisie devoted to ostentation and worldly pleasures and very afraid of death.

Those who visited the metropolis during Porfirio Díaz's regime went back home with the notion that the modernization of Mexico was a patent and swift-moving reality. In this period, art served the purposes of the church only sporadically; in most instances it was at the service of the state, which needed an increasing number of government buildings (called palaces), prisons, public buildings, and statues of presidents of the republic, governors, and generals. Moreover, the audio-visual aspects of culture were not overlooked. In all the town squares, music boxes or kiosks appeared, where wind ensembles would boom out their tunes every Sunday. In the larger cities, theatres were built where opera singers brought in directly from France and Italy would warble for the well-to-do.

Mexico came to produce composers of operas such as Cenobio Paniagua, but their numbers never equalled those of the journalists, novelists, poets, playwrights, and silver tongues. Despite the fact that the government headed by Porfirio Díaz opened only a few new schools, in the cities the written word eventually predominated over the spoken word. Twenty-five of every hundred people learned how to read and write and took to reading French authors translated into Spanish, Spanish authors and even Mexican ones. The sentimental poets (Guillermo Prieto, Manuel Acuña and Juan de Dios Peza), a whole range of *costumbristas* (depicters of regional or national mores) from Joaquín Fernández de Lizardi to Angel del Campo, and several playwrights described in their work the life-styles of the Mexican nation. Only the last minority of the Liberal epoch, in which figures such as Manuel Gutiérrez Nájera, Manuel José Othón, Luis G. Urbina, Amado Nervo, Federico Gamboa, and Salvador Díaz Mirón were active, attempted – in the words of José

Luis Martínez – "to step forward at the same pace as contemporary culture, to be men of their time as well as of their particular homeland . . ."

Mexican culture, the culture of the nineteenth century and of a large part of this century, paid little heed to poetry. The culture of modernity had a higher regard for the novel. The passion for poetry exhibited in the Baroque period was transformed in modern times into a passion for novels. This genre, together with the newspaper, thus became the major vehicle of culture, one that was just as important then as the cinema and television are nowadays. I do not recall who said: "Novels are going to do away with everything else." But I *do* remember that my parents, who had first-hand contact with the culture prior to ours, and even with the one prior to the eighteenth century, saw in the imaginary and sentimental world of the novel the origin of all modern evils. Even the supposedly good novels were bad in their eyes. They would say that the good ones should be used as fuel to feed the fire burning the ones that upset the apple-cart of our traditional values. Just like novels, the newspapers grew in number, but did not "stoop" to reach the masses. Rather, they merely served as cultural nourishment for the élite and for a growing middle class.

The proliferation of newspapers during this period is hard to believe – there were literally hundreds of them. Not only in the country's capital could one find (more or less voluminous) dailies and weeklies: even towns of 5,000 to 15,000 inhabitants came to have one or even two periodical publications. In Mexico City, aside from the *Monitor republicano*, *El siglo XIX*, *Le trait d'union*, *El pájaro verde*, *El imparcial*, *La voz de México* and *El país*, many more were published. In any event, with the relative exception of the newspapers for the workers, the expenses of all of these papers were borne by the parties of the ruling class and their articles were written for readers belonging to that dominant group. The number of copies printed was very limited: many printed no more than 1,000 copies, or less, and only in rare instances did they exceed 20,000. On the other hand, newspapers were very expensive: more than a worker's daily wage. Thus, modernization as disseminated by periodicals was unable to reach a populace that continued to hang on to every word uttered by the priest in his sermon.

Another phenomenon that barely touched the populace was the transition from a personal code of ethics dictated from the pulpit and the confessional to one prescribed by one's individual conscience, and from a public code of ethics originating in the "royal will" of the authorities to one stemming from written law, the product of congresses made up of representatives of the secular social élite. During the Liberal era, the first civil and penal codes at the national and state level were promulgated and legislation calling for absolute respect for private property was enacted, though there was "many a slip 'twixt cup and lip" in the observation of such laws.

Avarice for material wealth, which had been considered a vice in the old regime, became an end in itself, a major goal. As in the case of Protestant countries, the Mexican élite of the Porfirian period proposed to restrain the Christian ethic upholding equality and give greater impetus to the bourgeois doctrines of progress and freedom. They also promoted love for one's country instead of for mankind, and nationalism in the place of Catholicism. Without relinquishing its moral code shaped by Catholicism, the populace – and especially the peasantry, which lagged even further behind – became enthusiastic partisans of an exaggerated form of patriotism nurtured by stirring speeches, parades of *charros* (trick horseback riders), and pyrotechnics.

At the height of this period, the scientism of the eighteenth century was once again adopted. As the revolutionary surge began to wane, attention turned again toward intellectual adventures, pursued along more critical and precision-oriented lines. Since science was the favourite pastime of the period, the nickname of *científicos* was applied to outstanding individuals under Porfirio Díaz's regime. Since scientism caused such a stir, one might have expected Mexico quickly to make up lost ground in the fields of physicomathematics, biomedicine, and the social sciences. However, in the natural sciences there were only isolated flashes, sparks, and extremely short-lived advances. In the area of the human sciences, sociology and economics were launched as intellectual disciplines, but seldom did they go beyond their initial "flash of lightning." The most significant scientific achievements were made in history, the Cinderella of scientific activities. Overall, scientific activities remained on a very minor plane, inhibited by lack of equipment and appropriate bibliographical resources.

The common people remained devoted to their priests and to their religious traditions. In the words of Amado Nervo: "Clearly, to the chagrin of the masses in the country, we have a liberal constitution: with obvious repugnance on the part of the people . . . we established the independence of church and state and we secularized the education provided by the government." The Juárez and Lerdo regimes came very close to setting off a plebeian uprising because of their penchant for Protestant propaganda, the establishment of the freedom of worship, and the suppression of religious orders. The handful of positivists in Porfirio Díaz's regime wanted to put an end to the theological and metaphysical ethos prevailing in Mexico and to initiate the era of positivism, offering no other religious cult than that of Auguste Comte, already initiated in Brazil under the name of "the religion of humanity." But the *vox populi* did not allow the minority of devotees of Comte to have its way. The revolution of the eighteenth century, launched from the heights of society, still could not descend to the level of the people a full hundred years later. Perhaps this was because the revolutionary aristocrats – the apostles of this licentious, scientific-technical, and capitalist brand of modernity – did not deign to stoop to the filthy and ignorant strata of the population, as the apostles of Christianity had done during the sixteenth century. The culture brought over by the Spanish priests took root quickly – without the need for genocide – among the indigenous élites and, above all, among the native masses. In contrast, the culture imported by intellectuals since the Enlightenment was transformed only partially into a commodity of the masses and that happened as of the revolution, during the twentieth century.

The Mexican Revolution

With the insurrection led by Madero in opposition to the dictatorship of the *científicos*, we witnessed the birth of an era we have agreed to call "the Revolution," although it should rightfully be called "the Second Reform" since, contrary to the current official view, it never intended to break with the epoch whose eponyms were Benito Juárez and Porfirio Díaz. Although there was no lack of movements in favour of breaking away – such as the one led by Zapata, who sought to return to the pre-enlightened and pre-liberal epoch – the victors, the constitutionalists of Venustiano Carranza, only aimed to eliminate the abuses of Díaz's dictatorship and not the culture of modernity.

During the phase of the Mexican Revolution, two leading minorities were responsible for the advancement of the modernizing process. Luis Cabrera referred to the members of the first of these minorities as "the revolutionaries of yore" and to those of the second as "the revolutionaries of the present." Others have chosen to distinguish them in terms of "the revolutionary group" and "the generation of 1915." I attempted to characterize both dominant groups in *La ronda de las generaciones*, and with regard to the group that guided the destiny of our country between 1911 and 1935 I wrote the following:

> The revolutionary group included a great number of illustrious men of humble, rural extraction. It also welcomed into its ranks a higher percentage of persons of common breeding than the minorities which preceded it. For that reason, no previous group ever came closer to the masses than the revolutionaries. It was a human minority, an excessively human one, with a dearth of ideologists. It had many characters straight out of the pages of a novel and, also, good novelists. It had a great deal of presence, and outstanding painters adept at capturing it on canvas. The first movie director Mexico ever had belonged to this group; that is why we can still see, on the silver screen, the comings and goings of the violent stage of the Mexican Revolution. It created a new atmosphere in Mexico, another epoch which accepted such adjectives as "nationalist," "modernizing," on occasions "peasant," but usually "urban." In the new phase of Mexico's modernization, the minority which conducted the Revolution between 1910 and 1935 ended up playing the role of a fix-it man: it destroyed more than it managed to build.

The group governing the generation of 1915 and also the period of Mexican life from 1936 to 1958 was somewhat different from the group described above.

It destroyed the myth of Mexico's natural wealth; it viewed the peasants and inhabitants of lower-class urban neighbourhoods as oppressed, although not totally without hope. It did not conceal its pessimistic form of nationalism nor its meagre share of xenophobia. Like the populace, it too suffered from Yankeephobia, and yet without the vehemence of those of the revolutionary era. The ruling minority of 1915 exhibited a considerable degree of refinement. Its nationalism existed alongside feelings of admiration for the countries playing a major role in modern culture, i.e. France, England, Germany, Russia, and the United States. In any event, the men at the crest of the epirevolutionary wave never renounced Mexican-style authoritarianism, always defending the virtues of a patriarchal system. They evidenced a perfectly clear inclination towards a state which was active, meddlesome, watchful, precautionary, wholesome, regulative, moralizing, the author of popular organizations and political parties, the prefect of the great majority of our schools, and the guardian of national life.

Perhaps the most outstanding feature of the protagonists of 1915 was their constructive zeal, their feverish enthusiasm for establishing institutions. Over a span of 20 years, they made fashionable that oh-so-modern way of being miserable, consisting of always being in a rush, dashing this way and that, and taking very seriously the country's efforts to move forward rapidly in pursuit of modernization.

With the exception of the vanguished reactionary "revolutions" led by Emiliano Zapata and Pancho Villa, the other reformist "revolutions" – designers of the Constitution of 1917 – only purported to afford greater appeal and popularity to the values of "modernity" that had been circulating in Mexico since the eighteenth century. And with that hypothesis in mind, we should look more closely at the period from 1910 to 1958, when the population came to espouse republican institutions and a system based on a combination of social classes and ethnoses; our civilization was strengthened through agro-industries (collective or individual), private industries, state industries and many other enterprises of all kinds, with some domestic skills and techniques and many others obtained on lease, and with the support of a government that was building dams, irrigation channels, technological institutes, fields for agricultural experimentation, oil wells, oil pipelines, power plants, highways, airports, and radio broadcasting stations.

In so far as ethical, aesthetic, scientific, philosophical, and religious values are concerned, the Mexican Revolution did not represent a break with Porfirio Díaz's regime, the Reform, the Independence period and the century of Enlightenment. In some respects it consolidated previous achievements, and in others it served to unfold and extend developments such as those that occurred in the field of health, for example, a decline in mortality in a context in which physicians gained a definitive advantage over priests and witch-doctors. In addition, a close familiarity with death is something that has become less common in the past half-century. Dying with resignation, making fun of the *calaca*, playing with the *pelona* (both terms for death), eating a special kind of bread decorated with skulls and crossbones and skulls made of sugar or chocolate for the Day of the Dead, are all customs that are fast disappearing. Both the Mexican government and society in general claim to be proud of the increasing decline in the number of "little angels" and in the overall mortality rate. The "governments arising from the revolution" have won major victories over death thanks to the campaign against malaria, vaccination against smallpox, chemotherapy, vitamins, antibiotics, the discrediting of witch-doctors, the greater number of physicians and their distribution throughout the entire country, public sanitation, health clinics and hospitals . . . Since the people have come to fear death almost as much as the common American, they have collaborated in health campaigns. Bread and soap are becoming more widespread. Bathing has come to be viewed favourably and accepted because it is both pleasurable and healthy. Physical fitness through sports and the fight against obesity bear witness to the efforts being made to revitalize essential values among the inhabitants of urban centres, especially among the dwellers of the chic, tree-lined neighbourhoods.

With regard to aesthetic issues, the true mixing and mingling of the élite and the masses was not fully attained until after the year 1958. Be that as it may, from the third decade of this century on, it became fashionable among some of our artists to use, as a source of inspiration, the handicrafts and literature of the lower classes. In 1922, Dr. Atl élitized Mexican folk art with his book *Artes populares en México*. Shortly thereafter artists and men of letters, banded together in groups such as LEAR, BOI, and *agoristas*,[1] devoted themselves to imitating popular art, popular music, poetry born on neighbourhood streets and in saloons, folk dances such as the *sandunga* and the *jarabe*,[2] and *pastorelas*.[3] From its inception, Mexican cinema catered to popular tastes with films about *charros*, *peladitos*,[4] and Indians. All in all, many of the worthwhile art forms of the revolution drew on currents that had little or no nationalistic and folk elements in them; witness the school of the contemporaries and others who distinguished themselves by their diversity, universality, and excellence. The Mexican artistic élite opened up a small window shedding a little light on the common people and a huge one on the world, letting in the styles in vogue among the international élite. The government made great strides in eliminating illiteracy, and yet the abundance and variety of literary fruits came close to driving the new readers crazy. The new species of "professional writer" did not care about the tastes or the level of understanding reached by the masses who had only recently learned to read.

From its beginnings, and through its intellectuals, the revolution claimed to be just. And this revolutionary form of justice, "with its hoarse, pectoral voice" called upon the well-to-do to give the peasants, workers, and aborigines a helping hand. The Constitution of 1917 added to the liberal ethics of the Constitution of 1857 three new sets of obligations whose labels were "agrarianism," *laborismo*, and *indigenismo*. The first of these justified and provided for the handing over of *parvifundios* (small plots of land) to those who worked them with their own hands; the second established workers' rights in industry; and the third declared that it was a matter of utmost urgency to incorporate the copper-coloured marginal groups into democracy, civilization, and national culture as practised in Mexico. Almost all the members of the élite were in agreement concerning these three aims. Perhaps the greatest amount of discord was to be found in the victims of the three "-isms," for their opinions were not taken into account when efforts were being made to do them justice. Since the eighteenth century, our ethics have no longer been produced in Fuenteovejuna:[5] they have been the result of the "royal will" of sovereigns who made children out of the people, and of legislators who believed that the common masses are like children who cry when they are bathed.

Perhaps owing to its eagerness to find solutions to problems affecting the masses, the revolutionary family took a long time before it set science, which had been relegated, to work for it. As late as 1965, an inquiry into research in the natural sciences in Mexico revealed that only a few individuals were promoting research in the physicomathematical and biomedical domains. More recent reports indicate that greater advances are now being made and that many monographs and doctoral dissertations are being written; but we have yet to witness the kind of performance needed to place us on a par with the countries that generally receive the Nobel Prize for physics or chemistry. Periodic surveys in the field of the social sciences have been less disheartening. Some groups, in particular historians, are already conducting highly valuable theoretical research.

In contrast to science, and along a different path, philosophy made its appearance very early in the panorama of the revolution. First, it attacked positivism; then, it created huge intellectual configurations and devoted itself to clarifying our national realities. On the eve of the collapse of Porfirio Díaz's regime, the young men of the *Ateneo de la juventud* stated that the official philosophy "was too systematic and too definitive to avoid making mistakes." Later, as adults, three thinkers of the *Ateneo* designed original philosophical systems, none as vigorous and unique as that of José Vasconcelos, who was responsible for "the philosophy of co-ordination." The disciples of the members of the *Ateneo* and of the Spanish philosophers who had come to reside in the New World since 1939 set about deciphering *El perfil del hombre y la cultura en México*. They also produced a copious literature, which they referred to as the "philosophy of that which is Mexican," and their detractors expressed themselves in *El mito del mexicano*. Actually, none of the great philosophers of the revolution was a prophet in his own land. The local élite was to fulfil its philosophical needs with materialisms, idealisms, vitalisms, and existentialisms of European origin. The custom continued to consist of letting oneself be taken in by any form of symmetry with a semblance of order, so long as it had been created in the Old World. Modernization in Mexico remained dependent.

Since the eighteenth century, the élite has been concerned with the religiousness of the masses. In the mid-nineteenth century this was considered one of the nation's greatest defects. The belated religiousness of the greatest philosophers of the revolutionary era could not prevent the anti-religious assault launched by the foremost leaders of the revolution. Those of us who are now in our fifties were able to see, with our own eyes, the ill-will of the man at the top towards religion as practised by the people and their clergymen. We witnessed the closing of churches, the anti-clerical speeches, the challenges made to God, the burning of religious images, the hidden priests, the teachers who tried to wipe out fanaticism, the closing of religious seminaries, the Catholic martyrs, and the satanization of believers. And we had occasion to observe (many of us only as children) the popular response to religious persecution; we also witnessed the Cristiada[6] upon which the peasants embarked in opposition to those who stood for impiety. Our modern culture has repeatedly smashed up against the rocks of the Mexican people's religious devotion.

The Mexican Revolution was still unable to bring the cycle of modern culture to its summit in 1958, the last year of the fourth phase of the modernization of Mexico's cultural values.

Notes

1. Liga de Escritores y Artistas Revolucionarios (League of Revolutionary Writers and Artists); Bloque de Obreros Intelectuales (Bloc of Intellectual Workers); the *agoristas* were poets whose works were to be understood even by the illiterate and were a kind of anti-poetry or natural prose. An example of an *agorista* was Gutiérrez Cruz.
2. The *jarabe* is a Mexican dance similar to the Andalusian *zapateado* (Spanish heel-tapping dance and its music).
3. A pastoral play, the main theme of which is the announcement that the Archangel Michael makes to shepherds concerning the birth of the infant Christ.
4. A lower-class, poor, uncultured person who nevertheless is usually likeable.
5. The author is referring to a historical drama written by Lope de Vega around 1618, in which the inhabitants of Fuenteovejuna murder a tyrant and, when questioned by the investigating judge as to who had committed the crime, claim that it was Fuenteovejuna . . . all of them.
6. The Cristero rebellion, a political and religious movement which took place in the 1920s, started as a violent defence of the right to worship against anti-religious measures taken by the government.

THE PEASANTS AND THE NATION-STATE IN JAPAN, MEXICO, AND RUSSIA (1860–1940)

Michiko Tanaka
El Colegio de México, Mexico City, Mexico

Introduction

Within the overall framework of comparison between the socio-economic transformations which occurred in Mexico, Japan, and Russia as of the 1860s, this paper attempts to compare the processes of the formation of nation-states from the standpoint of the states' policies regarding peasants. It also takes into account the specific nature of each peasant society, its culture and "mentality," and its tradition of protest, things that had a bearing upon the course of the formation of the nation-states, giving them their particular characteristics. The paper also discusses other important factors such as international circumstances, domestic economic and political conditions, and the nature of the leadership. The task is complex and requires broad knowledge of each of the processes. My aim is to contrast images of the three societies as they follow their own course in history, so as to enrich the interpretation of each process. Once criticism of the paper has been received, a new agenda for research on each case will be developed.[1]

The three countries examined are "non-Western," in the sense that they do not constitute the hegemonic centre of Western civilization and that they have built nation-states and carried out industrial revolutions under pressure from outside. They adopted the "Western model" of civilization as of the middle of the nineteenth century or before.

Today, however, "the Western model," "the myth of the perpetually expanding industrial society," and "the developmental model" are subject to serious reconsideration since, if the model were to be applied in a universal and effective manner, the whole world would be threatened by the depletion of non-renewable resources and the destruction of the physical and mental conditions necessary for human life. In contrast, the limited application of this model in one part of the world implies the perpetuation of backwardness and misery in the rest of the world. In Mexico and in Japan, as in many other parts of the world, there is a growing awareness of the need to improve on this model, since it would turn out to be catastrophic over the long term. It is therefore necessary for historians to re-examine "modernization" processes and to remember once again that which has been forgotten – suppressed desires and values, lost traditions or heroes and movements that have been marginated in history – so as to open the way for the adoption of more viable options for the future. It is hoped that this paper will contribute to that reappraisal.

The three countries examined have a long agrarian tradition and were predominantly peasant societies in the middle of the nineteenth century. The majority of the peasants lived in communities that were worlds in themselves, as well as being administrative units connected to the government. One criterion for measuring the depth or impact of the social transformations in these countries could be the degree to which the agrarian communities were affected by, or incorporated into, this process.

The Formation of Nation-states in Japan, Mexico, and Russia

The nation-state, a particular kind of state, a government for a nation, emerged in the period of European expansionism under the impact of mercantile capitalism, but it was consolidated as a political entity under industrial capitalism. In the period of the imperialist wars, from the last decades of the nineteenth century on, the nation-state came to be almost the only viable model of an independent country, and continues to be the current and predominant concept of a state despite the numerous times it has been questioned.

The two basic aspects of the consolidation of the nation-state are: the formation of a state sovereign vis-à-vis other states and supra-state organizations such as the church or transnational corporations; and the national integration process which involves the concentration of power in a central state, the dissolution or reduction of political, economic and especially military autonomy, and the limitation of the cultural autonomy of infra-state units.

Although one precedes the other, these two aspects are interrelated and must be studied together. Therefore, before moving to an analysis of the national processes whereby the peasants were integrated, we shall outline the major features of the processes of affirmation of national sovereignty and the consolidation of a centralized state.

Of the three cases under review, Mexico is the one that had to overcome the greatest obstacle in order to achieve and maintain national sovereignty. The Mexican state is relatively young; it emerged as a result of the independence wars less than two centuries ago, and was based on the colonial political unity and the developing Hispanic-indigenous cultural community. The new central government arose under the conservative Creole leadership which came to power by defeating the radical democratic leaders. Iturbide's empire and his conservative Constitution, both short-lived, did not meet the needs of the social contingents mobilized in the fight for liberation: the Creole *hacendados* and priests with their mestizo and Indian peasant followers. Even after the establishment of the republic, the reforms decreed by J.M. Morelos, who headed the radical wing of the independence movement – the abolition of slavery and discrimination by caste, and the paternalistic legal separation of indigenous communities – were only adopted in a formal manner. For over half a century, the new state had to face different challenges to its sovereignty – US expansionism, European intervention, and the instances of regional separatism which presented a very real threat to the integrity of the country. Constant changes in the head of state reflected the weakness of central power. For that reason, it was necessary to resort to military leaders such as Santa Anna to serve as president. The institution of the Reform laws and the Constitution of 1857 appeared to put an end to this political chaos and introduce a liberal national strategy. However, the European intervention in support of the conservative programme, at France's initiative, once again interrupted the process. The victory of the republic over Maximilian's empire meant the failure of Napoleon III's imperialistic intentions and was of decisive importance for consolidating national sovereignty and the central government. Juarez's Liberal government left two major political inheritances – presidentialist centralism and the principle of non-intervention in international politics. Nevertheless, this political achievement did not lead to a definitive solution to the problem of national sovereignty. The preservation of political independence did not mean the exercise of full sovereignty in Mexico's case. Under the dictatorship of Porfirio Díaz, the country began to fall into economic and cultural dependence. The political leaders, dominated as they were almost totally by Western influence in the form of positivism, liberalism, and social Darwinism, looked outward rather than inward for the solution to problems. In their eagerness to attain "civilization," they tried to take short-cuts by importing capital, technology, technicians, and even workers. The progress made under Porfirio Díaz – railways, petroleum, mines, commercial agriculture, and foreign financing – was the source of the external pressure exerted during the years of the revolution and subsequent reforms. The confiscation of real estate held by foreigners during the revolution and the nationalization of petroleum in 1938, based on Article 27 of the Constitution of 1917, represented a milestone in the consolidation of the economic sovereignty of the Mexican state. The implementation of national, popular educational and cultural policies as of the revolution contributed to the formulation of a national cultural strategy that tended towards the creation of a Mexican cultural identity.[2]

In contrast to Mexico, Russia and Japan had existed as relatively centralized sovereign states for several centuries. The Russian state had subjugated the Orthodox church by means of the reform of worship as far back as 1660 and the government of the tsar was not dependent upon the approval of any external or internal authority for its existence. Similarly to the case of Spain, the desire to reconquer the Tartar-Mongols and Lithuanians turned into the impetus for territorial expansion, except in this case in the Euro-Asian continent. Specifically, as of the reign of Peter the Great, a very active expansionist policy was adopted and, during the first half of the eighteenth century, exploration was conducted as far as the coasts of the western Pacific. The new territories that were conquered made it possible to grant lands to the nobles working for the state and also to distribute land to retired army veterans so as to settle them as militarized colonists and to open new agricultural frontiers. The Napoleonic War of 1812, in contrast, did not produce spoils or other benefits to anyone, despite the united resistance of the army and the people. The expectations of social reform – the emancipation of the serfs – which had increased under the influence of the French Revolution and been heightened by the co-operation of the people in the war, were soon frustrated, since the Russian Empire was the leader of European post-revolutionary reaction. It was necessary to experience defeat in the Crimean War in order to recognize the need for emancipating the serfs.

Peter the Great also gave a decided impetus to the policy of "Westernization" in order to implement the national autocratic modernizing strategy. He instituted a series of reforms of military and bureaucratic organization; he promoted industry on the basis of servile labour; and he established an absolutist regime by placing the feudal lords under his authority, requiring them to serve in the government and reinforcing the servile labour system. This "Westernization" of the aristocracy by force created a significant gap between the culture of the governing élite and that of the popular masses, especially the peasants.

Russia preserved a special position in the European "world" market because it had its own Eastern trade route and was self-sufficient in basic foods and light industrial goods. Its financial, technological, and administrative dependence upon France and Germany increased as a result of an active economic policy of heavy industrialization and infrastructural development at the end of the nineteenth century, within the framework of the absolutist state. The rapid expansion of railways and the increase in metal-mining and manufacturing were nevertheless not enough to prevent Russia's defeat by Japan in the War of 1905. The popular revolution of that same year was ruthlessly suppressed by the government, though the government was forced to adopt a series of political and socio-economic reforms at the insistence of the liberal leaders. The national autocratic structure designed during the reign of Peter the Great experienced major changes under the leadership of a bourgeois constitutional monarchy. The belated liberal reforms, instead of having the expected effect, provoked even greater economic differentiation and sharpened social contradictions. The weakness of the tsar's regime became evident when the empire entered the unpopular European war and had to face popular protests in the cities, in the countryside, and at the front. Under these conditions, the February bourgeois revolution overthrew the monarchy; but in October it was superseded by the alliance of the democratic and popular social revolutionary forces. The political and economic chaos at the beginning of the Soviet regime, and the external danger to its survival from the military interventions of different powers, resulted in the consolidation of a highly centralized regime under the dictatorship of the proletariat. With the retreat of the Japanese army from the north of Sakhalin in 1925, the Soviet state established its sovereignty in a large part of the territory of the Russian Empire.[3]

The Tokugawa shogunate was a centralized feudal regime that was established in 1600, after a century and a half during which political power had been divided. The threat of Spanish conquest, whether real or imagined, in any case served as a pretext for adopting a policy of "isolationism" for two and a half centuries – a measure that assured monopolistic control on the part of the central government not only in trade but also in cultural contacts with the outside world. The "danger" of the penetration of Christianity also served as a pretext for instituting ideological control in the form of an annual registry of religion. News of the arrival of Russian explorers in the second half of the eighteenth century alarmed scholars and the leaders who were best informed about the outside world, leading to the promotion of exploration in the north and the colonization of the island of Hokkaido, home of the Ainu.

The crisis in national sovereignty created in Japan by the arrival of Commodore Perry, a man who had gained his experience in the wars against Mexico, had a profound impact on the leadership of the country. Later, after the conclusion of the unequal treaties, this concern was shared by a broader spectrum of the population, including the lower officials of the seigniorial governments and local leaders, consisting of the small bourgeoisie of the cities (*gōshō*) and the countryside (*gōnō*). The proposal by the government of Napoleon III to finance a project to transform the shogunate into an absolutist state, the punitive military expeditions of the Western powers, the temporary occupation of the island of Tsushima by the Russian navy – all these factors weakened national sovereignty but helped strengthen national consciousness and stimulated the unification of the anti-shogun forces.

The defeat of the power of the shogun in the Meiji Renovation (*Meiji ishin*) meant that the shogunate's concept of a dependent nation-state was definitely rejected in favour of independent status. At the beginning there were different proposals for national strategies, reflecting the participation of different forces in the Meiji Renovation; one of these was the democratic strategy of the Movement for Freedom and Popular Rights. However, after thoroughly familiarizing themselves with the political, economic, and social organizations of the Western powers, the political leaders in power opted for an autocratic strategy that implied the conversion of the country into an imperialist power. The autocratic constitutional monarchy promoted the colonization of the islands of Hokkaido and Ryukyu and initiated the interventionist and expansionist policy towards Korea, Taiwan, and China. The victory in the war of 1904–1905 with Russia evidenced the emergence of the Japanese state as an imperialist power. By the time of the First World War, Japan had heavy industry, a chemical industry, and capital goods industries.

The military impact felt in the middle of the nineteenth century was so strong that it left no doubt in the minds of the leaders inside or outside the government as to the need to assimilate Western civilization. With that purpose in mind, compulsory universal basic education was implemented and a system of higher education was established for a select minority who would devote themselves to assimilating the sciences, technologies and general knowledge of the West. At the same time, the government tried to inculcate ethnocentrism in the population by means of the institution of *tennō* (emperor) worship and the exaltation of traditional values in classrooms and army barracks.

Under these circumstances, the radical ethnocentric opposition gained strength and, with the support of part of the army, forced itself on the Westernizing and conciliatory leaders and initiated an active imperialist policy. The 15-year war that began with the occupation of Manchuria in 1931 was to end with the catastrophic defeat of the country that represented the end of the national imperialist strategy outlined during the middle of the nineteenth century.[4]

The Peasantry before the Reforms of the Mid-nineteenth Century in Japan, Mexico, and Russia

In the mid-nineteenth century, in all three countries, the peasantry constituted the majority of the population as well as the production base. Central power was located in the densely populated agricultural zone. Nevertheless, the natural and historical conditions germane to each country differentiated the social position of the peasants – their relationship with the state, their participation in the market economy, and their cultural communication with the rest of the population. In comparative terms, the following are the most important characteristics.

Geographic Distribution, Communications, and the Agricultural Frontiers

The linking of the country's territory by means of land, sea, and river communications and the agricultural use of the land was most intensive in Japan, an insular country that is relatively small and has a high population density. Outside the big cities, the population was distributed throughout the country on the narrow coastal plains and in the river valleys. With the exception of Hokkaido, which began to be colonized at the end of the eighteenth century, there were no more major agricultural frontiers remaining in the whole country. In contrast, Mexico and Russia had populations that were of a relatively low density, concentrated in the areas near the capitals or in areas where commercial crops were cultivated (wheat in Chornazem and henequen in Yucatán, for example). Except for certain suburban areas, the use of the soil was generally extensive and production increases were obtained by means of the colonization of new lands. Despite the existence of a network of major highways with transport and mail services, communications in Mexico were still quite uncertain. The majority of the peasants travelled by foot, and muleteers used droves of donkeys to transport loads. Land travel in the extensive semi-desert plains of the north was difficult even on horseback, and the same was true of the tropical jungles along the coasts and in the south. Neither the rivers nor the ocean were of use in overcoming the difficulties of intercommunication since the population was concentrated on the upper plain.

In Russia, communications improved a great deal during the months of snow. In addition, the existence of large navigable rivers and of canals on the broad plains facilitated contact and transportation in the southern and south-eastern regions.

Both Mexico and Russia suffered modifications to their land areas on various occasions during the nineteenth century. The drastic reduction in Mexico's territory created an awareness of the need to incorporate and colonize the then scarcely populated north, and led to the settlement of militarized colonists in the border zone. Nevertheless, there remained much arable land that was used only marginally for grazing. Russia, whose territory was growing, always had available new and very extensive agricultural frontiers. In the second half of the nineteenth century, one part of Siberia – the legendary Ural region – began to be exploited by militarized colonists and free peasants.

Agriculture[5]

From the standpoints of climate, types of basic crops and agricultural systems and technologies, the three countries present major contrasts. Each country had a set of agricultural traditions adapted to its specific natural conditions and based on popular customs. Mexico was basically characterized as the corn culture, although wheat and other commercial crops were already being grown in large areas. Corn is a relatively stable crop, adapted to differing climates and types of land, and requiring little care, but it exhausts the soil if it is cultivated continuously. Long- or short-term fallowing, combined with grazing and crop rotation, in accordance with the pre-Columbian method, were necessary to preserve the fertility of the soil. The use of the land and the task of preparing the soil, in the case of slash-and-burn agriculture, were regulated and carried out collectively by the peasants.

In contrast, Japan was considered the rice culture. The cultivation of rice in a flooded field is a stable method of production and conserves the productivity of the soil. By controlling the water, the same field is utilized for cultivating other cereals, yielding two or more harvests annually. Aside from rice, important commercial crops such as cotton, black mulberry trees, oilseeds, and vegetables were grown in rotation. Overall, the Japanese agricultural system required a great deal of care and extensive use of fertilizers. The regulation of the use of water and forests needed communal agreement.

Russia belonged to a mixed agriculture culture. The cultivation of cereals, mainly barley and wheat, was undertaken by ploughing the land two or three times a year and combining fallowing with grazing. Only in the Chornazem region (black land) in the south of the Ukraine was continuous cultivation practised. The use and periodic redistribution of the land were regulated by communal agreements.

In all three countries, commercial production was fairly widespread by the middle of the nineteenth century, although there were differences in the nature of the market. While Russia and Mexico were integrated, to a greater or lesser degree, in the external market – Russia with wheat, Mexico with henequen, coffee, vanilla, cattle and leather, and so on – Japan was oriented solely towards its domestic market. Moreover, the expansion of commercial production was achieved in different ways: in Japan, following the already existing tendency, production increases were attained by intensifying the exploitation of the land and strengthening family production units, despite the fact that there was concentration in land ownership. In contrast, in Russia and Mexico, production increases were achieved mainly by extending the land under cultivation, through colonization.

Ownership Systems and Forms of Land Exploitation

In Mexico, both in the colonial and post-independence periods, there were three types of ownership of agricultural land: communal ownership by Indian villages, where the land was worked by a combination of communal and family labour; small private ownership, where land was mostly worked by the family; and large private ownership (haciendas) where the land was worked by wage labour, slaves, or debt peonage. Following independence, under the system of absolute private ownership, the latter type of land ownership expanded rapidly; village lands were fenced in and rent was demanded for their use. This system also encouraged the accumulation of debts in the *tienda de raya*, or hacienda store, as a means of binding labour that was legally free.

In Russia and Japan, the feudal property system prevailed. In Russia, seigniorial lands and land worked by the peasants existed side by side. The former tended to disappear in areas of low productivity, but in the fertile region where wheat was raised for export it remained and even tended to increase. Other than the seigniorial farms and land for dwellings, the farmlands, forests, and water were considered communal property and their use was regulated communally. In many places, such resources were subject to periodic redistribution so as to maintain equity among the communal farmers. The land was usually worked on a family basis. In marginal regions and in those within the domain of non-Russian lords, there were also properties held by peasant families.

In Japan, with the exception of the rural warriors (*gōshi*) in a few domains, the land was worked only by peasant families. There was no competition between peasant and feudal exploitation either for the land or for labour. Feudal policy was to maintain a stable number of small areas worked by peasants and to avoid possible economic differentiation between the contributing producers. However, despite the fact that the sale or "permanent mortgage" of the land was prohibited, the latter occurred frequently and, in fact, was officially recognized in order to protect the interests of the landowners. The concentration of land among the rich peasants and merchants did not lead to commercial exploitation of the land with the use of wage labour, but rather to the expansion of the land tenancy system.

Status of the Peasants

In Mexico, slavery and legal discrimination on the basis of race were abolished in the war for independence, and individual liberties and equality were proclaimed. Nevertheless, the preponderance of indigenous people among the peasant population and their distribution among over 50 ethnic groups, often monolingual, put them at a disadvantage vis-à-vis the landowners (*hacendados*) and merchants of Spanish or mestizo extraction. The indebted slaves, called *peones acasillados*, did not see any improvement in their situation and their indebtedness tended to increase. Political leaders in this chaotic transition period had little in common with the Indian peasants. Both the centralist Conservatives and the federalist Liberals considered the customs and institutions of the "Indian" peasants to be backward, and believed it was necessary to civilize them. In addition, political anarchy helped increase the power of the caciques, or local bosses, who frequently were landowners or members of the clergy, and who maintained taxes that had officially been abolished (tithes, per capita tax, sales tax, etc.) and viceregal services without modifications. It was not until the Reform Laws and the Constitution were put into effect under the Liberal central government of the restored republic that the colonial social order began to be affected.

In Russia, as well as in Japan, the peasants had a subservient status, although the terms varied. In Russia, with the exception of a small number of liberated peasants and militarized colonists, the entire peasant population belonged to one of two categories of serfs: those of feudal lords and those of the state. Although those of the state generally enjoyed better conditions, none of them were free. Although the feudal lord could not kill a serf and, when selling him, tended not to break up the family or separate the serf from the land, he could use the serf's person and the product of his labour virtually without any limits beyond those of his own conscience and economic need. If the serf fled, he was pursued by the government of the tsar. The fact that there were certain cases in which serfs became wealthy enough to buy their freedom and that of their families, and even became important merchants or industrialists, or that some small impoverished lords lived almost as poorly as their serfs, does not change the overall picture. Only in the regions annexed by the Russians and inhabited by Lithuanian and Polish lords or German colonists did the government of the tsar apply a more liberal policy towards the peasantry.

In Japan, the peasant had to be registered in a village, and in order to move had to obtain permission from the village head. The shogun or lords exercised dominion over a given territory and could transfer to their vassals the right to collect taxes and demand services from the population. But they could not control the peasants nor sell them, with or without the land. In contrast to the Russian serf, the Japanese peasant held a relatively high status in the social hierarchy – below the warrior and above the merchant and artisan. Towards the middle of the nineteenth century, a marked socio-economic differentiation was to be observed in the most economically advanced areas of the country. On the one hand, there were the wealthy peasants, who were landowners, moneylenders, rural entrepreneurs, and local notables; on the other, there were poor peasants who were tenant farmers, debtors, and semi-proletarians and who were marginated from power in the village community. Some wealthy peasants performed administrative functions in their respective domains and bought lower-level titles to warrior status.

Another important aspect in comparing the status of the peasants was their access to arms and military training. In Japan, arms for combat had been the exclusive prerogative of the warrior since the founding of the Tokugawa shogunate. The peasant, like the artisan and merchant, could not carry any arms other than a short sword for personal defence when travelling. Only after the confrontation with external armies was military training of the peasants initiated on a limited scale in the dominions of the shogun and of some lords.

In Mexico, the Indian peasants did not have access to arms either, only to work tools. In the central and southern regions, riding horseback and handling a rifle were the exclusive privileges of the landowners and their men. In the border zones of the north, however, lived the militarized colonists; and the farmers carried firearms for defence against intrusions by Yaqui or Apache nomads. The military mobilization of the villages during the war for independence left a deep imprint on the peasant population in many regions, and created links with the officials of the liberating army who began their military career in that war. Some military leaders, retired or on active duty, exercised local sway and became men of influence and eventually leaders of popular rebellions.

In Russia, as of the period of Peter the Great, military service for serfs was instituted. The service was long and demanding and, despite the promise of freedom and the granting of a plot in the new agricultural land for veteran soldiers, the job was considered onerous. However, experience in the army, as well as temporary migration to the city in search of additional income – which was especially common among the peasants of the central region – offered the communal peasants the opportunity of seeing a world beyond their native town and of making contacts with people of different social extraction (*raznochintsui*): the Russian middle class. At the same time, military service served as a vehicle for instilling patriotism and faith in the authority of the tsar.

The Peasant Community and its Outside Links

In all three countries, the peasant community that existed can be characterized as a "closed corporation" (Eric Wolf). The community constituted a world in itself for the majority of the peasants, who spent most of their lives there. It also constituted an autonomous unit which was, in large measure, self-sufficient. By the mid-nineteenth century, this community was under the influence of the market economy in all three countries. Consequently, the tendency towards greater economic and social differentiation produced growing domestic tension. The concentration of land in the hands of the big landowners and the migration of the poor in search of additional income were already widely evident.[6]

The relative self-sufficiency of the peasant community did not mean that the peasants lived in isolation. Despite poor communications, there were numerous links with the world beyond the communal limits. Vertical linkage – that is, an asymmetrical relationship – existed between the community and the different levels of political, economic, and religious power. In Japan and

Russia, where there was a feudal system, the vertical linkage was between the community and the central or seigniorial government. The peasant community constituted the basic administrative unit, with a given territorial extension and officially recognized authorities who were usually elected by its members. The community had official status as a *mura* (Japan) and *dirievnya* (Russia). In Mexico, where the colonial order was preserved virtually intact in local administration, the vertical relationship between the central and state powers and the community (village) through the *villa* or *pueblo cabacero* (head village of the municipality) was still not overcome. The relationship between the peasant community and the powerful landowner also tended to be vertical, because economic dependence was combined with physical coercion exercised by the private guards. The horizontal linkage consisted of the relationship of symmetrical interchange of men and women (most frequently as spouses), goods, labour and services, and cultural and recreational elements. This linkage tended to increase together with the expansion of the market economy. Trade relationships could also be asymmetrical or unequal under conditions of social discrimination and colonial or neo-colonial feudal privilege.

In order to evaluate the internal cohesion of the society, it is important to examine the vertical and horizontal ideological links of the community with the outside world. The vertical link is the hegemony that the ruling class or classes exercise over the peasantry by means of religion, the moral code, or the value system advocated for the maintenance of the established hierarchical order. In Japan, at the beginning of the Tokugawa shogunate, the vertical articulation of the communities with the feudal powers was established and the horizontal link was limited as much as possible in order to increase the degree of control. However, this situation did not last long and, as of the middle of the eighteenth century, in parallel with the expansion of the market economy, the following phenomena occurred: the migration of labour, the movement of specialists, artisans, and artists, and the dissemination of an urban culture which promoted a taste for "luxury" (according to the feudal government, everything that was not strictly for subsistence was considered a luxury) as well as a hedonistic attitude towards life. The government of the shogunate tried in vain to control these new relationships and attitudes; finally, it had to adapt to the new reality and turn for co-operation and guidance to the rich peasants and educated merchants who had assimilated the Confucian moral code. During the crisis of the shogunate, a few of the latter offered their services to help the feudal government overcome its economic difficulties, and assumed technical administrative and financial functions. At the same time, when they discovered the hypocrisy of the ruling class, which required frugality only of the masses but not of itself, the educated peasants began to question the feudal authorities. This was one of the sources of the loss of legitimacy of the shogunate.[7]

In Russia, the fact that the tsar's government collected per capita taxes and required military service of all the peasant population, including those who belonged to the nobles, and that the tsar was head of the Orthodox faith, suggests the existence of greater direct vertical control than in Japan. The Russian feudal government also used the peasant community as its administrative base and tried to reinforce it by institutionalizing the authorities and communal customs such as *starasta* (elders) and periodic distribution of farmlands. Despite the community of faith and the possibility of indoctrinating serf soldiers so as to make them identify with both tsar and country, the links between peasant culture and the aristocracy were obstructed by the growing Westernization and secularization of the latter. As this cultural gap widened, there emerged as a reaction people who idealized the peasantry and considered the peasant community as the repository of authentic Russian traditions. Others who were more realistic recognized the need to abolish the subservient status of the peasantry and to better its economic situation through improved agricultural and industrial development. These critics tended to be of diverse social origins (*raznochintsui*), but usually did not have direct links with the peasantry. The tradition of ideological opposition to the tsar existed in the heart of the peasantry and also among the urban merchants. That tradition was upheld by the heretic religious community of the divisionists (*raskolniki*), which originated in the religious reform of the seventeenth century.

In Mexico, after Independence, the peasant community (Indian people) found itself in a worse position than before in view of the fact that, under the viceregal regime, it had enjoyed official status, local autonomy, and the territory and natural resources for subsistence and cultural continuity. Invasion by landowners or religious institutions, which was not unusual, was punished, albeit always belatedly and after much red tape and numerous petitions. The existence of conflicts of interest between the different levels of colonial power or between secular and religious authorities allowed the communities a certain leeway. However, during the decades of political anarchy after Independence, the community was faced with the need to defend itself by its own efforts and with the support of neighbouring communities.

National cultural unity did not yet exist. Owing to linguistic diversity, it was difficult to form a cultural-ideological link between the indigenous peasant communities and the urban masses or the governing class. The colonialist psychosis of the mainly Creole governing class of the post-Independence period saw in every indigenous peasant mobilization a manifestation of the caste war (or war of the races). The religious link, which constituted one of the most important links of viceregal society, was severely weakened, since in the Catholic church a conflict emerged between the high clergy, who identified themselves with colonial authority, and the landowners and low clergy, who identified themselves with the indigenous people. During the Independence period, the radical leaders – including members of the low clergy such as Hidalgo and Morelos – were excluded from the new government, but they nevertheless preserved important social and cultural functions in the national society. However, neither the Liberal leaders of the centre, generally anti-clerical, nor the Conservatives who relied upon the high clergy, managed to establish linkages between the peasant communities and the new centralized state.

Peasant Movements

It is commonly believed that peasant movements are destructive events of short duration. However, other than in the marginal regions where effective control by the central power does not exist or in periods when the legitimacy of the central power is questioned, peasant movements among villages linked to the central power begin with actions that are within the law and show a respectful attitude towards the authorities. They often begin with a petition or legal appeal, persisting in these actions and waiting with great patience, often for more than a generation, until their legal resources are completely exhausted. Only then, on a step-by-step basis, do they turn to more radical actions.

The patient and continuous fight through legal petitions was transformed into a collective demand, accompanied by direct actions such as marches, meetings, demonstrations, the destruction of goods and documents, and confrontations with seigniorial or public forces. In general, instances of protest were undertaken as group ventures under the direction of the communal authorities or, if the community was socially differentiated, of the people with the most experience and knowledge from outside the community. Along with this radicalization, the territorial extension involved in the movement tended to increase and eventually the movement resorted for leadership to some local civil or military chief.[8]

In Japan, the Tokugawa shogunate achieved some 250 years of relative stability precisely because it made the social and physical separation of the warriors and peasants its constitutional principle, adopting different measures to avoid the unification of the peasant movements with the discontented warriors. Therefore, with the exception of the first few decades of the shogunate, there were no peasant rebellions led by warriors. Nevertheless, the internal contradictions in the domains, for example the fight among different factions for succession, offered the possibility of a temporary alliance. In the civil war of 1868–1869, the anti-shogun leaders tried to utilize peasant uprisings in the pro-shogun domains as a tactical measure. In Russia, the rebellions of the militarized colonists (*kozaki*), whose leaders proclaimed themselves the true tsars, as in the case of Pugachov, achieved peasant adhesion and support. In Mexico, as of the Independence period there were intermittent civil wars, as well as those waged against foreign invaders. This circumstance set the stage for an alliance between military men of different political affiliations and the communal peasants, who tried to defend their lands against the private guards of the landowners – as in the cases of the peasants in the states of Morelos and Guerrero with General Juan Alvarez of the Liberating Army of the South, or the peasants in Veracruz with Santa Anna's Lieutenant Colonel, Mariano Orlate.

In Japan prior to 1868, the legal order of the shogunate prevailed and the official ideology proclaimed the peasantry as the foundation of society. The shogun's decree of 1649 stated: "Rulers come and go, but the peasants remain and work the same land from generation to generation." At the same time, the greatest tax burden fell on the peasants' shoulders, and obedience to the hierarchical order and the prohibition of any acts of popular protest were strictly enforced. It was under these circumstances that the peasant movement emerged in the three districts of Heii, lasting for three generations – from the end of the eighteenth to the middle of the nineteenth century – and finally achieving its proposed objective. In Mexico, as of the colonial period and even in the state of anarchy after Independence, the communal peasants insisted on compliance with the law. The Indian villages, which brought lawsuits against the clergy or the landowners who were invading their communal lands, demanded respect for their original rights to the land, first before the colonial authorities and later before the Mexican authorities. The legality established by the central power could not always be imposed throughout the national territory, nor was its priority that of defending the interests of peasant communities. Nevertheless, the communities did not stop protesting to the legal authorities. They even produced "viceregal deeds" as a legal basis for their claims within the new system of private property, in order to reinforce their right based on custom.

The great caution of the peasant movements, especially communal ones, served to ensure the internal cohesion of the community and the legitimacy of leadership at each step. Even when they failed, peasant movements constituted a learning process for the peasantry. They educated peasants as to the structure and functioning of power and the hierarchy of the authorities. They evidenced the need to act in an organized and disciplined manner, and also served to establish a tradition of protest among peasants, with their own heroes and symbolic and practical collective memories. Peasant movements were a means of popular expression, a method of communication with the different levels of power on a basis of equality, even if this was only momentary.

One of the most effective forms of peasant struggle has always been flight. In Russia and Mexico, and in Japan until the seventeenth century, the availability of new lands made flight an effective tool. The emergence of communities of runaways (fugitive slaves of African origin) in the coastal areas of

Mexico during the colonial period and the establishment of settlements of fugitive serfs in Siberia are just two examples. The attempt by the tsar's government to impose ever greater restrictions on the personal freedom of the serfs and the resort to indebtedness by Mexican landowners in order to retain their peons only serve to confirm the importance of flight as a method of protest. In Japan, as of the eighteenth century, there was little possibility of real flight. It was only practised as a symbolic communal action in which the peasants abandoned the domain to which they belonged to draw the attention of the shogun to the repudiated feudal lord.

In agricultural border zones and in areas with poor quality land, the small farmers – among them the fugitives – needed to establish a link with the state in order to protect themselves against the invasions of the lords or the incursions of nomadic peoples. The state, in turn, had an interest in safeguarding its territory and in promoting productive exploitation and, therefore, in protecting the marginal population. Under these circumstances, the link that was established in the marginal regions tended to be more symmetrical. The need to arm the peasants or the impossibility of disarming them certainly served as the basis for armed rebellions in areas that were peripheral to the central power.

In all three countries, the peasant movement had a bearing on the evolution of official policy and became one of the major sources of concern to the governments of these fundamentally agrarian societies. Through the experience of the peasant movements, there emerged among the peasants local leaders who began consciously to assume the role of linkage agents among the communities, or between these and the different levels of power, including the religious hierarchy and the market.

National Integration of the Peasantry

Economic Integration

The abolition of feudal or colonial restrictions in favour of individual freedoms was the basic premise for the integration of the peasantry into the national society and, in particular, into the domestic market. In Mexico, the abolition of slavery and of social discrimination dating back to the colonial period was formally proclaimed in the Declaration of Independence of 1821; in Russia, with the Great Reforms of 1861–1865, the process of emancipating the serfs began without the abolition of the status of the feudal nobility; and in Japan, the reforms following the Meiji Renovation abolished feudal statuses and restrictions, although they established new ranks of nobility with certain privileges within the framework of the bourgeois monarchy.

Originally, the nation-state was constructed on the individualistic principle; this principle was modified in order to ensure the development of absolute private ownership, which is fundamental to capitalist society. The market economy, which functions on this basis, mobilized the individual initiative of the peasants for a greater intensity of labour and profit. The nation-states that attempted to strengthen themselves by competing with foreign hegemonic powers tried to create the same bases and faced different problems.

In Mexico, the system of absolute private ownership began to operate at the time of Independence, when the colonial restriction that "protected" the communal properties of the Indian peoples was eliminated. The Law of Lerdo de Tejada, which set down the legal basis of the system of private property for the purpose of disentailing corporate property, still recognized the communal lands held by the villages as exceptions. But Article 27 of the Constitution of 1857 made the principle of private ownership absolute. Together with the religious corporations and others, the peasant communities lost the legal basis for preserving communal lands. The Liberal central government's primary interest was in the productive use of the land, which to them meant commercial exploitation. In order to achieve that end, they even resorted to colonization, by European and Asian immigrants, of the lands expropriated from the indigenous peasant communities.

Despite unfavourable legislation and the official policy of harassment, the peasants continued their efforts to defend the communal lands against invasions and expropriations, demanding that they be returned to them. This constituted the prelude to the Revolution of 1910–1917. During the nineteenth century, the number of dependent agricultural workers (*peones acasillados*) increased, as did that of share-croppers and tenant farmers, as a result of the dispossession of the communal peasants' lands and the expansion of the haciendas. These landless peasants were later to demand that the revolutionary government carry out land distribution.

The revolutionaries of 1910–1917 criticized the consequences of the Liberal national strategy of 1857, and proposed a new national plan that was to guarantee political, economic, and cultural independence, as well as meet the basic demands of all the social forces that took part in the revolution. Without a doubt, the peasantry participated in the revolution as an important social force and the agrarian issue was always present in discussions regarding the new national strategy. This situation was reflected in Article 27 of the Constitution of 1917, which laid the basis for agrarian policies. However, a careful study of the original article, its later amendments, and agrarian laws and statutes of different periods leads one to conclude that a unified agrarian plan was not formulated, but rather that there were various parallel plans that were not always in agreement with one another. According to their view of the world and their expectations regarding Mexico's future, different leaders of the revolution proposed different agrarian plans: large-scale commercial agriculture; collective or co-operative commercial agriculture; family subsistence agriculture to complement wages, etc.

In all cases, the leaders of the new state were basically concerned with integrating the peasantry into social production, so as to be in a position to supply the cities and industry, and not allowing peasant production to be limited to subsistence agriculture for home use. In contrast, the basic concern of the peasants was to own and cultivate a large enough area of land to be able to lead a dignified life. Under the capitalist system, the market regulates the relationship between these two goals, the national and the peasant goal, which do not always coincide. In Mexico, where an attempt was made to partially socialize agricultural production in order to reconcile the various goals, the state utilized, not always successfully, the distribution of land (*ejido*), the granting of credits and technical assistance, agricultural infrastructure projects, and the control of commercialization through guaranteed prices. In theory, all of this was to induce peasants who were petty landholders to follow official policy, but in reality it served the purposes of the commercial farmers. As a result, the communal peasants or *ejidatarios* had to intensify their labour and complement it with non-agricultural jobs in order to support themselves as peasants, owing to the effects of the market economy, which tends to lower the prices of agricultural products and necessitates greater consumption.[9]

In Japan, the principle of absolute private ownership was established through the abolition of the seigniorial rights of territorial dominion in 1871, the Land Tax Reform, and the cadastre conducted throughout the country in 1873–1876. Large extensions of communal land or of land for communal use, mainly woods and wastelands, became the property of the *tennō*, the Japanese monarch, and of the central, prefectural, and municipal governments. There were also individuals who appropriated communal lands. Only part of the said lands were preserved as the property of each district (*ku*), equivalent to the village (*mura*) of the shogunate, under the condominium system of the communal members. However, since socio-economic differentiation developed among the inhabitants of the district, a few landholding families directed local politics and tended to abuse district resources. Under the Tokugawa shogunate, the sale or "perpetual mortgaging" of land was formally prohibited. Perhaps for that reason, there was a custom whereby original peasant owners frequently could mortgage the lands without any time limit and could demand their return if they paid for them. As of the Land Tax Reform, there was no longer a legal basis for such a demand and the concentration of land in the hands of absentee landowners made the application of the law more mechanical. This reform and the deflationary policy of Matsukata initiated in 1885, which caused the bankruptcy of a large number of rural agricultural and industrial units, stripped a significant number of peasant landowners of their land and, at the same time, accelerated the expansion of land tenancy. Peasant organizations emerged, such as the Brotherhood for the Restitution of the Land (Tochi Fukken Dōshikai), which from the end of the nineteenth century on demanded agrarian reform. The guarantee of perpetual tenancy constituted one of the principal demands of numerous tenant movements that continued to spring up even in the latter years of the Fifteen Years' War (1931–1945). After the victory in the Russo-Japanese War and the expansion of colonial domains, there arose the possibility of importing basic foodstuffs such as rice cheaply from Taiwan or Korea in order to supply the greater demand created by growing Japanese industrialization. This new circumstance caused discrepancies on agrarian policy between the industrialists and landowners, who constituted the two basic classes in power. Under the landowning system, with its high rents, the petty tenant farmers barely participated in the market. Only the large landowners and part of the small landed farmers constituted factors in the national market as suppliers and consumers. At the initiative of the reformist current within the government, some measures geared to converting tenant farmers into landowners were adopted, though these could not solve the problems of the majority of tenant farmers. With the impact of the Great Depression of 1929–1933, the industrialists as well as the landowners supported the policy of expanding into Manchuria, adopted by the government under pressure from the military as a way out of the crisis and as a solution to numerous problems, among them the agrarian one. It should be pointed out that the Japanese peasantry, even the poorest, also accepted the policy of colonizing Manchuria without protest. Nevertheless, this solution did not alleviate the agrarian situation of the peasant majority and required large human sacrifices owing to the prolonged war with the Chinese and other peoples. Only with the post-war agrarian reform was the Japanese peasantry fully integrated into the national economy, becoming one of the factors in the Japanese "miracle" of economic development. However, the very mechanism of rapid economic growth that gave priority to industry and to the external sector undermined the economic and social foundations of the peasantry which, by 1980, had been reduced to a minority sector.[10]

In Russia, the Great Reforms delimited the lands of the landowning aristocracy and of the "emancipated" peasants. The new status of the latter was that of serfs of the state until such time as they had paid off their debt to the tsar's government, which had covered the compensation given to the feudal lords for their land. In this and later agrarian reforms, official policy made the payment of the debt and taxes and the utilization of the land the responsibility of the community as a whole, and not of the peasants as individuals. This was an attempt to abolish the serf status without significantly affecting either the labour system or the availability or cost of labour for the seigniorial farms. The petty landholder peasant who was in debt to the state was obliged to work the land of the lord under lease or as an agricultural worker on his farm, under the collective responsibility of the community as before. Nevertheless, the expansion of the market economy in the countryside, and the opportunities for non-agricultural jobs towards the end of the nineteenth century in the central and Ural regions, allowed some peasants to save money and acquire land without fear of being stripped of it by the lords, as had occurred before. This tendency became more pronounced as of Stolypin's reforms of 1906, which finally established the principle of absolute private ownership and tried to sell off the seigniorial and state farms by auction. In the course of several decades, the Russian peasantry underwent a rapid process of social differentiation which resulted in a small number of wealthy peasants, independent middle-class peasants, and numerous poor landless peasants, tenant farmers, and day labourers. There was an increase in the number of village conflicts in which not only landlords, but also newly rich peasants, were accused of enhancing their personal wealth and of failing to bring any benefit to the community. The old communal standard imposed itself on these occasions in violent outbursts. In the Revolution of 1917, the Land Decree which granted the usufruct of the land to those who worked it was of decisive importance in making the peasantry adhere to the revolutionary government. The peasants achieved their goal: the agrarian law of February 1918 guaranteed them enough land of their own to live well. Nevertheless, the destruction of the distribution network and the decrease in the industrial production of consumer goods under conditions of civil war and foreign intervention led the peasants to produce only what they consumed themselves. This obliged the Soviet authorities to resort to coercion to obtain agricultural products. The new economic policy adopted to correct the fall in production and commercialization resulting from the policy of forced distribution during the civil war allowed for the private accumulation of capital and caused a reappearance of the socio-economic differentiation that had been checked by the agrarian reform of the revolution. The *nouveau riche* peasants who re-emerged tried to resist the re-establishment of the socialist regime in the countryside, by taking advantage of the fact that they controlled most of the machinery, animals, work tools, and technical and commercial know-how. Towards the end of the 1920s, when the socialized industrial sector was consolidated and the Soviet government was recognized internationally, forced collectivization occurred, through the mobilization of the stratum of poor peasants, to put an end to small peasant production. On the government's initiative, and in accordance with the centralized plan, the countryside was mechanized and the application of chemical fertilizers was begun. These measures, together with the continued policy of colonization of new lands in Central Asia and Siberia, once again raised agricultural production, which had been at a low level for a period. With collectivization, the collective farms (*kolkhozes*), together with the state farms (*sovhozes*), constituted units of agricultural and partly industrial production as well as administrative social units. The Soviet peasantry was thus integrated vertically into social production. The problem of supplying basic goods to the population was apparently solved, even in wartime (1939–1945) and during the post-war period. Once the tasks of the war and reconstruction were completed, however, the new problem was the difficulty of mobilizing initiative, especially to improve the variety and quality of agricultural production; different measures, such as material incentives, the partial restitution of the family parcel of land, and the free market were adopted to solve this problem.[11]

Political-institutional Integration

Another of the basic conditions for the integration of the peasantry into the nation-state is the dissolution or reduction of the autonomy of agrarian communities and the reorganization of the population within the framework of national institutions. In the three countries under comparison, as of the reforms of the mid-nineteenth century the central government tried to take an active part in the peasant world by means of the establishment of a centralized bureaucracy; an improvement in the communications network; the formation of centralized public power (the armed forces and the police); and the institution of a system of public education. Consequently, communal authority was subject to either radical or gradual decline, depending on the particular case, and the public functions of the internal organizations of the community diminished.

In Japan, the Meiji government attempted, at the start, to radically reorganize the system of local administration so as to establish direct, vertical control over the population. With this purpose in mind, it carried out the most complete general registry of the population ever and mechanically grouped a given number of families into the minimum administrative unit and a given number of these units into a larger administrative division, and so on. Through this administrative division, the central government tried to impose the will of the state on the local organization of the population. The attempt failed in the first instance because there were various peasant uprisings in protest against the new system. In 1879, the old order was provisionally restored with modifications that were only formal in nature. However, the government soon reorganized local administration, grouping various village communities (*mura*), known from then on as districts (*ku*) into a municipality (*son*) with offices, post office, police, etc., in the municipal seat. A dual administrative system began to operate in which the centralized bureaucratic system controlled public matters down to the level of the municipal government, where the landowners, public officials, merchants and professionals took part in policy-making and even the national political parties participated. However, the majority of the rural population did not play an active role in this political-administrative world at the municipal level because the electoral system, according to the census, did not allow them to participate, and their links with the local bureaucracy were sporadic. In contrast, at the district level the traditional communal authorities, whose members partially coincided with the municipal leaders – for example, in the case of the landowners – used their traditional method of government by consensus to administer matters vital to production (the use of water and forests) and community life.[12]

Nevertheless, under these conditions of political-administrative duality there was a centripetal force that tended to integrate the peasantry. Two institutions that were of particular importance in this regard should be mentioned: the system of public education that included basic education lasting four (later six) years, established in 1872, and compulsory military service for men, decreed that same year. The Japanese state utilized the modern peasant organizations that were based on traditional horizontal linkages for the purposes of national integration. In the first half of the Meiji era, an important political movement arose whose social base consisted of the rural middle class and the peasantry, and which objected to the autocratic modernizing strategy of the state and proposed an alternative liberal-democratic approach.[13] Under the influence of this Movement for the Freedom and Popular Rights, different rural youth groups emerged with civic or political aims; these were called *seinenkai* (association of youths) modelled after the traditional *wakamono nakama* (village youth organization), which performed basic communal functions. In contrast to the *wakamono nakama*, the *seinenkai* tended to relate to the other organizations in a horizontal manner and they came to form a local or regional federation. However, this initiative of creating a larger network of organizations was considered very timely by the central government, which was trying to build a system of national mobilization and support. The manipulation and intervention of the federation of youth organizations which was then called *seinendan* (youth league) occurred, on the one hand, because of the directed socialization that young people had received through their schooling, military service, or mass media campaigns and, on the other hand, because the advisors to the youth leagues were generally teachers, municipal officials, or veterans of the armed forces who tended to adopt the official line without much questioning.[14]

After various years of political mobilization, universal male suffrage was approved in 1925. At the same time, the Law for the Maintenance of Public Security was passed, reinforcing the state's ability to repress political movements opposed to the regime. Under these conditions, various worker or peasant-based political parties emerged which, in reality, were unable to obtain the support of the peasant masses or of the tenant farmers, except in a few instances. As long as these opposition parties operated in the national political milieu with which the communal peasants had no links, the state retained certain institutional links and continued to manipulate local organizations.

In Mexico, beginning with the restoration of the republic in 1867, an effort was made to achieve the unification and centralization of the legal-administrative system. Nevertheless, during the entire Porfiriato,[15] the traditional communal authorities and the private authorities of the haciendas (caciques) and mining, colonizing, railway, and other types of companies coexisted with the public administration authorities. The linkage and relative importance of these local authorities varied from one region to the next. In traditional agricultural regions with a large indigenous peasant population in the central plain and the south, the traditional political organization of the communities constituted the basis for local administration and was linked to the central government through the municipal seat. There were established the public offices, the church and eventually the school, which employed Creole or mestizo officials and teachers. The haciendas and national and foreign companies employed labour from the villages on a regular or seasonal basis in addition to the regular, often dependent workers who lived on company land in what was virtually a town. These companies tended to wield influence over local and regional civil and military officials, a circumstance which worked in their favour in the event of lawsuits or conflicts over land or water with neighbouring villages.

Only well-educated, Spanish-speaking people with considerable financial resources participated in national politics. The peasant masses were excluded from electoral politics and their participation prior to 1910 was limited solely to occasions of peasant or indigenous rebellions or military mobilizations against them. These rural masses were virtually untouched by the ambitious plans for national secular education and technical-agricultural or industrial development proposed during the Porfiriato. The factors that can objectively be considered to have contributed to the integration of the peasants were, on the one hand, the construction of the network of railways, which made possible regular communication between the capital and remote regions of the country and, on the other, the creation of the national army in which the peasants were forced to serve by levy and whose officers and veterans at times enjoyed prestige among the peasant population, advising them and even organizing petitions, lawsuits, or peasant rebellions.

The Revolution of 1910–1917 appears to have removed a large part of the peasant population from this political-administrative marginalization, since they had contributed to the installation of the new power, and the new electoral system guaranteed the participation of all the male population. The national institutions of defence, public education, communications, and social security began to include the rural population as well. Above all, the system of distribution of lands for communal use (*ejido*), along with a series of agricultural measures geared to strengthening peasant use of the land (including collective measures), were adopted during the years 1936–1939, and created vertical agrarian links between the state and the peasantry. Yet the peasants did not participate in the power alliance that developed after the revolution. Only for a brief period did the pro-agrarian leaders exert influence, and a limited influence at that, on the central government's agrarian policies. Cárdenas' administration, which tried to direct the class struggle through institutional channels in order to avoid civil war, adopted a series of radical agrarian measures and, at the same time, implemented the policy of agricultural development which in the long run benefited the business sector in the countryside. Despite the formal inclusion of the peasant sector in the governing party (CNC-PRM/PRI), the agricultural and agrarian policy of the Mexican revolutionary regime was determined mainly by the interests of the agricultural and industrial bourgeoisie, the workers, and the state bureaucracy. The asymmetrical, vertical link of the peasantry with the state tends to repress peasant initiatives to organize themselves independently and horizontally for productive or political purposes. New caciques emerged who were local leaders of the centralized peasant organization or local officials who, in contrast to the landowners, linked the peasant population with the state.[16]

In Russia, the tsarist government adopted the Great Reforms for the partial emancipation of the serfs and the political-administrative reforms of the 1880s in order to reach a definitive solution of the serf problem and to open the way for limited peasant representation in the prefectural government. Nevertheless, in these reforms the government of the tsar tried to preserve the agrarian communities which were considered the basis of social stability and to make use of their traditional authorities and institutions. This approach was not very viable since the expansion of the market economy in the countryside, spurred partly by these very reforms, contributed to a rapid social differentiation within the communities. The number of rural conflicts increased and peasant protest was no longer directed solely against the landlords or large farmers, but also against the *nouveau riche* peasants who amassed family fortunes by means of usury, mediation, and the leasing of land without fulfilling their communal obligations in a degree corresponding to their wealth. This same circumstance also caused an increase in the temporary or permanent migration of peasants to cities and industrial centres. The military mobilization of the peasants due to frequent tensions with such powers as Great Britain or Japan on the Asian borders of the Russian Empire made it necessary to modernize compulsory military service by reducing the period of service but increasing the number of peasants recruited. The construction of the railways in the closing decades of the nineteenth century also favoured the movement of rural inhabitants and their contact with other sectors of the population, especially with professionals and men of different occupations (*raznochintsui*) who introduced them to a range of revolutionary ideas – anarchist, socialist, and social-democratic.

The rebellions of the peasant communities and the insurrections of the soldiers in the Revolution of 1905 were of great political significance. Stolypin's reforms, which permitted peasant participation in the election of the members of the Duma (the Russian parliament), were merely palliative measures, adopted to safeguard the tsarist regime. Nevertheless, rural conflicts did not disappear and the opponents of tsarism gained support among the peasants. After the fall of the Russian monarchy in February 1917, in May of that same year the First Pan-Russian Congress of Peasant Representatives, covering 242 local assemblies, proposed agrarian legislation that required the expropriation of the properties of the nobles and the equitable distribution of land for the entire peasant population. This petition, presented to Congress, was taken into account in the Land Decree issued on 26 October 1917, and was transformed into the Agrarian Law of February 1918. Even before the October Revolution, the rural soviets, which were the new local centres of power, emerged. These soviets were linked to the new state through the higher soviets; the traditional communal political organizations which often combined religious functions were replaced by new committees and assemblies. Public power was reinforced (the Red Army, the militia, and the state security police), and a system of compulsory, secular public education was established; a literacy campaign for peasants and other sectors of the working population was also conducted. However, the new Soviet state faced major difficulties in the area of provisions, in the face of wartime conditions, inadequate communications, and the peasants' decision to maintain a decorous self-sufficiency rather than contributing to social production. In instituting the system of forced hand-over of food, the government relied on the Committees of Poor Peasants, and the hegemony of the Bolshevik wing of the Social Democratic Party (Communist Party) was consolidated in the countryside as well. There was resistance to the agrarian policies of the Soviet government in the south of the Ukraine. In this region, the communal peasants had carried out a guerrilla struggle, under the leadership of the anarchist Nestor Majno, against the Austro-Hungarian intervention in support of the counter-revolutionary forces of General Denikin, which was prolonged as a result of the signing of the peace treaty of Brest-Litovsk. When the revolutionary regime was finally installed in this area, this armed peasant movement opposed the centralization of power and was defeated as a counter-revolutionary force. The collectivization instituted in 1929 had a profound effect upon the rural political order, since not only the *nouveau riche* peasants who had reappeared during the New Economic Policy, but also a good number of small, individual farmers who objected to the changes, were sent to forced labour camps. Grouped in new productive, administrative, and social units (the *kolkhozes*), the peasants were linked to the state vertically and the agrarian communities ceased to function as they had before.[17]

Ideological-cultural integration

Another basic condition for the consolidation of the nation-state is the creation of a collective consciousness among the population through public education and other alternative means of directed socialization, such as indoctrination through military service; the mobilization of public opinion through mass media campaigns; the celebration of national holidays and the appeal to patriotic feelings related to war, etc. Religion was one of the important traditional cohesion factors in all three societies. The nation-state tries to utilize the influence of religion for the purpose of integration or to substitute it with a new faith, be that nationalism, developmentalism, or socialism.

In Japan, not one but several religious traditions such as Confucianism, Buddhism, and state and popular Shintoism coexisted under the shogunate, despite the fact that it promoted neo-Confucianism as its official ideology. However, the task of the Meiji state was to create a new religion that would shape Japanese nationalism. This new religion was created by a combination of ethnocentrism (*tennō* worship as the maximum expression of national identity) and of the respect for Western civilization. The sense of inferiority in the face of aggressive European-US industrial capitalism was translated into chauvinism towards the neighbouring peoples, "caught in Asian stagnation." This new religion was propagated among the peasant population through the schools and military service. The victories in the wars with China and Russia, which were so widely disseminated by the press, came to constitute a collective memory that was converted into the nucleus of the new state religion. This religion managed to mobilize practically the entire population in order to conduct an imperialist war that was sustained for 15 years, beginning in 1931. For this spiritual mobilization, the Yasukuni sanctuary was erected in 1879, and there the souls of those who have died in combat – a total of over 2.4 million by the time of the 1945 defeat – are venerated. The dead of each community, who, in accordance with the deeply rooted popular custom, were worshipped at one of the annual popular Shintoist celebrations, were thus centralized and used as one of the pillars of the new state religion.[18]

In Mexico, the consolidation of the nation-state came with the fight of the Liberal leaders against the high clergy, who, allied with the landowners and prominent merchants, supported dependence and favoured European intervention. Here, too, the wars spurred a strengthening of national consciousness, but in the opposite direction from the Japanese case. The mobilization of the population, including the peasant masses, in defence of sovereignty, created a national consensus against the expansionism, interventionism, and chauvinism of the great powers. Despite the fact that in the struggle for independence, as in many of the peasant rebellions of the nineteenth and twentieth centuries, some clergymen and religious symbols with national associations (such as the Virgin of Guadalupe) had great importance, the anti-clerical, positivist, liberal current persisted in the leadership of the Revolution of 1917. The anti-religious campaign that was carried out in the 1920s and 1930s was really aimed at weakening the popular religious tradition and the autonomy of the peasant world. This provoked the most tenacious peasant resistance – more so than the high clergy's objections to government policy – and led to the mass rebellion of Cristeros between 1927 and 1929. Although the rebellion was repressed, the state had to give up its radical anti-clerical policy and adopt, instead, an enlightening, materialistic educational programme.[19]

In Russia, the empire expanded on the basis of "Great Russian" chauvinism, in which the figure of the tsar was identified with the fatherland, exercising political, institutional, and religious charisma. The orthodox religious tradition served to reinforce Russian nationalism among the peasant soldiers. Nevertheless, this policy provoked the resistance of different Asian peoples who lived within the boundaries of Russian territory but had their own national aspirations. With the defeat of the monarchy and the Socialist Revolution, which was at the outset decidedly anti-religious, Russian orthodoxy was discarded as the ideology for achieving social cohesion in the nation. In fact, even the heterodoxical current of *raskolniki* – which partly contributed to the fall of the tsar – was not held to be of value: the new regime hailed Communist internationalism as the new ideological base which would enable it to defend the unity of the Soviet multi-national state in the face of foreign intervention, and which would also serve to extend its model to the rest of the world, converting the new state into the "mother country of the world proletariat." This contributed to the creation of a Soviet identity different from the Russian one, but for the majority of the Russian peasant population it meant a break with their own traditions. This fact perhaps explains in part the problem of the lack of peasant initiatives, despite the introduction of the new ideology through collectivization, education, the party, mass organizations, etc. For the peasants, socialism was presented in the form of changing agrarian policies; production standards established by others; machines, chemical fertilizers, new work equipment and a system of distribution with which they were unfamiliar. During the Second World War, there was a partial rehabilitation of the traditional national and religious symbols, as was illustrated in the film *Alexander Nevski*.

The creation of a national consciousness was often associated with the adoption of an official language. The use of Spanish in Mexico, the adoption of Russian as the *lingua franca* in the Soviet Union, and the standardization of the language on the basis of the Tokyo dialect in Japan, all evidence the same trend to a greater or lesser degree. As the rural provincial population, the peasantry tends to be situated on the margin of this linguistic unification, especially if it belongs to an ethnic minority. The policy of assimilating minorities, especially nomads, also characterizes the nation-state: the Mexican state in the nineteenth century with the Yaquis; the Japanese with the Ainu; and the Soviet state with the Tartars, Mongols, or Kirgis, who at one time or another were settled in new lands. This policy met with stiff resistance until, in some cases, it was revised. It also caused the disappearance of some ethnic groups.

National identity is often linked to peasant tradition when the state attempts to achieve the cohesion of the entire nation. As we indicated previously, in Japan prior to 1868 the Confucian tradition, which was the official ideology, assigned a dignified status to farmers. The shogunate fell after the success of the peasant uprisings in 1866, and the people received the new government hoping for a total change (*goisshin*). As programme of the Aizu peasant uprising of 1868 demanded, or as the leaders of the Batallion of Red Lances (Sekihōtai) promised, the peasants expected the new government to cut the annual land tax in half, to cancel debts, and to ensure an equitable distribution of wealth and local autonomy.[20] When the peasants saw that the Meiji state had adopted an autocratic system of government, that the industrialization policy was undertaken at their expense and that Westernization implied the rejection of their traditional values, a series of peasant uprisings demanding the renovation of the world (*yanaoshi*) took place. Even the 1884 rebellions of the "Poor of Chichibu Party" and others against the autocratic government were legitimized on a pre-modern moral basis, as Yasumaru Yoshio points out. This peasant aspiration for a just world in communal terms was again espoused by the radical agrarian platform of the renovationist movement of the Shōwa era, known as the period of Japanese Fascism, which attempted to reconcile the interests of the poor or landless peasants with those of the landlords or industrialists, at the expense of the neighbouring Asian peoples. Once it was totally incorporated into the ideology of the imperialist state, the peasant aspiration was converted into a programme of oppression towards other peoples.[21]

In Russia, the culture of the Westernized governing élite stood in contrast to popular culture, especially traditional Russian peasant culture. "Rural" meant Russian, and for the modernizing reformers in the tsar's government as well as for the majority of the 1917 revolutionaries, "Russian" was the equivalent of "oriental stagnation." The aspirations of the Russian peasantry expressed in the peasant rebellions of the nineteenth and twentieth centuries – land, equality, and freedom – were synthesized, to some extent, in the agrarian programme of the First Pan-Russian Congress of Peasant Representatives, which later became the first agrarian programme of the Soviet state. Nevertheless, the original peasant programme was conceived within the framework of communal autonomy. For the Soviet state, which assigned priority to industrialization and was eager to get away from "oriental stagnation," there was no room for the communal ideal of the peasants' agrarian plan. Besides, the Soviet state was making efforts to consolidate itself as a multi-national state on the basis of the new principle of proletarian internationalism so as to overcome "Great Russian" chauvinism and nationalisms and regionalisms of the multi-ethnic population. The communalism of the Russian peasants was considered anti-Soviet. The radical anti-religious campaign of the Soviet state also had its main impact on the peasants, since their community and social relations centred around religious celebrations and rites. Lastly, the process of collectivization led to the displacement of those peasants who opposed the changes, and this again affected the horizontal social integration of the Russian peasantry. Their integration into the new Soviet culture had as a social cost the sacrifice of part of the peasant tradition.

In Mexico, for the Porfirian ruling class – which identified itself with liberal, positivist, and scientific Western civilization – the "Indian" peasant masses represented a major obstacle to progress. The laws on the disentailment of corporate property, which included communal property, and the laws on colonization were to dissolve the agrarian communities which, according to them, remained stagnant. The leaders of the Mexican Revolution, in contrast, adopted as their own part of the agrarian ideology. The goals of the peasant struggle from the colonial period on – the restitution of Indian village lands that had been invaded by the big landowners – as well as the new demands for land for dispossessed peasants and for the expropriation of large tracts of land concentrated in the hands of "landowners, *científicos*, and caciques," were expressed in the Plan of Ayala of 1911. Later, with the incorporation of agrarian leaders into the revolutionary government, those popular goals legitimized the government in the eyes of the people. Nevertheless, among the leaders of the post-revolutionary state, the conviction persisted that in order to build a developed nation-state it was necessary to integrate the "Indian" peasants, who were in a state of "Egyptian immutability" (Manuel Gamio), into modern industrial civilization. While some preferred to adopt a new proletarian or socialist terminology for it, what this implied, of course, was Westernizing them. Thus, the policy of gradual assimilation of the indigenous population through basic education in Spanish and the provision of basic services was carried out.[22]

Conclusions

Prior to the emergence of the nation-state, the impact of the state on the daily life of the peasants was not very great, being more or less limited to tax collection and the suppression of peasant movements. A declaration of war, an infrequent but characteristic action of the state that could directly involve the population, only affected the area of combat and not the whole of society as it does today. This situation changed radically with the emergence of the integrated and modernizing nation-state. Its laws, institutions and ideologies came to have a more direct influence on the lives of the peasantry. Specifically, war, which has been the expedient almost inevitably used by the nation-state to establish and maintain its sovereignty or to extend its boundaries at the expense of others, has also enabled it to penetrate ever more deeply into the peasant world. When the war was of a liberating nature, against colonial domination for example, its power to integrate the peasants was that much greater. The threat of intervention by the Western powers in Japan in the mid-nineteenth century, the foreign interventions in Mexico during the nineteenth and twentieth centuries, and the foreign intervention in the USSR in the post-revolutionary years produced a crisis affecting national sovereignty in each of these countries. At the same time, by overcoming that crisis, the state was able to integrate the population, including the peasants, more effectively.

In pre-modern Japan, the centralized feudal regime developed an institutional and ideological framework to incorporate the peasants. However, the physical separation of the other urban classes and the absence of war for more than two and a half centuries had favoured the relative autonomy of the peasant world. There, new local leaders emerged who linked the peasantry with different levels of feudal power, of the market and of the new urban cultures. Nevertheless, the leaders of the new centralized state that arose out of the crisis of national sovereignty chose an autocratic national strategy as the means to modernize the country quickly. Consequently, they limited democratic participation and only partially integrated the peasants into national society. The peasantry contributed to industrialization and to the building of the armed forces with economic and human resources, but did not enjoy political participation, and their traditional leaders faded from view. The local leaders who retained influence – landowners, public officials, and professionals – no longer belonged to the peasant world.

In Russia, as of the early eighteenth century, the strengthening of the serf system and territorial expansion through wars combined to implement the modernizing and autocratic national strategy. Industries were established with servile labour and the largest army in Europe was formed on the basis of serf soldiers. The tsarist government tried to preserve and utilize the communal peasant tradition for its own ends. Nevertheless, this programme had to be modified, starting with the Great Reforms of 1861–1865 and, especially, after the unsuccessful revolution of 1905. In Stolypin's reforms, an attempt was made to integrate the peasantry into the capitalist economy and the liberal regime. Despite these measures, the tsarist national programme was discarded after the revolution of February 1917. During the period between this revolution and the October Revolution, a broad gamut of alternative programmes emerged, among them the agrarian programme of the Congress of Peasant Representatives. Even afterwards, for a period of about a decade, the new national programme underwent considerable changes as far as agrarian issues were concerned. The definitive Soviet national programme tried to integrate the peasantry directly into social production by means of collectivization and planning. Not trusting the peasants because of their *petit bourgeois* tendencies, it tried to liberate them from "feudal"or "bourgeois" influences by purging the "rich" peasants and by the militant atheism campaign. The declaration of war in 1939 reinforced this centralist tendency. Consequently, the autonomy of the peasant world was radically reduced.

In Mexico, from the colonial period on, the indigenous peasant world maintained relative autonomy although it had to fight continually against the invasion of its lands by large landowners and religious establishments. During the Porfirian period, under the system of absolute private ownership and positivist liberal policies, the landowners and local and foreign colonizing companies enclosed the land and exploited the labour of the communities. The local landowners represented an obstacle to the linking of the peasantry with national society and the market, since they tried to create a self-sufficient world around their estates. The peasantry constituted one of the main forces in the 1910–1917 Revolution, and its agrarian demands were at the heart of the national programme of the new government. The peasantry was linked to the state through the distribution of land and through measures to promote agricultural development. Cárdenas' government tried to revive the revolutionary process and achieve the integration of the peasants into the nation-state, initiating a revolutionary mobilization through the distribution of arable farmlands and the establishment of collective *ejidos*. Nevertheless, through the institutionalization of the class struggle for the sake of national unity, the peasants' political participation was controlled and tended to be limited to the sphere of action of the CNC-PRM (the National Peasant Confederation and the Mexican Revolutionary Party). The *indigenista* policy[23] and a policy of norm-based standardizing public education also contributed to the weakening of the autonomy of the peasant world.

Notes

1. There are various works that analyse these societies in comparative terms. Some authors study them as examples of the "success of modernization," whose model is the Euro-American industrial society"; Cyril E. Black et al., *The Modernization of Japan and Russia* (Free Press, New York, 1975), and Angus Maddison, *Crecimiento económico en el Japón y la URSS* (Fondo de Cultura Económica, Mexico City, 1969) are examples. The first, which includes several authors, analyses these processes and also tries to identify the economic and institutional conditions that paved the way for modernization. Other authors, such as Barrington Moore, Jr. (*Social Origins of Dictatorship and Democracy. Lord and Peasant in the Making of the Modern World*, Beacon Press, Boston, 1966), Eric Wolf (*Las luchas campesinas del siglo XX*, Siglo XXI, Mexico City, 1972), and Michio Shibata (*Kindaisekai to minshū undō*, Iwanami, Tokyo, 1983) attempt to explain the reasons for the

differences in the political trajectories of the nations – on occasion catastrophic – with special attention to the role of the popular masses.

2. *Historia general de México*, 3rd ed. (E1 Colegio de México, Mexico City, 1981); *Historia documental de México*, vol. 2 (UNAM, Mexico City, 1964).
3. Jerome Blum, *Lord and Peasant in Russia* (Princeton University Press, Princeton, 1961); Carsten Goehrke et al., *Russia* (Siglo XXI, Mexico City, 1975).
4. *Iwanamikōza nihon rekishi*, vols. 10–21 (Iwanami, Tokyo, 1976); J.W. Hall, *Imperio japonés* (Siglo XXI, Mexico City, 1978); Paul Akamasu, *Meiji 1868. Revolucíon y contrarrevolución* (Mexico City, 1977); M. Tanaka, "La renovación Meidyi y la formación del proyecto nacional del Japón moderno," *Relaciones internacionales*, no. 30 (1982), pp. 21–38.
5. On the characteristics of agriculture and the peasant community in the three countries, one can consult: Iinuma Jirō, *Nihon nōgyō no saihakken* (NHK Books, Tokyo, 1982); E. Wolf, *Los campesinos* (Ed. Labor, Mexico City, 1971: Arturo Warman, . . . *Y venimos a contradecir* (Ed. de la Casa Chata, Mexico City, 1976); Blum (note 3 above).
6. On the nature and history of peasant communities: Wolf (note 1 above); George Forster, *Tzintzuntzan. Mexican Peasants in a Changing World* (Little, Brown, Boston, 1967); Oscar Lewis, *Life in a Mexican Village. Tepoztlan Revisited* (University of Illinois Press, Urbana, Ill., 1951); Kimura Motoi, *Nihon sonrakushi* (Kōbundō, Tokyo, 1978); Emori Itsuo, *Nihon sonraku shakai no kōzō* (Kōbundō, Tokyo, 1976).
7. Yasumaru Yoshio, *Nihon no kindaika to minshū shisō* (Aokishobo, Tokyo, 1975); Takagi Shunsuke, *Meiji ishin sōmō undōshi* (Keisōshobō, Tokyo, 1974); Michiko Tanaka, "La ambivalencia del estrato medio. Los *gōnō* en Shinano en la época de la crisis del shogunato Tokugawa," *Estudios de Asia y Africa* (El Colegio de México), vol. 13, no. 1 (1978), pp. 1–39.
8. On pre-modern peasant movements: Blum (note 3 above); B.F. Porshniev, *Feudalism i narodnuye massuy*, (Nauka, Moscow, 1964); Leticia Reina, *Las rebeliones campesinas en México* (*1819–1906*) (Siglo XXI, Mexico City, 1980); Jean Meyer, *Problemas campesinos y revueltas agrarias* (*1821–1910*) (Sepsetentas, Mexico City, 1973); Aoki Kōji, *Hyakushō ikki no nenjiteki kenkyū* (Shinsensha, Tokyo, 1970); Yokoyama Toshio, *Gimin* (Chūōkōronsha, Tokyo, 1970); Mori Kahei, *Mori Kahei chosakushū*, vol. 7 (Hōseidaigaku Shuppankai, Tokyo, 1974); M. Tanaka, *Movimientos campesinos en la formación del Japón moderno* (El Colegio de México, Mexico City, 1976).
9. Andrés Molina Enríquez, *Grandes problemas mexicanos* (Mexico City, 1908); Jesús Silva Herzog, *El agrarismo mexicano y la reforma agraria* (Fondo de Cultura Económica, Mexico City, 1959); Friedrich Katz, *La guerra secreta en México* (Era, Mexico City, 1982); J. Wormack, *Zapata y la revolución mexicana* (Ed. de Ciencias Sociales, Havana, 1971); Héctor Aguilar Camín, *Fronteras nómadas de México* (Siglo XXI, Mexico City, 1977).
10. Akimoto Masao, "Chiso kaisei to chihō seiji," *Iwanamikōza nihon rekishi*, vol. 14 (Iwanami, Tokyo, 1975); Kaino Fukuju, "Matsukata zaisei to jinushisei no keisei," ibid., vol. 15; Nishida Yoshiaki, "Nōmin undō no hatten to jinushisei," ibid., vol. 18; Nakamura Masanori, "Daikyōkō to nōson mondai," ibid., vol. 19; Mori Takemaro, "Senjika nōson no kōzō henka," ibid., vol. 20; Aoki Koji, *Nōmin sōjō no nenjiteki kenkyū* (Shinsensha, Tokyo, 1967).
11. H. Carr, *Historia de la Rusia Soviética* (Alianza, Madrid, 1974); Blum (note 3 above); Isaac Deutscher, *La revolución inconclusa* (Era, Mexico City, 1967); S. Seráev, *El socialismo y las cooperativas* (Progreso, Moscow, 1981).
12. Ochi Noboru, "Nihon kindaika to chiiki shihai," in Kamishima Jirō, ed., *Kindaika*

no seishinkōzō (Hyōronsha, Tokyo, 1974), pp. 83–113; Barrington Moore, Jr. (note 1 above).

13. Irokawa Daikichi, *Shinpen. Meiji seishinshi* (Chūōkōronsha, Tokyo, 1976).
14. Dainippon rengō seinendan, *Wakamono seido no kenkyū* (Tokyo, 1938); Hirayama Kazuhiko, *Nihon seinenshūdanshi kenkyū josetsu* (Tokyo, 1982).
15. The regime of dictator Porfirio Díaz, 1885–1911.
16. Paul Friedrich, *Agrarian Revolt in a Mexican Village* (Prentice-Hall, Englewood Cliffs, N.J., 1970); Romana Falcón, *El agrarismo en Veracruz. La etapa radical (1928–1935)* (El Colegio de México, Mexico City, 1977); A. Gilly, *La revolución interrumpida* (Ed. El Caballito, Mexico City, 1971); A. Warman, *Campesinos, hijos predilectos del régimen* (Nuestro Tiempo, Mexico City, 1972); Moisés González Navarro, *CNC* (Costa Amic, Mexico City, 1968); E. Wolf, *Las luchas campesinas en el siglo XX* (Siglo XXI, Mexico City, 1976).
17. Deutscher (note 11 above); C. Goehrke (note 3 above); Wolf (note 16 above).
18. Yanagita Kunio, *Meiji Taishōshi. Sesōhen* (Heibonsha, Tokyo, 1972); Irokawa Daikichi, *Meiji no bunka* (Iwanami, Tokyo, 1970).
19. Jean Meyer, *La Cristiada* (Siglo XXI, Mexico City, 1974).
20. M. Tanaka, "Yonaoshi-ikki. Movimientos campesinos en la crisis del shogunato premoderno," in P. Muhkerjee, ed., *Movimientos agrarios y cambios sociales en Asia y Africa* (El Colegio de México, Mexico City, 1974), pp. 181–240; Sasaki Junnosuke et al., *Yonaoshi ikki. Nihon minshū no rekishi*, vol. 5 (Sanshōdō, Tokyo, 1874).
21. R.J. Smethurst, *A Social Basis for Prewar Japanese Militarism. The Army and the Rural Community* (University of California Press, Berkeley, 1974).
22. Manuel Gamio, *Forjando patria* (Porrúa, Mexico City, 1916).
23. The state policy for the economic, social, and cultural integration of the Indian population, which was implemented in the late 1930s.

THE REGIONAL IMPACT OF THE MEIJI RESTORATION AND THE MEXICAN REVOLUTION

Alfredo Romero-Castilla
Universidad Nacional Autónoma de México, Mexico City, Mexico

This paper represents an initial attempt to explore the influence of the Meiji Restoration and the Mexican Revolution on their respective regional contexts. Our interest in conducting this research springs from two different sources of motivation. The majority of the historians and social scientists who have studied these processes have done so from the perspective of each nation's individual history, assigning less importance to aspects involving the interaction of the two. Nevertheless, such interaction has been perceived, to the extent that for some authors the qualities possessed by both movements constitute a model capable of being transposed to other social settings.

This essay, therefore, proposes to explore various issues related to the interaction of the above-mentioned movements, for the purpose of explaining the types of contacts that existed between these societies and their respective neighbours and of ascertaining whether they had a regional impact and what, if any, direction it took. This is a problem germane to the study of international relations, an understanding of which involves the comparative study of the following three aspects: (1) definition of the nature of both movements; (2) familiarization with the essential attributes and development of the links existing among the peoples of Asia as well as those of Latin America; and (3) establishment of the fact that the possible influence wielded through diplomatic relations, intellectual contacts, the dissemination of ideas, migratory flows, trips of important personages, etc., are above all expressions of the internal social evolution of those countries.

In other words, these contacts are forms of human communication eliciting responses in other social ambits which do not always prove to be appropriate; nor do they constitute, per se, a transferable model, for one should not lose sight of the fact that since such links are expressions of autonomous or original phenomena, they are characterized by a degree of specificity and, therefore, evidence a dissimilar evolution which varies from one society to the next.

Viewing the issue from this standpoint, we need to clarify the nature of the processes to be analysed and to delimit the concepts of "modernization" and "revolution" utilized to define both processes. The theoretical meanings of these concepts are not analogous. The commonly accepted notion of modernization is based on three assumptions: a conviction regarding progress, the establishment of rational societies, and the fundamental importance of industrialization. These constitute an analytical framework for studying the process of social change. The latter is conceived of as the transition from a "traditional" society to another, "modern" one, qualitatively distinct from the previous society, whose paradigmatic model turns out to be that of the advanced *Western* countries, and, most particularly, the United States.

This ethnocentric backdrop inherent in the theory of modernization represents an obstacle to a full understanding of these phenomena and also affects the possibility of arriving at a suitable comparison of these processes for which – given the characteristics of Asian and Latin American historical development – the criterion of modernization is not entirely appropriate.

Something along those lines also be applied to the concept of "revolution." This term also has a general connotation that is applied to a phenomenon of radical convulsion in a political–military sphere, the result of which is a profoundly different pattern of institutional organization, considered to be more progressive than the one existing during the epoch immediately preceding. However, in research on social change the use of the term "revolution" has been extended to refer to substantial transformations in economic and social structures, and some authors have in fact gone so far as to speak of a scientific and technological revolution. While this concept modifies the relations of power and institutional balance, it does not comprise per se the basis for social transformation, which rather is to be found in the driving social forces of change.

This whole complex series of elements, outlined in a schematic fashion, has a bearing on the path we follow in making these comparisons, since such a path includes searching for and explaining the similarities and differences between these apparently analogous phenomena. For this reason it is necessary to determine, in the first place, the distance separating Japan from Mexico and, in the second place, the distance dividing both of these societies from other Asian and Latin American nations. In this regard, one should bear in mind the fact that, from their beginnings, all of these societies have had distinct social structures.

1

Modern Japan emerged after breaking with its feudal past and, in the opinion of some authors, its development has represented the only case of the formation of an industrialized society in Asia, achieved in the space of less than one hundred years thanks to the successful adaptation of Western technology and economic and political institutions.[1] In contrast, other authors claim that the major features of this movement are its capitalist structure and the interests of its hegemonic class, the direct inheritor of its feudal past.[2]

Contemporary Mexico, for its part, grew out of the experience of being a colonized and dependent society. Its revolutionary movement has been thought to possess both the traits of a liberal, nineteenth-century revolution, insofar as the establishment of a constitutional and democratic government is concerned, and, at the same time, precursory elements of the first twentieth-century socialist revolution.[3] However, according to a different assessment, the Mexican Revolution proved to be a consecutive stage of a single historical undertaking: the development of capitalism, to which was added a series of social problems never before brought to light.[4]

This first distinction leads us to consider other concomitant aspects. The historical conditions accompanying the birth of "modern Japan" have been referred to in various ways. Most frequently in texts written in English the term "Meiji Restoration" has been used to speak of the process stemming from an internal structural crisis – exacerbated by pressures from abroad – which allowed for the re-establishment of imperial power and the creation of a state favouring economic growth. But that process has also been referred to as a "revolution," "transformation," or "reform."

In this regard, it is worth mentioning the opinion expressed by Michiko Tanaka,[5] who points out that this series of terms calls for a more detailed explanation. In texts written in Japanese, there has been confusion owing to the indiscriminate use that has been made of the words *fukko* (restoration) and *ishin* (renovation).

The term "revolution," for its part, stresses the structural changes that occurred during those years and the displacement of the dominant feudal-bureaucratic group by a new group that objectively represented a capitalist tendency regardless of its social origin – which, among others, could be that of the samurai, officials of the feudal bureaucracy. In contrast, the terms "transformation" or "reform" indicate the persistence of privileges among the members of the old ruling class within an absolutist power structure, which was gradually transformed into a new class.

These dichotomous categories, Tanaka adds, are useful in drawing up generalizations, which at times are necessary, but they do not help us reach a full understanding of the event in all the specific ramifications of its meaning. Consequently, if "renovation" is the correct translation of the word *ishin*, this term is appropriate, as well, for denominating the event, since it has a connotation of "revitalization," a basic concept in Japanese consciousness, even at the present time.

In the case of the Mexican Revolution this problem, of a conceptual nature, is not present. Here the word *revolution* denotes a radical, political, and military-type movement leading to a pattern of organization of institutions varying very markedly from the one that existed in the preceding epoch. In this sense, just like other social movements in Latin America, the Mexican Revolution has attempted to achieve certain social goals, striving "to destroy, on the one hand, feudalism and colonialist liberalism and, on the other, to oppose penetration by the new form of imperialism. That is to say, they have been and continue to be anti-traditionalist and anti-imperialist."[6]

In other words, on the one hand the Mexican Revolution was a widespread agrarian uprising directed against large rural land ownership and, on the other, it was also an institutional political movement in which the class struggle within the rural structure caused a confrontation between peasants and large estate owners and a weakening of the dominant class.

Therefore, we find that the Meiji Restoration and the Mexican Revolution are not identical historical processes, owing to the dissimilarity of conditions from which they arose and the goals they pursued. Strictly speaking, in Japan there was no revolution in the sense of the term as presented here, whereas in Mexico the revolution did fit the definition.

Nevertheless, whether the changes that took place are interpreted as a modernization process or as a movement promoting capitalism, it is evident that the latter element is present in Japan as of 1868, judging by its orientation toward industrialization and its tendency to favour big business, which was soon to make it another member of the group of major industrial-capitalist powers operating on an international plane. In Mexico, the land issue was the main motivating factor of the revolution and the problem of industrial development was deferred until a later era.

With regard to the links between Japan and Asia for one, and Mexico and Latin America, for the other, we should point out several factors. The three regions that are denominated South Asia, South-East Asia, and East Asia do not comprise a homogeneous historical bloc. In these regions various forms of societal life have been developed, by distinct means, such as: a marked persistence of agrarian society in the case of India, China, Korea, and other places in South-East Asia; the early appearance of feudalism in Japan; different colonial experiences and varying political options after the gaining of independence. Among these conditions, foremost are the problems of underdevelopment and dependence which still plague several of these societies.

In this respect, Japan proves to be less "typically Asian" than its neighbours, for it has distinguished itself because of "the less acute nature of underdevelopment . . . the importance of social democracy, the high level of industrialization [and] the fact that it was to be found outside the sphere of liberation movements and that on occasion it actually opposed such movements".[7]

In so far as the question of Mexico and Latin America is concerned, it is also assumed that there is close affinity between the peoples of the region, which is not an accurate picture either, since the area is characterized by "extreme heterogeneity,"[8] being fragmented according to the nations that have sprung up since the Independence period. Despite the fact that they have common features such as language, religion, and systems of social and national authority and that all of them "have fought against common enemies ranging from Iberian colonialism to US imperialism, the structures of each country's society and of each one's state exhibit characteristics and specific features" which make for significant differences in their respective configurations.[9]

From all of the aforementioned considerations, we can derive two statements related to regional impact, on the basis of which we can attempt to compare both processes: (1) the Meiji Restoration was a political movement that produced changes in institutional power and balance, preserving the old order, from which arose a state that favoured capitalism and social change; (2) the Mexican Revolution represented a revolutionary political experience which generated essential changes in the country's economic and social order, for the purpose of continuing the process by one path of captialist development.

Thus, it is on the basis of these considerations regarding the internal characteristics of both movements that we can trace possible lines of influence so as to determine the impact of the Meiji Restoration, particularly on China and Korea, and the significance attributed to Mexico's revolutionary movement in the region of Latin America. To this end, the following elements will be taken into account: (1) diplomatic contacts; (2) migratory flows; (3) social reforms framed as a model transferable to other societies; and (4) the strengthening of ties of inter-regional solidarity.

2

As we have already stated, the Meiji Restoration entailed, in the first place, a break with the feudal state which, besides involving a recognition of the social forces that participated in it, reinforced a nationalistic consciousness that strove to achieve the fortification of Japan vis-à-vis the "Western" powers and the development of its economic strength.

The restoration of imperial power demanded, of necessity, a restatement of foreign relations, and the following measures were adopted: (1) the exercise of control over foreign policy in the person of the emperor; (2) respect for the treaties entered into by the Bakufu government; and (3) the establishment of an office in charge of foreign relations.[10] All of these measures were specifically directed toward the United States and the European powers, although this plan also had repercussions upon the country's closest neighbours.

Japan's diplomatic relations with China and Korea after the Restoration were carried out in three phases: the first one covered the period 1868 to 1871, the year in which the initial treaty with China was signed. The second involved a shorter period of time, from 1872 to 1873, and was characterized mainly by outbursts of Japanese expansionism, underlined by the *sekairon* (debate concerning the invasion of Korea). The third phase commenced with the expedition to Taiwan in 1874, which culminated in the Kanghwa Treaty, signed in February 1876.[11]

With the signing of the Kanghwa Treaty, Japan witnessed the beginning of a transitional decade distinguished by the pressing need to modernize, its influence over the destiny of Korea, and its confrontation with China. In this period, migratory flows and the exchange of ideas also played an important role.

For China's part, the migration of Chinese started at the beginning of the Meiji period when Chinese merchants arrived in Japan and participated in the modern transformation of the country, working as business representatives of foreign firms set up there. The following wave of emigrants comprised a very heterogeneous group of diplomats, students, travellers, and political refugees whose attitude with regard to Japan varied greatly. On the one hand, there was disdain on the part of official representatives and, on the other, interest shown by those who felt that they could learn lessons from the Japanese model and apply them to China.[12]

The opening up of Korean ports enabled different Japanese sectors to express their individual points of view regarding what shape relations with Korea were to take. For some, this was a problem of security, for others a zone of economic expansion, and for yet others an opportunity to contribute to the modernization of another Asian country.[13] The first Japanese immigrants were merchants who launched an economic offensive,[14] and were so successful that during the 1880–1905 period, there was a total of 42,460 immigrants including peasants, small businessmen, soldiers, and officials.[15]

Related to the above-mentioned movement, there was also a group of Korean immigrants made up of students, who found in Japan a favourable atmosphere for learning about advances in different fields of knowledge and for observing what was taking place there. Forming part of this group were Kim Ok-kyun and Pak Yong-hyo, reformers who viewed the Meiji Restoration as a model worth imitating. With the support of certain Japanese political groups and prominent figures such as Fukuzawa Yukichi, in 1884 they planned a coup against the old Confucian order prevailing in Korea; this was a total failure.[16] As a result of this "incident," strong anti-Japanese sentiment was generated in Korea, followed by a series of clashes between the two countries, but this did not manage to stop the exodus of young Koreans who sought to further their intellectual development in Japan.[17]

As regards China, after the military defeat inflicted by Japan certain intellectual sectors advocated change, and these were divided into two groups with different tendencies: the reformists and the revolutionaries. The former sought to harmonize Confucian tradition with a knowledge of "Western" technology. One of the most outstanding advocates of this idea was Kang Yu-wei who, in 1898, proposed to modernize China within the framework of the imperial regime. Like others of his contemporaries, Kang viewed Japan as proof of the fact that "modernization meant more than guns and ships, and with his colleagues he worked to develop a synthesis of Chinese and Western ideas that would provide a stable foundation for modern society."[18]

In this manner, Japan began to have an effect on the life and thought of some sectors in China. More recent studies have identified the 1898 movement and the Meiji Restoration as two expressions of a specifically Asian mode of transformation, i.e. *ch'ingni* (movement in favour of restoration), which involves the action of an authentic intellectual movement operating outside the range of the centres of power and seeking political change. This type of movement had appeared in China in other epochs in the face of domestic economic or political crises and, more specifically, in the face of external threats.[19]

Thus, one can see why Chinese reformers recognized the movement embodied in the Meiji Restoration as a model for internal reconstruction from which valuable lessons could be learned. However, "the promoters of the movement never once considered transforming the very foundations of Chinese society (whereas the monarchical reformers of the Meiji period had broken with the patterns germane to Japan's 'feudal' economy) . . . for which reason this attempt to modernize China 'from above' met with failure."[20]

During the same era in which reformers were building their programme, the revolutionary course of action represented by Sun Yat-sen made its appearance. According to some research findings, this revolutionary pioneer and Father of the Republic sought outside help for his movement, especially in Japan, where he managed to obtain "the invaluable contribution" of several of his Japanese friends, among them Toyama Mitsuru, Inukai Ki, Miyasaki Tōrazo, and Kayano Chōchi.[21]

They were all important political figures and all of them were convinced of the need to unify Asia under the protection of Japan. Moreover, their interest in China's problems was in keeping with a scheme to introduce a pattern similar to the Japanese one. They were sure that if they were successful, a friendly relationship with a new Chinese government would be guaranteed and would lead to the adoption of measures beneficial to all, since the introduction of a model of this nature would undoubtedly be effective, constituting as it did a perfect synthesis of East and West, that is to say, a pattern that represents "the surest path to modernization for all Asia . . ."[22]

Sun Yat-sen was not alone in following this direction. During the First Republic other Chinese leaders also maintained links, albeit less overtly, with Japan. This was the case with the young activists of the T'ungmeng Hui group: Liang Chi-chao, another admirer of the Meiji reforms, Yuan Shi-kai, and Tsao Ju-lin.[23]

Lastly, associated with the above, we should refer at somewhat greater length to Pan-Asianism, since this was the last phase of Japanese influence upon the region during the period we are concerned with. At the beginning of the Meiji Restoration, there was a pronounced tendency to imitate and outdo Europe, while denying at the same time any possible identification with Asia. This rejection of all that was Asian was more apparent with regard to its closest neighbours, China and Korea. Philosophers such as Fukuzawa Yukichi considered those societies to be reactionary and to be doomed to lose their independence once progress had taken hold in their respective territories and they had no choice but to advance side by side with Japan in a common effort to become part of the process of civilization.[24]

This notion laid the foundations for what was later to be a regional-level scheme which, with Japan as its guiding light, would attempt to achieve Asian unity and, therefore, it was hoped, create supporters among national movements in Asia. The result was the announcement of the so-called "sphere of Asian co-prosperity," which served as a frame of reference for collaboration between the Japanese and the nationalists in their opposition to the presence of Europe during the Second World War.

3

The task of examining the actual manifestations of the influence of the Mexican Revolution proves to be complex. Documents dealing specifically with this issue are not available, for the greater part of research is devoted to "assessing Mexico's accomplishments as of the 'Revolution'."[25]

However, it is generally accepted that the Mexican Revolution was "the first authentic and outstanding social revolution in Spanish America,"[26] a notion which one should trace so as to verify the possible influence of the Revolution on other societies and to ascertain whether the social movements that have taken place in Central America or in Argentina, Chile, and Uruguay are "patterns that are outgrowths of the Mexican phenomenon."[27]

The outline proposed in the preceding section should be observed with regard to two factors: (1) the influence of US foreign policy and (2) the influence of the same on the rest of Latin America.

Mexico's geographical proximity to the United States has been a dominant element characterizing the country's existence from the nineteenth century on. The revolutionary movement carried out during the period 1910–1920 was affected by the political actions taken by the US government. As Berta Ulloa has indicated, the Mexican social movement commenced as a "revolution with outside interference" which created a crisis by doing away with the status quo maintained in Mexican-US relations during the 30 years of the

Porfiriato.[28] As of that time, Mexico was "subjected to constant pressure from abroad to impede the possible success of revolutionary efforts to effect decisive changes in the situation whereby foreign investors, especially from the US, predominated in Mexico's economic system."[29]

This confrontation gave rise to military as well as diplomatic disputes, as is evidenced by the 1914 invasion of Veracruz and the continual and frantic efforts of the different revolutionary governments to be recognized. In 1917 the problem was no longer one of the progress made by the armed campaign but, rather, concerned the fact that when the new Constitution was approved, "it had included a program of reforms that involved, among other things, the destruction of *latifundia* and the elimination of control over the most dynamic sectors of the economy, especially the oil sector, but these measures were faced with numerous kinds of pressure."[30]

At the beginning of the 1920s, power was taken over by the Sonora group. While this did not entail a significant change with regard to the socio-political scheme of the revolution, it did foster in the US a willingness to negotiate to the point that by "the end of World War I, Mexico came to be situated unequivocally within the US sphere of influence."[31]

Nevertheless, socio-economic policies adopted subsequently, during President Lázaro Cárdenas' administration, once again jolted foreign interests, which felt they had been negatively affected by land reform and by the elimination of the privileges and exemptions that the oil companies had enjoyed.[32] All of these occurrences were the object of several detrimental actions, which provoked a response in defence of the principles and ideas of the revolution on the part of Mexican and Latin American intellectuals.

In the 1920s President Alvaro Obregón – in the face of pressures demanding an amendment to the Querétaro Constitution and of the campaign to discredit the movement – decided to send outstanding intellectuals as diplomatic representatives for the purpose of "carrying out a policy of solidarity with the other Spanish-speaking nations on this continent which were subject to the same conditions vis-à-vis Saxon imperialism."[33] An illustration of the above was the Special Mission headed by the philosopher Antonio Caso, who attended the festivities commemorating Peru's Centennial of Independence and later toured Argentina, Brazil, Chile, and Uruguay to give lectures.[34]

Thus, it was during the process of defending the revolution that its significance was acknowledged among the peoples of Latin America. Or, to quote Hubner:

> The Mexican Revolution is one of the most interesting social-political movements of this century. Its major importance proves to be undeniable for the rest of Latin America. To a great degree, it is exemplary and worthy of being imitated. The conditions under which it originated, the particular trajectory it took, the legal forms under which

it has come to take shape, the economic and social milieu in which it has evolved, the repercussions of its Latin Americanist action. . . .[35]

In order to comprehend the potential scope of these measures, it is necessary to examine in some detail the legal aspects and the Latin Americanist action of the Mexican Revolution. In the first case, what is involved is the series of claims made by the peasant and working classes, from which arose "the first Declaration of Social Law embodied in Articles 27 and 123."[36] The second aspect refers to the fight against US imperialism initiated by Madero and continued by Carranza, who understood "before others did, the future awaiting Latin America in the strength of the international solidarity of its Republics."[37]

We could also phrase this in another fashion: the state that arose from the revolution intervened forcefully in the distribution of land and in labour relations. Article 27 of the Mexican Constitution "is categorically opposed to latifundia and to the monopolization of land and ensures the peasant class the ownership of lands to be cultivated, taking care that through the system of *ejidos*, such lands continue to be in the hands of the peasants and that a new landlord class does not arise. . . ."[38]

In so far as labour relations were concerned,

through Article 123 of the Constitution, [the state] puts considerable limitations on conflicts between capital and labour, by imposing minimum norms which neither of the parties can change or renounce. By making the total amount of salaries dependent upon prior negotiations before they can be modified, it establishes a policy of fixed salaries, as opposed to the policy of variable salaries, which were subject to market fluctuations in the capitalist economy.[39]

Such victories are significant for a social ambit such as Latin America, owing to their feasibility of application "to several republics that call themselves democratic and are no more than feuds of the former owners of the land, administrators of religious faith, individuals who control credit and those who reap the benefits of the raw materials found in the country."[40]

Solidarity throughout the Continent appeared linked to internal politics and led the governments of the revolution to put forward "anti-imperialism" as one of the principles of foreign policy. What is entailed here is a concept "of Pan-Americanism as Latin Americanism in a counter-offensive,"[41] one of whose most indefatigable promoters was Lázaro Cárdenas. This Mexican form of Latin Americanism is of an active nature.

It involves the fight against imperialism, the economic and spiritual federation of these peoples, the creation – among them – of a new brand of civilization and culture which does not attempt to be either European or Indian, but exclusively American. It put forth the idea of continental unity. Before any other country, it shaped what nowadays is called "continental nationalism," the American *zollverein*,[42] the customs and economic union of the peoples of Latin America.[43]

These expressions of "Latin American nationalism," produced in the very heart of a Mexican intellectual movement and geared to counteract the influence of a campaign to discredit the revolution – a campaign that portrayed it as a paragon of dangerousness and even went so far as to describe it as "Mexican-Soviet"[44] – generated an intellectual tendency that went even further, proposing the need to search for "American solutions" to the region's problems. Views such as these were elaborated by philosophers like José Vasconcelos in Mexico and José Carlos Mariátegui in Peru, to mention just two examples.

Vasconcelos proposed the need for each country to produce "its own philosophical expression" as a way of ensuring the peoples of the region a place in history, and stated that upon defining its ethnic movement it would also be necessary to endow it with its "own cultural scheme."[45] For his part, Mariátegui noted a unity of Indo-Spanish America because it sprang from a single source, the Spanish Conquest, which "standardized the ethnic, political, and moral anatomy of Spanish America," and observed in the "Mexican Revolution, with its destiny, with its ideology, and with its proponents, the solidarity of all the new men of America."[46]

Lastly, we should mention other facets: the possible influence of the Mexican Revolution on Latin American political exiles who have resorted to Mexican hospitality at difficult times and, upon returning to their countries of origin, have proposed certain social reforms. Similarly, one could do research on the influence that can be observed in the realm of art and literature, specifically the Mexican muralist school, which found adherents in several Latin American countries.

To a certain extent, this whole flow of ideas could be considered to have encouraged a series of nationalist movements which occurred in Latin America after 1910, such as the ones led by Hirigoyen in Argentina in 1916; by Getulio Vargas in Brazil in 1930; by Peron in Argentina in 1945; and by Arbenz in Guatemala in 1954. Nevertheless, strictly speaking, it would be difficult to regard these as direct repercussions of the Mexican Revolution, although they do have similar ideological, social, and nationalist foundations.

Therefore, the possible influences of the Mexican Revolution should be sought in the thought and actions of certain Latin American political leaders and in the fact that some of them took refuge as exiles in Mexico, where they recuperated in order to be able to continue with their social struggles. To this effect, we can mention the cases of Victor Raúl Haya de la Torre, promoter of nationalist-revolutionary trends in Peru and founder of the Alianza Popular Revolucionaria Americana (APRA); Augusto C. Sandino, head of an armed front opposing US occupation of Nicaragua; and Fidel Castro in Cuba.

These issues have not received much scholarly attention and deserve to be looked at more carefully. In the case of Haya de la Torre, of interest is his appeal for collaboration between the classes which, inspired by nationalism and integrated into a single political party, would achieve the creation of an anti-imperialist and anti-oligarchical state. This position was in keeping with the one put forth, in the case of Mexico, by Vicente Lombardo Toledano, who proposed the strengthening of a state which " would represent national interests, to the extent that it nationalized enclaves and did away with agrarian feudalism. Such a state would be open to national classes, establishing an alliance between them, which it would co-ordinate by means of the representation of functional interests; that is, formalizing a corporative state."[47]

In theory, this attempt at a revolutionary programme is similar to Mexico's – at its most radical point in the 1920s – but, as Abelardo Villegas points out, its political praxis is quite different. In Mexico, the Partido de la Revolución (Partido Nacional Revolucionario, or PNR) "arose after the armed movement was over, for the purpose of reconciling the interests of the different caudillos who had been victorious, ensuring continuity in the regime and hindering outbursts from reactionaries."[48] First, in 1924, Haya de la Torre founded the APRA (American Popular Revolutionary Alliance), whose most important political goal was to gain power through "electoral means, rejecting armed uprisings."[49] This was contrary to the process followed by the Mexican Revolution.

The decade of the 1920s also witnessed the rise of Augusto C. Sandino, who left his native country when he was very young, became a blue-collar worker, and later held several administrative posts in US firms in Central America and Mexico. There, he worked in the South Pennsylvania Oil Co. and in the Huasteca Petroleum Co. in Tampico. Sandino's first contact with Mexico was brief (1923–1926), but he had many experiences in that country, finding there a climate of revolutionary effervescence, marked by the political and ideological actions of the workers, anarcho-syndicalist groups, the agrarianism of Zapata, socialism and, above all, great nationalist fervour manifested in the support given to the Mexican government in its attempts to claim sovereignty over its subsoil resources according to the terms set down in Article 27 of the Mexican Constitution, the fundamental purpose of which was to put an end to the highhandedness and abuses of foreign companies, in particular US firms.

Incidentally, Mexican petroleum played an important part in the fight in Nicaragua and in the movement led by Sandino. The animosity of the US government that arose because of the decision of Calles' government to apply the laws on foreign status and oil became more intense when, in 1926, a movement developed against the illegitimate government established in Nicaragua with the help of the US, and a "Mexico-Nicaragua" operation was put into effect. Mexico not only gave shelter to Nicaraguan political refugees but also, once the possibilities of an armed revolution had increased, provided the exiles with arms so they could attempt the operation and allowed soldiers to be recruited in Mexican territory."[50]

In the United States, that action was interpreted as if "the Mexican government was determined to undermine US prestige and influence in Central America, increase its own external power and thereby spread the doctrines of nationalization of foreign property and Bolshevism."[51]

Sandino left Mexico in 1926, when the revolt against Chamorro and Díaz broke out, immediately becoming a military leader with extraordinary strategical abilities who, at the head of an organized group, won some victories, giving continuity to a popular guerrilla struggle which was not to end until his death by treason in 1934.

Nevertheless, Sandino's experiences in Mexico and the fact that he had the support of the government of Plutarco Elías Calles did not combine to promote a movement similar to the one that occurred in Mexico. The Sandinist movement, according to Amaru Barahona Portocarrero, was an anti-colonial movement for national liberation, since its main goal was to expel from its national territory the occupying US troops; it was characterized by the combined effort of different classes, being "comprised of peasants (small landowners or tenant farmers from latifundia in the northern part of the country), blue-collar workers (especially the ones in US mines and plantations in the northern and eastern regions of Nicaragua), some medium landowners, and intellectual workers.[52]

Given these social foundations, it is evident that Sandino's movement was distinct from the Mexican one and, in view of its characteristics and strategy, it also had a different outcome.

> No transformation in the relations of production of society was proposed . . . nor did it draw up a political programme or plan congruent with the assumption of state power. The organization of the movement revealed a contrasting duality. In its military aspect it reached an optimum of rationality, if we take into account the guerrilla form of fighting that it adopted and the resources it had at its disposal. On the other hand, politically the movement was dependent upon the kind of caudillo leadership afforded to it by Sandino, who was systematically opposed to giving it a structure based on a particular party or programme.[53]

Thus, once the departure of the invading army had been achieved in 1933, the absence of social revolutionary objectives hindered the continuity of the struggle, because Sandino "was not ready to decide that the evacuation of US troops merely entailed a substitution of the extreme – colonial – forms of imperialist domination by other, more subtle forms of a neo-colonial nature, and that the essence of the said domination remained unchanged.[54]

In this way, the influence of the Mexican Revolution on the Sandinist movement turned out to be episodic. In the case of Fidel Castro and the Cuban Revolution, it is even more insignificant. In contrast to Sandino, Castro spent his time in exile in Mexico in a historical atmosphere dominated by the reformist trend that the Mexican Revolution had adopted by that time, which made any influence more improbable.

Whereas on the one hand Fidel Castro and his colleagues enjoyed the sympathy of certain sectors of Mexican society, which helped them in organizing the movement to overthrow Batista, on the other the government and the police kept them under constant surveillance. This official attitude demonstrated the fact that by the end of the 1950s, the 1910 Revolution was no longer meaningful for those looking for change on the Latin American continent.[55] For that reason, Castro had to move towards another line of revolutionary action which "was a novelty in Latin America, where reformism continued to occupy the attention of the most outstanding politicians . . . liberalism was then being considered an inadequate and inefficient means for solving Cuban and Latin American problems . . . and socialism was appearing as the only valid path."[56]

In other words, after Cárdenas, when the Mexican Revolution had lost the sense of a break with traditional society and confrontation with US imperialism, it no longer appeared as a revolutionary model. As a result, it can be inferred that the current Cuban and Nicaraguan revolutions represent, by their very importance, other means for reformulating revolutionary thought and action in Latin America.

4

In the light of the above, it remains to offer some general considerations which can serve as a conclusion to this paper. As we have stated, our interest in conducting a comparative study on the regional impact of the Meiji Restoration and the Mexican Revolution stems from a desire to determine the degree of influence wielded by these movements in their respective regions, and we are attracted especially by the fact that the status of "models" has been ascribed to both of these.

Throughout this paper, we have explained that the geographical proximity and the historical and cultural links of both societies vis-à-vis their neighbours indicate that there was in fact such an impact, viewed in terms of diplomatic interactions, the exchange of ideas, and migratory flows. However, none of those contacts managed to further processes of social change analogous to the two models.

This finding poses a very significant problem, referred to by Jean Chesneaux as "the untransferability of models"; according to this notion, the evolution of history is of an uneven nature, not allowing for the artificial adaptation, in a given social formation, of structures and elements of collective life taken from another social formation for the purpose of patterning the former after the latter.[57]

This failure of transferral is more evident in the case of the attempt to modernize China and Korea from the top down, and arose from to the distinct social characteristics that both societies exhibit. The ascendancy of Japan over Korea was only made possible through annexation, and thus the amalgamation of both societies was achieved under the influence of colonial domination, an aim which in the case of China was not realized successfully. For its part, the Mexican Revolution was not in a position to present itself as a model. Owing to the pressures and threats it was subjected to, it was unlikely that plans would be made to promote another, similar revolution in Latin America, for that would also imply that in these societies there were historical conditions similar to those giving rise to the Mexican movement. Nevertheless, one fact remains clear: the ill-will directed against the revolution elicited a defensive campaign within Mexico itself and in the rest of Latin America, which kept the meaning of the movement alive.

Despite these considerations, it is also apparent that the successful capitalist transformation of Japan continues to arouse interest and to be viewed as a guide not only for Asia, but for other developed societies, such as the United States and, more recently, Africa.[58] Similarly, once the stage of danger and rejection of the Mexican Revolution had been overcome, it was redeemed as an exemplary movement for Latin American countries, especially as of the 1960s under the plan "Alliance for Progress." Recently, its status as a prototype has been reaffirmed by the Kissinger Report, where it was presented as an example of a genuine people's revolution which sprang entirely from "indigenous roots."[59] In the face of such appraisals, there is a continued need for extensive research into the influences that have been outlined in this paper.

Notes

1. Edwin O. Reischauer, *Japan: Past and Present* (Charles E. Tuttle Co., Tokyo, 1971).
2. Jon Halliday, *A Political History of Japanese Capitalism* (Pantheon Books, New York, 1975).
3. Raúl Cardiel Reyes, "La democracia social," *Cuadernos americanos*, vol. 226, no. 5 (1977), pp. 55–74.
4. Arnaldo Córdova, *La ideología de la Revolución Mexicana. Formación del nuevo régimen* (Ediciones Era, Mexico City, 1973).
5. Michiko Tanaka, "La renovación Meidyi y la formación del proyecto nacional del Japón moderno," *Relaciones internacionales*, vol. 9, no. 30 (1982), pp. 21–22.
6. Abelardo Villegas, *Reformismo y revolución en el pensamiento latinoamericano* (Siglo XXI, Mexico City, 1972), p. 83.

7. Jean Chesneaux, *Asia oriental en los siglos XIX y XX* (Editorial Labor, S.A., Madrid, 1969), p. 209.
8. Tulio Halperin Donghi, *Historia contemporánea de América Latina* (Alianza Editorial, Madrid, 1972), p. 7.
9. Pablo González Casanova, ed., *América Latina. Historia de Medio Siglo, América del Sur* (Siglo XXI, Mexico City, 1977), p. vii.
10. Kim Key-hiuk, *The Last Phase of the East Asian World Order: Korea, Japan and the Chinese Empire, 1860–1882* (University of California Press, Berkeley, 1980), p. 110.
11. See note 10 above, p. 11.
12. Noriko Kamachi, "The Chinese in Meiji Japan: Their Interaction with the Japanese before the Sino-Japanese War," in Akira Iriye, ed., *The Chinese and the Japanese. Essays in Political and Cultural Interaction* (Princeton University Press, Princeton, 1980), p. 58.
13. Richard H. Mitchell, *The Korean Minority in Japan* (University of California Press, Berkeley, 1967), p. 7.
14. Cho Kijun, *Hanguk Kyongjesa* (History of Korean Economy) (Seoul, 1962).
15. Gregory Henderson, "Japan's Chosen: Immigrants, Ruthlessness and Development Shock," in Andrew C. Nahm, ed., *Korea under Japanese Rule* (Center for Korean Studies, Western Michigan University, Kalamazoo, Mich., 1973), p. 264.
16. Harold F. Cook, *Korea's 1884 Incident. Its Background and Kim Ok-kyun's Elusive Dream* (Royal Asiatic Society and Taewon Publishing Co., Seoul, 1972).
17. See note 13 above, p. 10.
18. George M. Beckmann, *The Modernization of China and Japan* (Harper & Row, New York, 1962), p. 179.
19. John E. Schrecker, "The Reform Movement of 1898 and the Meiji Restoration as Ch'ing-i Movements," in Akira Iriye (note 12 above), pp. 96–97.
20. See note 7 above, p. 57.
21. Marius B. Jansen, *The Japanese and Sun Yat-sen* (Harvard University Press, Cambridge, Mass., 1954), pp. 2–4.
22. See note 21 above.
23. Ernest P. Young, "Chinese Leaders and Japanese Aid in the Early Republic," and Madeleine Chi, "Ts'ao Ju-lin (1876–1966): His Japanese Connections," both in Akira Iriye (note 12 above), pp. 124–160.
24. Bunsō Hashikawa, "Japanese Perspectives on Asia. From Dissociation to Coprosperity," in Akira Iriye (note 12 above), p. 329.
25. María de la Luz Parcero, *Introducción bibliográfica a la historiografía política de México, siglos XIX y XX* (National Autonomous University of Mexico, Mexico City, 1982), p. 125.
26. Mauricio Magdaleno, *Escritores extranjeros en la Revolución* (Biblioteca del Instituto Nacional de Estudios Históricos de la Revolución Mexicana, Mexico City, 1979), p. 209.
27. See note 26 above.
28. The regime of dictator Porfirio Díaz. See Berta Ulloa, *La Revolución Intervenida (1910–1914)* (El Colegio de México, Mexico City, 1976).
29. Lorenzo Meyer, "El primer tramo del camino," in *Historia general de México*, vol. IV (El Colegio de México, Mexico City, 1976), p. 263.
30. Lorenzo Meyer, "La encrucijada," in *Historia general de México* (note 29 above), pp. 146–263.
31. See note 30 above.
32. Tzvi Medin, *Ideología y praxis política de Lázaro Cárdenas* (Siglo XXI, Mexico City, 1984), p. 190.

33. Juan Hernández Luna, *Antonia Caso. Gran explosión de México* (Sociedad Amigos del Libro, Mexico City, 1963), p. 12.
34. See note 33 above.
35. Manuel Eduardo Hubner, *México en marcha* (Editorial Zig-Zag, Santiago de Chile, 1935), pp. 8–9.
36. Mario de la Cueva, *El nuevo perecho mexicano del trabajo* (Editorial Porrúa, S.A., Mexico City, 1978), pp. x–xii.
37. See note 35 above, p. 525.
38. Cardiel Reyes (note 3 above), p. 67. *Ejidos* are common lands.
39. See note 3 above.
40. See note 35 above, p. 528.
41. See note 32 above, p. 191.
42. German word indicating a customs union established among the German states in 1834 (under Prussian leadership). It created a free-trade area and was an important step in German unification.
43. See note 35 above, p. 525.
44. Julio Cuadros Caldas, *México-Soviet* (Santiago Loyo, Editor, Puebla, 1926), pp. 6–7.
45. Rafael Moreno, "La cultura y la filosofía iberoamericana de José Vasconcelos," in Alvaro Matute and Martha Donís, eds., *José Vasconcelos: De su vida y su obra*, Textos de Humanidades, 39 (National Autonomous University of Mexico, Mexico City, 1984), pp. 102–115.
46. José Carlos Mariátegui, "La unidad de la América Indoespañola," in Rubén Jiménez Ricárdez, ed., *José Carlos Mariátegui. Obra política* (Ediciones Era, Mexico City, 1984), pp. 281–283.
47. Julio Cotler, "Perú: Estado oligárquico y reformismo militar," in Pablo González Casanova, ed., *América Latina: Historia de medio siglo*, vol. 1 (Siglo XXI, Mexico City, 1977), pp. 382–383.
48. Abelardo Villegas, *Reformismo y revolución en el pensamiento latinoamericano* (Siglo XXI, Mexico City, 1972), p. 173.
49. See note 48 above, p. 174.
50. Gregoria Selser, *El pequeño ejército loco. Sandino y la operación México-Nicaragua* (Bruguera Mexicana de Ediciones, S.A., Mexico City, 1980), p. 9.
51. Robert Freeman Smith, *The United States and Revolutionary Nationalism in Mexico, 1916–1932* (University of Chicago Press, Chicago/London, 1972), p. 236.
52. Amaru Barahona Portocarrero, "Breve estudio sobre la historia contemporánea de Nicaragua," in González Casanova (note 47 above), vol. 2, p. 387.
53. See note 52 above, p. 388.
54. See note 53 above.
55. Herbert Matthewes, *Castro, A Political Biography* (Allen Lane, London, 1969), pp. 176–177, 280.
56. See note 48 above, p. 272.
57. Jean Chesneaux, *¿Hacemos tabla rasa del pasado? A propósito de la Historia y los historiadores* (Siglo XXI, Mexico City, 1979), pp. 170–179.
58. William G. Ouchi, *Theory Z. How American Business Can Meet the Japanese Challenge* (Avon Books, New York, 1981) and "Japon un modèle pour l'Afrique?" *Jeune Afrique*, no. 2 (1984), pp. xx–xxiii.
59. *Informe Kissinger (contra) Centroamérica*, introduction, notes, and comments by Gregorio Selser (Sociedad Cooperativa Publicaciones Mexicanas, S.A., Mexico City, 1984), p. 220.

THE CHINESE AND MEXICAN REVOLUTIONS: AN OVERALL COMPARATIVE ANALYSIS

Victor Lopez Villafañe
Universidad Nacional Autónoma de México, Mexico City, Mexico

Introduction

The purpose of this paper is to make a conceptual analysis of the similarities and differences between China's and Mexico's respective revolutionary processes. We are faced with the usual space limitations imposed upon papers of this sort and are thus obliged to synthesize – perhaps to an excessive degree – and to offer statements which may seem too categorical to the meticulous specialist, for we do not place either of the above-mentioned revolutionary processes in a precise historical context.

With regard to the most fruitful method of comparative analysis, we consider it best to concentrate on two or three issues we believe are fundamental to each case and to determine points of convergence and divergence for each one.

Revolutionary Processes: Origin, Social Forces, and Insertion in Contemporary Society

In academic tradition, comparative analyses almost always take as their starting-point the greatest social difference, which, in turn, is derived from theoretical formulas we use to classify economic-political systems. Thus we would have to state, for instance – in keeping with this tradition – that whereas in China peasant rebellions culminated in the creation of a socialist state, in Mexico the same type of uprising led to the establishment of a state which, although it enjoyed greater autonomy, did not manage to remain outside the sphere of relations forming part of the international capitalist system. Naturally, we are not opposed to wide-ranging definitions and classifications, yet we *do* note that in many cases the features observed are strikingly distinct from established classificatory models; the Chinese and Mexican revolutions are cases in point, the former being far removed from the typical socialist revolution and the latter also far removed from the classical model of a capitalist bourgeois revolution.

In view of this, we feel there is a kind of hiatus regarding the theoretical foundations of twentieth-century revolutions in backward countries, both in Marxist and non-Marxist thought, which could clarify for us – with a certain measure of objectivity – the historical and conceptual meaning of these revolutionary transformations in a non-European context, particularly the one germane to Latin America, Asia, and Africa. Having made this clarification, we perhaps need to justify the degree of conceptual liberty that we take in attempting to analyse China and Mexico's revolutionary processes.

If we take into account a long span in the history of both countries (between 200 and 300 years prior to the outbreak of revolution), we find that a characteristic common to both is the struggle they underwent to become part of the modern industrial world during the latter part of the nineteenth century and the twentieth century. As in almost all backward nations, this change entails the modification of the traditional mode of subsistence of the ancient agrarian community and the ties joining together that community and the old political order, in a transition toward the creation of a new state, a new ideological conformation, and the creation of a new logic in the relations among the social forces for economic development.

Another common trait in this transition is the fact that these transformations were foreshadowed by a long series of peasant struggles led by small nuclei of intellectuals and, subsequently, by leaders who in time developed a revolutionary ideology, offering an alternative to the struggle of the masses. In China, this culminated in the establishment of the programme of the Chinese Communist Party, and in Mexico in a progressive application of the principles of classic liberalism and the organization of democratic-bourgeois forms, with significant sections of the law relating to the new role of workers in society.

Nevertheless, the first major difference we find is the way in which their specific origins determined the course of these revolutionary processes. In China, transformations were preceded by the breakdown of the old imperial system, whereas in Mexico the imprint of colonialism was to mark the entire transformation. The revolutionary process was initiated once it became possible to dismantle the whole bureaucratic structure of Spanish colonization, after almost three centuries of domination. With the independence movement of 1810 we witness the birth of a cycle of revolutions in Mexico that only culminate in the fourth decade of this century.[1]

In Mexico neither the Independence nor the Reform period of the mid-nineteenth century allowed for the creation of a national political power, but they did constitute major links, helping set new horizons for society and paving the way for the Mexican Revolution of 1910. Thus, in Mexico exogenous factors were to play a key role in the configuration of the new society. They are a challenge that has always been present, and explain the exemplary nationalism of the revolutionary ideology of this century. In a historical perspective, the constant battling against foreign elements explains, to a certain extent, the radical nature of some of the reforms, but it also accounts for the limited impact that these reforms have had in the long run, especially in the realm of economic independence. So many years of direct colonization and struggle against the European powers, and later the US, led to the emergence of a political conscience that was radical in some respects, but geared to negotiating, owing to the impossibility of Mexico's achieving full political and economic independence; and this tendency became a central factor in the ideology of the new state.

In China, the external factor played a different role. For one thing, that country was never colonized in the political sense of the term and, however minimal it might have been, a certain pride in its national culture was preserved. Secondly, the external factor was always of an economic rather than a political nature, that is to say, it tended to accentuate China's position as a backward nation.[2]

With respect to one of the questions we deem to be most significant in this comparative study – the social forces which made possible the path of transformation – here also the two countries share a common feature: the lack of economically and politically structured social groups which could have allowed for revolutionary movements similar to those that occurred in seventeenth- and eighteenth-century Europe. Perhaps this explains, more than any other factor, the almost explosive aspiration to create a strong and centralized type of state with a markedly nationalistic ideology that was to arise in those countries after innumerable trials and failures. The social forces seem to appear less in the typical form of a social class or important segments of various upward-bound classes, but more as a mixture of diverse groups and sectors within highly controversial alliances (such as Zapata–Villa–Carranza in Mexico and the Kuomintang–Chinese Communist Party in China). Involved here are revolutions supported by the peasant masses: landless peasants, exploited wage labourers, blue-collar workers, and the urban sectors. Possibly the most significant distinction consists in the fact that in Mexico, in the end, the hegemony of a middle-level agrarian sector was imposed under a liberal programme which, nevertheless, found it necessary to substantiate its legitimacy by making major concessions to the masses of workers and peasants. On the contrary, in China those same concessions were transformed into the very heart of the revolutionary struggle, and in that struggle one could observe a remarkable continuity between the programme of Sun Yat-sen and the proposals of the Chinese Communist Party during the period of the Japanese invasion and the second civil war.

The problem that both revolutionary processes would eventually have to deal with was the transposition of the traditional rural community to the conditions and demands of the international capitalist economy and new world politics. As we have already pointed out, in Mexico the said community was eroded by a lengthy colonizing process and, in China, by a type of disruption that caused increasing disarticulation between the central power of the imperial bureaucracy and the rural community. It has been mentioned that a possible cause of this disruption was China's inability – despite its enormous growth in the fields of science and technology – to implement a commerical-industrial expansion scheme that would have formed the basis for the country's modern development.[3]

Within the framework of rural transformations on an international plane, the cases of China and Mexico appear as agrarian revolutions in the underdeveloped world, the product of the failure of policies to meet the land-related demands of the vast masses of peasants. In another way, they also reflect the absence of an alternative path of social transformation, such as results from the development of commercial farming and the creation of an urban manufacturing class that can act as a pivot for change, and which was experienced by European countries to different degrees and in different ways.

For example, in Mexico one of the "big businessmen" of the nineteenth century was the church, which ended up suppressing initiatives favouring any sort of transformation. Thus, the first attempt at land reform was made when the governments of the Reform period launched an ideological programme involving agricultural modernization that would strip the church of its numerous tracts of idle land and begin a process of economic development in the country. Yet those to benefit from this were not the representatives of a new class of businessmen but, rather, long-established estate owners and foreign companies. The process of land concentration was to be consolidated in the period known as the Porfiriato (1877–1910), and this gave rise to a landless peasantry destined to fuel the revolutionary movement that would begin in 1910.[4]

On the other hand, a regional power managed to evolve; later it was to serve as an incubator for the forces leading the revolution, especially in those regions where the development of capitalist forms had spread quickly, taking advantage of gaps in the domestic market that had not been covered by foreign capital. In the northern part of the country, especially, an economic and political force arose that was to challenge the old dictatorship, a force that owed its strength to its activities in the fields of mining, agriculture, and business. In contrast, in the south of the country conservative estates predominated, tying down and subjugating the peasantry. To all of the above we would also have to add the significant presence of foreign companies, which exploited their workers. For that reason, the Mexican Revolution represented a convergence of the peasants' struggle for land and the fight waged by groups of workers to better their living conditions; it was also a dispute between the old agrarian structure and a new social force which sought to modify the traditional structure of political power, a struggle grounded on colonial vestiges that one hundred years of independence had been unable to do away with (estate owners, the church, military caciques, etc.).

In China, also, no particular social stratum headed the revolutionary process from the end of the empire until the era of the struggle by the Communists to gain power; this strife, again, was expressed in terms of major class and group alliances. The basic social element was, as in the case of Mexico, the landless peasantry, supported by urban workers and led by intellectuals and political representatives of the upper strata of the country's bourgeoisie.

Let us take a closer look at the status of Chinese peasants. China did not have a feudal structure similar to the one found in Europe; it was not even like the Japanese one. It could, in fact, be said that cohesion in the world of the peasant community itself was much less pronounced than in Mexico where, above all, the ancient communal ways of life had survived the colonizing process and, in the long run, constituted one of the motivations of the peasants' struggle up until the time of President Lázaro Cárdenas' agrarian reform (1934–1940).

China's agrarian history is that of a majority of landless peasants (only 30 per cent were landholders) who tilled the fields of landowners under leasing arrangements. The latter contributed the land and the former the labour. Crops were divided up between the two, the proportion depending upon the terms of the contract. The situation varied greatly throughout the country; it was more favourable in those regions which were near large cities and thus benefited from the market economy. The conditions of the peasants were bad: they could not support themselves solely from farming and were forced to work in crafts industries in order to subsist. However, those peasants who were unsuccessful in combining agricultural work with crafts activities were compelled to borrow money from the landowners, thus increasing their dependence and giving way to a process of indebtedness that often culminated in suicide. The middle-level peasants were also subject to disadvantageous conditions in the market, since they were usually forced to sell at lower prices after the crop had been harvested, because they had to meet their payment of taxes and loans. On the other hand, the landholders took advantage of this situation, hoarding the grain which they could later sell at higher prices. Worth noting is the fact that this situation varied from one region to the next and, particularly, in the areas near large cities, where resident landowners were rare. In fact, one phenomenon to evolve was the existence of the absentee landowner, who would usually collect his rents in cash.

Thus, a commercial economy located in the areas most affected by the presence of foreigners undermined peasant property and, in general, made their lives more difficult. Similarly, in areas ruled by military caciques, the exploitation of peasants by landholders, grain merchants, and the caciques themselves worsened. In extensive areas of China, the end of the imperial regime did not produce fundamental changes in the political and economic role of the rural upper classes; as far as the peasants were concerned, it meant a deterioration in their situation. Therefore, the first attempt to modernize and provide solutions to China's political problems stemmed from the revolution headed by Sun Yat-sen, which failed in 1915 when the government of the military caudillos was reinstated.

Later, the doctrine of the KMT, as Chiang Kai-shek formulated it, ruled out the inclusion of any social and economic programme to solve China's problems. From the standpoint of its domestic framework, perhaps that was what served as the grounds for the struggle for ideological hegemony between the KMT and the Chinese Communist Party in the decade prior to the establishment of the Popular Republic. Here is the point where we should also situate the strategy of "nationalizing Marxism" within the realities of China and the policy of broad alliances that the Communists designed to conquer their enemies at home and abroad (i.e. the Chinese Communist Party was transformed, in reality, into the "Marxist" incarnation of the KMT).

In comparative terms, it may be said that the KMT's endeavours to hasten the transformation of China into a modern state by a reactionary path, based on a strong bureaucracy and supported by a coalition between sectors of the old agrarian ruling classes – whose political power was formidable but who were in a weak economic position – and a new commercial and industrial élite – with some degree of economic power but rather little political and social power – turned out to be a total failure.[5] In both instances, peasant insurrections and rebellions were a decisive factor in pushing the country toward the Communist path of modernization and not toward a Fascist one or toward the democratic variants of capitalism.[6]

Mexico's social nature was different from that of China. From colonial times, it was a constituent part of the world capitalist economy. Although it is still a topic of domestic controversy, we do not believe one can speak of a "feudal stage" as one can in the case of China; however, in Mexico there did exist greater cohesion and solidarity among the members of the agricultural community, an example of which was the relationship between the estate owners and the government. But we can also observe a gradual worsening of peasants' living conditions, which became acute at the close of the nineteenth century. During that period a class of aristocratic landowners arose in Mexico, possessing enormous latifundia that they had managed to acquire at the expense of village lands. The Mexican Revolution was an act of survival for the peasantry, which was pushed into taking up arms in order to regain the land it had lost. But what was to give the revolution a broader social dimension was the creation of an alliance of a faction of the governing bureaucracy itself, a sector of the liberal rural upper class, and the leaders of the peasant masses. Two factors should be pointed out here. First is the fact that the historical alliance of these groups took place even in the midst of armed strife between them for political hegemony; however, in that struggle very important aspects such as the ones that pitted the KMT against the Chinese Communist Party were not clarified.

The second question has to do with the ideological conformation of the Mexican variant of representative democracy, through the establishment of a new state that would give expression to a strong national unity composed of diverse social forces. This nationalist ideology was an important component of the new economic strategy, as well as of the type of "democracy" restored through the regime's political ruling party, the National Revolutionary Party, which as of its inception in 1929 unified and eventually controlled regional caciques. In 1938, it was transformed into the Party of the Mexican Revolution, and structured itself as a party in which peasant and worker organizations became its very nucleus.

Regarding the question of nationalism in China and Mexico, several brief remarks are in order. Nationalism as expressed through twentieth-century revolutions is very different, both in character and content, from the kind of nationalism which arose in the context of the creation of the nation-states, mainly in Europe. In both processes, nationalism emerged out of a need to confront new external economic and political forces which, on a domestic plane, constituted an obstacle to the construction of a modern state and which in the case of China were an essential factor in the configuration of the revolutionary ideology of the Communists in the 1930s and 1940s. This type of nationalism was also useful in defining the specific characteristics of the Chinese Revolution in the context of the socialist world taking shape, with the adaptation of Marxism to China's concrete realities.

In China, nationalism was an ideological force that was always present in revolutionary programmes, particularly in the ones drawn up by Sun Yat-sen and Mao Tse-tung. It was represented by the need to build a new China politically and economically independent from the imperialist powers. In China, nationalism was manifested in a more violent and radical fashion than in Mexico, owing not only to the acuteness with which the presence of foreign powers was felt in the economic ambit, but also because it came to express the conviction that a new society was possible only through a complete break with the world power structure prevalent between the First and Second World Wars.

Nowadays, the subject of just how much the presence of foreigners in China was a determining factor in the formation of its revolutionary conscience is still a highly controversial issue. The history of China's relations with the imperialist powers is one of subjugation from the sixteenth century on, this becoming much more intense after the first Opium War up until the

Japanese invasion. China was transformed into a "semi-colony," since it awarded economic and political concessions and rights to the colonizing nations – a situation that hindered the progress of China's domestic evolution. From an economic standpoint, the stifling of China's industrial development by the Western imperialist powers could not have taken place if it had not already been curbed by purely internal forces.[7] This hypothesis appears to be consistent if we observe what happened in Japan, where the political and economic unity achieved prior to the invasion of Western elements established different conditions in the new dealings demanded of Japan by the Western powers.

Without denying the effect that domestic "stifling" had on a domestic level, it seems to us that what was of greater import in determining the revolutionary conscience and the radicalism adopted by the Chinese Communists was China's status vis-à-vis the new balance of world power after the First World War and the Bolshevik Revolution. That period was characterized by a lengthy political crisis which was to result in US hegemony after the Second World War. In this sense, we believe that the Japanese invasion was not the only factor determining the increasing strength of the Communists.[8] That invasion was, in turn, the product of the military-ideological structure of Japan, that was to lead to the economic-political crisis that preceded the War of the Pacific.

We have already stated that the various political efforts to build a new Chinese state failed, from Sun Yat-sen's democratic revolution to the reforms made by Chiang Kai-shek's KMT government. In fact, the Communists under Mao's leadership made the revolutionary experiment practicable by taking advantage of the crisis of the imperialist powers and, on a domestic plane, capitalizing on the common ground between different sectors of the population. On the one hand, inverting Marxist theory, they turned the landless, oppressed peasantry into an extremely important revolutionary factor. At the same time, they tried to obtain the co-operation of the middle-class and rich farmers by means of a moderate agrarian reform, and, on the basis of their analysis of the development of capitalism, they reached the conclusion that the new revolutionary project should envision an alliance with the country's bourgeoisie, whose development had been hindered by the control and monopoly of industry and finance by foreign forces. The initial path taken by the new China was the result of a long struggle to become an autonomous and independent part of contemporary society, in which the old structures were torn down, with the participation of the masses in both the cities and the countryside.

The world crisis between the two major wars lent Mexican nationalism different characteristics. On an international plane, it had to confront and acquiesce to the United States' hegemony in the region. Within that framework, the reforms geared to regaining key sectors of the economy – such as the oil industry in 1938 – proved to be of great significance, although not of the same scope as the accomplishments of the Chinese Revolution.

In that context, one of the main objectives of the Mexican revolutionary process was to create a new state whose fundamental premise was the control of basic resources, which would provide it with a certain degree of internal political autonomy and legitimacy in the eyes of society.

The Mexican Revolution expressed the economic demands of a wide range of social groups, and its success involved a redefinition of the country's relation to foreign economic forces. A true national political power could not come into existence without first achieving a readjustment in development strategy which, as of the revolution, was to be based on the economic policies of the state (oil, transportation, electric power, etc.) and on the land reform introduced by President Lázaro Cárdenas. All of this linked the state indissolubly with nationalist policies that helped establish a power structure, including the participation of workers, peasants, and intellectuals. In its contemporary phase, Mexico's nationalism is qualified by the complex external relations that it needs to develop in the face of the United States' industrial and political power.

Conclusions

First, the roots of these revolutions were different. Three hundred years of Spanish colonization left a political-ideological imprint that was later to determine Mexico's revolutionary path. The issue of national political power revolved around that fact, i.e. the question of forming a new nation which could reconcile its heritage with the challenge of contemporary industrial society. In contrast, China – despite having suffered colonial oppression – had preserved its national culture, and the passage involved more directly a transition from the old agricultural community to industrial society via the establishment of socialism.

Secondly, another important difference is related to the political hegemony of the revolutionary groups. In Mexico, this hegemony was held during the first phase of the Mexican Revolution by the middle and upper sectors of the old liberal rural classes, whose most important achievement consisted in destroying the dictatorship and the economic oligarchy and establishing a development strategy that would entail a readjustment with other forces, especially those represented by the United States. In China, on the other hand, there was a more intense struggle for revolutionary hegemony, mainly between the KMT and the Chinese Communist Party, a struggle that culminated in the triumph of the latter on the basis of an extended alliance with wide sectors of peasants, workers, and the national bourgeoisie. To a large extent, that struggle was responsible for the very intensity and radicalism of those revolutionary efforts.

In both cases, thirdly, the impact of foreign influences was a very significant feature for revolutionary development, but perhaps the specific contexts were determining factors in the course of those transformations. In China the conflict was of greater proportions than in Mexico, since it formed part of the new configuration of world power in the twentieth century; that is to say, the conflict in China had an international impact, and the revolution was at the heart of a struggle over and a way towards the new world power structure. In Mexico, the revolutionary ceiling was delimited by the existence of US hegemony in the region. Within that context, there was formidable radicalism – which served as the foundations for the new state – but this was restricted by the persistent relation of subordination which ensured that the Mexican case was to be a variant, with very specific developmental traits, in the sphere of revolutions in backward countries.

Notes

1. The 1810 independence movement, the period of the Reform during the mid-nineteenth century, and the Revolution of 1910 are all considered within the cycle of the bourgeois revolution in Mexico. See Enrique Semo, *Historia mexicana. Economía y lucha de clases* (Ediciones Era, Mexico City, 1978).
2. China was part of the "external arena" of world capitalist economics in the sixteenth century, whereas the American continent was part of the periphery (see I. Wallerstein, *El moderno sistema mundial*, Editorial Siglo XXI, Mexico City, 1979, pp. 474–475). During subsequent centuries, economic pressures exerted by the Western powers to conquer China's market increased.
3. See Wallerstein (note 2 above).
4. By 1910, around 90 per cent of Mexican rural families had no land at all and approximately 85 per cent of the Indian communities had lost all their property. See Roger D. Hansen, *La política del desarrollo mexicano* (Editorial Siglo XXI, Mexico City, 1975), pp. 191–192.
5. In this respect China's experience is comparable to that of Russia, and in contrast to that of Japan and Germany.
6. See Barrington Moore, *Los orígenes sociales de la dictadura y la democracia* (Editorial Península, Madrid, 1976), p. 1969.
7. See note 6 above, p. 150.
8. See Chalmers A. Johnson, *Peasant Nationalism and Communist Power: The Emergence of Revolutionary China 1937–1945* (Stanford University Press, Stanford, Calif., 1967).

THE 1910–1917 MEXICAN REVOLUTION AND THE 1911 CHINESE REVOLUTION: A COMPARATIVE STUDY

Chen Zhiyun
Institute of Latin American Studies, Beijing, China

The 1910–1917 Mexican Revolution and the 1911 Chinese Revolution are two of the major historical developments of the beginning of the twentieth century. The Mexican Revolution inaugurated the modern history of the country by overthrowing Porfirio Díaz's dictatorship, which had lasted for 34 years. The Chinese Revolution put an end to the feudalistic imperial system under which China had lived for more than 2,000 years and raised the democratic-republican flag over the country. Both developments not only had a powerful influence in the evolution of the historical processes in these two countries, but also must be considered as part of a worldwide revolution. Therefore, a comparative study of these two cataclysmic events is called for, in order to define their role and their importance in the evolution of world history, and to shed light on their characteristics and subsequent effects. This paper will present a short analysis of the similarities and differences in the social changes brought about by these two events.

Mexico and China on the Eve of Their Revolutions

There were many similarities between Mexico under Porfirio Díaz (1877–1911) and China under Emperors Guanxu and Xuantong (1875–1911), the last two rulers of the Qing dynasty. Both nations were basically semi-feudal states, economically underdeveloped, and controlled by foreign capital. Capital and production concentration in Western Europe and North America reached an unprecedented level at the turn of the century. Liberal capitalism

Paper presented at the Conference on the Modernization Process in Mexico (1867–1940): The Social Transformations, co-sponsored by the United Nations University and El Colegio de México, Mexico City, 19–21 March 1985.

was moving towards monopolistic capitalism, and the export of goods was being gradually replaced by the export of capital. In order to maximize benefits, monopolistic capitalists were looking frantically for new colonies all over the world. At the same time, they used all available means to coerce some politically independent countries to be economically subservient to them. Under these new historical conditions, it was impossible for economically backward countries, such as Mexico and China, to implement a state-controlled modernization following the model set by Western European capitalism. As a consequence, faced with a massive penetration of foreign capital, they had to limit their efforts to a slow growth of their economies.

In the words of Mao Tse-tung, "Foreign capitalism played a very important role in the disintegration of the socio-economic Chinese order; on the one hand, it undermined the foundations of the natural economy, and ruined artisan industry in the cities and cottage industry in the rural areas; on the other hand, it sped up the development of a mercantilistic economy both in the cities and in the rural areas." Nevertheless, this "is only one aspect of the changes brought about by the introduction of imperialism in China. There is another concomitant but contradictory aspect: the collusion of imperialism and the Chinese feudal forces to avoid the development of a Chinese capitalism."[1]

Both China and Mexico initiated their transformation processes during the 1870s and 1880s with the introduction of foreign capital. Modern industry started with railway construction. In 1880 there were only 640 km of railways in Mexico, but by 1884 the total length reached 5,731 km, and by 1910 the figure was 19,280 km. The first railway in China between Guye and Tianjin was built in 1887. It was only 160 km long, but by the end of the century there was a tremendous boom in railway construction all over the country. The great powers, such as England, Russia, Germany, France, and the US, competed among themselves for the rights to invest in this industry, and by 1898 they had obtained rights to build 10,270 km of track. Similarly, modern transport by ships, mostly managed by foreign capital, displaced the traditional transport by sailing boats.

The modernization of communications fostered the development of industry and mining. In Mexico, not only such traditional metals as gold or silver were mined, but also other highly valuable minerals such as copper, lead, zinc, oil, etc., started to be exploited. The development of the electric power industry increased dramatically the demand for copper on a worldwide scale. Between 1895 and 1905 mining production in Mexico increased at an annual rate of 10 per cent, but the increase in copper production was 21 per cent. When an oilfield was discovered in Tampico, Mexico became the first oil-producing country in the world. In 1911, annual crude production reached 12,552,000 barrels. Manufacturing industries developed at a similar pace. Transformation industries using modern machines and equipment were established in the textile, leather, flour, and other fields. By 1910, there were 146 modern textile factories.

During the 1870s a few modern arms factories were established in China as a consequence of the development of the "foreignization" movement. The followers of this group also promoted the establishment of some civilian industries to substitute for military industries. Some bureaucrats, landowners, and merchants made investments and established modern enterprises in the fields of mining, textiles, marine transport, flour-processing, etc. The most important artisan shops, owned by small and medium-size Chinese interests, gradually introduced modern machines to replace their primitive utensils. Records show that in 1869 there were only five capitalistic enterprises in China, capitalized at 100,000 yuan; but by 1884 there were already 262, and their overall capital was 51,560,000 yuan.[2]

The construction and development of modern industries and communication facilities promoted the exchange of goods. Existing small local markets grew in size and became regional or even national markets.

Historical facts prove that both Mexico under Díaz and China by the end of the Qing dynasty had already started their modernization processes and that capitalistic production facilities were being smoothly developed.

But these processes differ from those followed by developed capitalistic countries. First, they took place under a massive foreign capital invasion, and, as a consequence, the development was in most cases subject to the interests of foreign capital. Second, both capitalistic and feudal or semi-feudal production systems coexisted in time and place; feudalistic systems were even more important than the modern system, and this was an obstacle for the development of capitalism in the cities.

Both Porfirio Díaz and his "scientists" and the Chinese group preaching "foreignization" promoted the introduction of foreign capital as an important instrument for economic development. For this purpose, and in complete disregard of national interests, they offered to foreign capitalists the rights to build railways, exploit mines, and transport goods by rivers and canals. As a consequence, the vital arteries of the national economy came to be controlled by foreign monopolistic capital. According to José Luis Ceceña, among the 170 major enterprises operating in Mexico in 1910 and 1911, 130 (that is, 77.7 per cent) were under foreign capital control. Their total paid-up capital was 1,288,000,000 pesos. Foreign capital was in control of oil exploitation (100 per cent), mining (98.2 per cent), agriculture (95.7 per cent), electric power (87 per cent), banking (76.5 per cent), and industry (84.3 per cent).[3] The Chinese economy during the 1880s was at an even higher degree of colonization. River and marine transport was almost totally controlled by foreign firms; customs was under British rule; railway construction rights had been given to foreign powers; 80 to 90 per cent of imports and 60 to 70 per cent of exports were controlled by Great Britain. By 1894 foreign capital had built in China some 100 industrial processing firms, producing textiles, paper, matches, cigarettes, etc., with a total paid-up capital of 35 million yuan.[4] After the Sino-Japanese war (1894), Russian, English, French, German, and American imperialists granted enslaving loans to the Manchu government as a tool for the future partition of China.

This large-scale foreign capital invasion prevented China and Mexico from building up their own modern capitalistic economies; on the contrary, both countries became markets for foreign goods and bases for the supply of raw materials to imperialistic countries. Low-priced raw materials such as copper, zinc, lead, oil, coffee, henequen agave (sisal), and chicle (gum of the naseberry tree, *Achras zapota*) from Mexico, and silk, tea, bristle, tobacco, and cotton from China were exported in great quantities, while cigarettes, clothing, thread, kerosene, iron and steel and other manufactured products flooded the domestic markets of these two countries. Thousands of traditional artisans went bankrupt, and the development of a national capital was constricted. The economic structure was unbalanced in such a way that while those sectors offering benefits to foreign capital were rapidly developed, all the other sectors continued to be highly underdeveloped.

The self-reliant natural economy of the rural areas was hard hit by foreign capital, but agricultural production for export developed rapidly. In Mexico local and foreign plantation owners undertook large-scale production of coffee, sugar cane, sisal, chicle, tobacco, etc. In Jiangsu, Zhejian, and other provinces along the Chinese coast raw silk production increased; farmers in Taiwan, Fujian, Hunan, etc., uprooted sweet potato fields to plant tea trees. But as Western capitalistic countries plundered the underdeveloped countries by unequal terms of trade, it was not possible for China or Mexico to improve their rural economies by an increase in the production of crops for export; nor was it possible for them to become well-established countries in the emerging field of capitalistic production facilities. On the contrary, foreign imperialism co-operated with the great local landowners in order to protect the feudal system and to exploit the farmers. The Law of Barren Lands, enacted by the Porfirio Díaz government in December 1883, sped up the process of despoliation of lands owned by the peasants. Surveying firms unscrupulously took over large tracts of land owned by Indian peasants, under the pretext that they were barren lands; during the last years of the Porfirio regime, over 95 per cent of the communal lands were expropriated. At this time, 97 per cent of all arable land in the country was the property of less than 1 per cent of the population, while there were some 3 million landless farming families, that is, 88 per cent of the rural population.[5] Most of these landless peasants could not be absorbed by the slowly developing industries, and were thus obliged to endure the most ruthless feudal exploitation; most of them became *peones*. Their debts were then handed down from generation to generation. In this way the large landowners managed to bind these *peones* to the land, making it impossible for them to escape.

In China, for more than 2,000 years feudal ownership of the land was the economic basis of society. The feudal system survived almost intact the Opium War (1840), and land leasing continued to be the main form of peasant exploitation. The development of a mercantilist economy and the bankruptcy of the small-scale farming economy did not bring substantial changes to the production infrastructure of the rural areas of China. Bankrupt farmers were unable to find jobs in the cities and were obliged to work as salaried rural workers serving the big landowners; when that failed, they had to get loans at usury rates and their exploitation and oppression was thus even greater.

Foreign capital invasion, the collusion between imperialism and feudal forces, the bankruptcy of farmers (comprising up to 70 to 80 per cent of the total population), and the worsening of the general condition of the nation and of its social classes to a degree never seen up to that time were the sources of social unrest on the eve of the revolution.

The external and domestic policies of the government of Porfirio Díaz and the Manchu represented only the interests of foreign capital and local big landowners. These governments, subject to imperialistic wishes, controlled the country with dictatorial powers, suppressed all peasant movements and opposed any kind of reform. Porfirio Díaz betrayed the promises he himself had made in the Tuxtepec Plan to oppose the re-election of the President, to reinvigorate national justice, to defend democracy, and to abide by the Constitution; he became a dictator for life. Under the slogan of "less politics and more administration," and with the support of a handful of generals, state governors and local bosses, he was a true absolute despot. Again, the reign of Empress Ci Xi (1861–1908) is the darkest period in Chinese history. Out of these national, social, and political contradictions, therefore, a strong anti-imperialistic and anti-feudal force emerged. The spear of these two revolutions was directed against the dictators: Porfirio Díaz and the corrupted Qing dynasty.

In short, we can see that the nature of society on the eve of the Mexican and the Chinese revolutions was basically identical: they were feudal societies with a profound dependence on external forces. The tasks of the revolutions were also similar: to overthrow dictatorship, to establish a democratic system, to end the feudal system of land tenure, to oppose the oppression and the exploitation by foreign imperialism, and to lay the foundations for the development of capitalism. Therefore, because of these characteristics, both the Mexican (1910–1917) and the Chinese (1911) revolutions are truly bourgeois democratic revolutions. But this type of revolution, in contrast to the bourgeois European revolution, is also part of national and democratic movements developed by colonies, semi-colonies, and oppressed nations and peoples against exploitation by international capitalism.

All such revolutions have always opposed oppression and exploitation by the international monopolistic bourgeoisie and that is the reason why they are always attacked by imperialist powers. As Lenin said: "Governing forces in Europe, the European bourgeoisie, have made alliances with all reactionary and medieval forces in China."[6] The awakening of oppressed peoples is marked by a series of revolutions at the beginning of this century, including the bourgeois revolution in Iran (1905–1911), the bourgeois revolution in Turkey (1908–1909), the democratic-bourgeois revolution in Mexico (1910–1917), and the Chinese Revolution (1911–1912). Lenin also said: "Hundreds of millions of people who were oppressed and deeply asleep in a medieval situation have been awoken, and now demand a new life and a new struggle in search of basic human rights and of democracy . . . The awakening of Asia and the widening of the proletarian struggle in Europe in search of power are the symbols marking the beginning of a new era in the history of the world."[7]

Differing Characteristics of the Mexican (1910–1917) and the Chinese (1911) Revolutions

Although the Mexican and the Chinese revolutions have similar traits, there are also major differences, mostly due to the different circumstances of the two countries. In Mexico the independence war against Spanish colonial dominion, and the reform movement headed by Benito Juárez, had brought about a certain degree of development of the capitalistic production system, and, comparatively speaking, local bourgeois forces were powerful. In contrast, the Chinese feudal system had already a history of more than 2,000 years and was deeply rooted in the country. Moreover, the oppression and exploitation of China by international capitalism was much worse. At the conclusion of the Sino-Japanese War (1894–1895), China was in danger of being partitioned among the great powers; the national bourgeois class was weak. These dissimilar historical conditions are at the root of the clear differences observed in the features of both revolutions.

In my view the basic differences between these revolutions are the following.

1

The Mexican Revolution was quite clearly an agrarian revolution, whereas the Chinese Revolution of 1911 was a political one, whose purpose was to overthrow the Qing dynasty.

In the Mexican Revolution a well-planned and well-conceived revolutionary programme was lacking. Francisco Madero, the Europe-educated son of a wealthy family, did not intend to unleash a revolution to change the face of Mexican society; all he did was to promise to implement, by means of a moderate protest movement, the slogan of "efficiency in suffrage and no re-election." This notwithstanding, and with the common objective of overthrowing the Porfirio Díaz dictatorship, all the different social classes jumped onto the revolution bandwagon, each of them insisting on their own demands. Peasant forces, especially those under Emiliano Zapata's and Francisco Villa's command, participated in the revolution demanding land. These forces played a decisive role in the revolutionary process and deeply influenced its orientation.

In order to gain the favour of the peasant forces, Madero presented his "San Luis Potosí Plan," a land reform plan promising to give back to the peasants the land that had been taken away from them during the Porfirio Díaz era. But when he gained power, Madero betrayed the peasants and failed to fulfil his promises. As a consequence, armed peasants continued their revolution with no outside support. On 28 November 1911 the revolutionary committee headed by Zapata issued the well-known "Ayala Plan," a land reform plan by which all lands, mountains, forests, and waterways expropriated from peasants during the Porfirio era by landowners, "scientists," and local bosses would be returned to citizens and to the villages. Landowners would be compensated for up to a third of the value of the confiscated lands. Moreover, the plan stipulated also that all those opposing such measures would have their property confiscated.

The Ayala Plan demonstrates that peasant armed forces participated in the revolution as an independent and well-organized party with its own programme of action. During the revolution the peasant army, fighting under the slogan of "land and freedom," expropriated the land and property of the wealthy. It was this slogan that impelled thousands upon thousands of peasants to participate actively in the revolutionary war.

The peasant revolutionary forces were finally destroyed and power fell into the hands of Carranza, who was the representative of the liberal bourgeois class, but the prestige and the influence of the peasants and of their struggle for their lands were such that even the bourgeois, when they took power, were obliged seriously to confront the agrarian question. Venustiano Carranza's government issued a new Agrarian Law on 6 January 1915. Article 27 of the 1917 Constitution prohibits latifundia (large estates) and protects three other forms of land tenure: Indian communal lands, common land, and the small private farm. Moreover, it stipulates that all lands and waters within the national territory are the property of the nation, and that the nation shall take all necessary measures to divide large estates into small lots to be given to population settlements in need of land. The Constitution also determines that land owned by the church or by members of the clergy shall become part of the national patrimony. It is true that these provisions in the 1917 Constitution on the agrarian problem were not implemented immediately, but this article of the Constitution was a great victory won by the peasants; it also laid the juridical basis for the agrarian reform which was implemented at a later stage on a national scale. In this sense, the Mexican Revolution of 1910–1917 had a profound impact in terms of social change.

The 1911 Chinese Revolution, in contrast, was a political one, directed by bourgeois revolutionaries, who used armed insurgency as their main instrument. The goal was the overthrow of the Qing dynasty. The Manchu government represented the feudal landowners of China, and its defeat was indeed beneficial with respect to the opening of capitalistic possibilities. But the democratic bourgeois revolutionaries did not formulate an agrarian programme that truly reflected the interests of the peasants. The great leader of the Chinese bourgeois revolution, Sun Yat-sen, was very sympathetic to the workers, and hated exploitation; to a certain extent he was aware of the agrarian problem, and that is why, in his "Three Principles for the People," the one dealing with the Life of the People guarantees equal rights to land. The essence of this idea was that, whenever land leasing prices went up, the state would buy all privately owned land at a low cost, thus nationalizing land ownership. This programme was criticized by Lenin, who said that it was a utopian land nationalization programme based on a subjectivist type of socialism. The programme was not attractive to the peasants, and the powerless bourgeois class did not dare to mobilize the peasants in a democratic bourgeois revolution against feudalism. This is one of the basic reasons for the defeat of the old democratic revolution in China.

2

The 1910–1917 Mexican Revolution was clearly anti-imperialistic. It fought and defeated two armed interventions by the US and it fostered nationalism. In contrast, the 1911 Chinese Revolution was more amenable to concessions to and compromises with imperialism.

As the 1910–1917 Mexican Revolution was a direct threat to the interests of foreign monopolistic capital, it was opposed from beginning to end by foreign imperialism. It was especially the target of interventions and sabotage by the US. All revolutionary forces in the various factions adopted a basically nationalistic attitude for the defence of national interests and the sovereignty of the state against all foreign intervention.

As the representative of the liberal bourgeois class, the Madero government tried to weaken the forces of foreign capital and to exploit the natural resources of the country using national means exclusively. This nationalist attitude was highly unacceptable to US monopolistic capital. The US ambassador in Mexico, Henry Lane Wilson, intervened directly in internal Mexican affairs by giving secret support to the coup d'état organized by Victoriano Huerta, and to Madero's murder. When Huerta showed a favourable attitude towards England, the US initiated in April 1914 an armed intervention and invaded the port of Veracruz. This operation was resolutely condemned by Mexico and other Latin American countries and the US forces were obliged to withdraw from Mexican soil. The constitutionalist group headed by Venustiano Carranza took power in 1914 and a series of measures to curtail foreign capital was introduced. A law issued on 7 January 1915 prohibited foreign firms from drilling oil wells or prospecting for oil without prior permission from the Mexican government. In March of that year, the Carranza government decided to collect progressive taxes from foreign mining and metal processing industries – measures that greatly displeased the American capitalists. Under the pretext of a frontier conflict, the American government conducted a second armed invasion on 9 March 1916, sending a "punitive expedition" under the command of John J. Pershing. This aggression was energetically resisted by the Mexican forces.

The articles of the 1917 Constitution gave juridical form to the nationalistic spirit of the Mexican Revolution. Article 27 declares that only Mexican citizens by birth or nationalization and Mexican societies have the right to own lands, water resources and their accesses, or to get permission for the exploitation of mineral and water resources or fossil fuels. These articles provided the juridical basis for the Mexican nation in protecting its national resources and the criteria inspiring future Mexican governments in their application of nationalistic policies.

Therefore, the banner raised during the 1910–1917 Mexican Revolution had a profound meaning for the defence of state sovereignty, for resistance against foreign intervention, and for the protection of national interests.

Bourgeois revolutionaries in China believed that the overthrow of the Qing dynasty was necessary to rescue China from its present condition, so that it would become independent and self-sufficient, and to avoid its partition among the great powers. In this sense the 1911 Chinese Revolution was deeply anti-imperialistic, which is why the revolutionary movement of Sun Yat-sen provoked the great powers into intervening in China. Backed by the machinations of the diplomatic missions, Yuan Shi-kai, the representative of the big landowners and the wealthy bourgeois classes, usurped power. This fact proves objectively that Sun Yat-sen's revolution was a revolution against the international capitalistic forces and that it was part of the national democratic movement for independence and self-reliance.

Nevertheless, Sun Yat-sen and his revolutionary comrades did not formulate a clear anti-imperialistic programme before 1924; they even had some hopes of gaining the sympathy of Western capitalistic countries. An external communiqué issued on 5 January 1912 by the provisional government, and signed by Sun Yat-sen as president, accepted the validity of all unequal treaties signed by the Manchu government, promised to fulfil all obligations related to foreign debts contracted by that government, and recognized the rights granted by the Manchu government to several foreign countries and individuals. The Nanjing government's intention in making these concessions was to obtain diplomatic recognition by Western countries. However, the Western powers gave their support to Yuan Shi-kai when he took power. In 1924, remembering the lessons of the 1911 Revolution, Sun Yat-sen said: "For a short while and under the pressure of circumstances, we were forced to pact with counter-revolutionary and autocratic forces. In fact such reconciliation is an indirect acceptance of imperialism, and this is the reason for the initial failure of the Revolution."[8]

3

The 1910–1917 Mexican Revolution managed to establish a relatively perfect democratic bourgeois system, and a new bourgeois Constitution was drafted, based on the 1857 Constitution but more democratic and better adapted to the circumstances. It included the principle of no re-election for the President. Article 123 guarantees the basic rights of workers: an eight-hour working day, elimination of all child work, equal pay for equal work without sex discrimination, and the right to strike and to organize labour unions. These articles were more democratically advanced than any other bourgeois laws in force at that time. The democratic system established by the Mexican Revolution has had a great influence on all future political reforms conducted in the country and on the maintenance of a stable political situation. All this created the necessary conditions for the development of capitalism.

The 1911 Chinese Revolution represents a new phase of the old-style democratic revolutions which took place after the Opium War; it is at the same time a bourgeois democratic revolution in the strict sense. Its great success was the overthrow of a 2,000-year-old absolute monarchy and the establishment of the first bourgeois republic in Chinese history. On 1 January 1912, a Provisional Government of the Republic was established in Nanjing, by which fact the Chinese bourgeois classes for the first time occupied the seat of power. But as they were still weak, the fruits of this victory fell into counter-revolutionary hands.

Besieged by a joint attack by imperialistic forces, the big landowners and the wealthy bourgeoisie, the bourgeois revolutionaries finally had to concede defeat and hand over the state to Yuan Shi-kai. Thus, the revolution ended in failure. The feudal monarchy had been abolished, but a new bourgeois democratic order failed to establish itself in China. The tasks of the bourgeois revolution were continued by another revolution, that of the new democracy under the direction of the proletariat.

Influence of the 1910–1917 Mexican Revolution and 1911 Chinese Revolution in the Modernization Processes of Both Countries

The Mexican Revolution overthrew the Porfirio Díaz dictatorship and weakened both feudal forces and imperialistic influences in Mexico. It also consolidated the bourgeois-democratic system in the country. These elements conditioned the development of Mexican capitalism, and accelerated the modernization process. However, owing to internal and external limiting factors, the revolution could not fully accomplish its anti-imperialistic and anti-feudal tasks. Articles 27 and 123 of the Constitution were not enforced immediately after the revolution, and large-scale agrarian reform and restrictions on foreign capital started only in 1934 under President Cárdenas. As a political revolution, the Mexican Revolution ended in 1917, but the task of social change was not completed during the revolution itself; rather, changes have been implemented through gradual reforms in the course of the following years. Therefore, some historians tend to prolong the revolutionary period until 1940 or even until the post-war period.

After the Mexican Revolution (1910–1917), and especially after the Cárdenas reforms (1934–1940), the capitalistic productive system developed rapidly, and gradually came to assume an important position in the country. But in this process it is possible to observe how the previous shortcomings affected the fulfilment of certain of the revolutionary tasks. These influences can be seen first of all in the profound dependency of the Mexican economy on foreign capital. Right after the nationalization of the oil industry, during the Cárdenas administration, direct foreign investments were greatly reduced, and after the war the proportion of foreign-owned capital within the total amount of investments in the country decreased, but the basic problem of dependence on foreign capital was not fully solved. This dependence is one of the major reasons for the deficiencies of the economic structure and the weakness of medium and small business in the country. All these factors had a negative effect on the modernization process.

Moreover, the agrarian reform responded only in part to the needs of the peasants and only partly promoted the development of productive forces. Those who received small plots of land as a consequence of the agrarian reform did not have the capacity to modernize their operations; in many instances, land was poor, the plot was very small, water was scarce, and financial resources were difficult to obtain. Moreover, the dualistic economic structure of agriculture after the reform impeded the development of productive agricultural forces. In brief, the agricultural modernization process could not catch up with general economic development. Farmers cultivating the common land and small-scale farmers producing grain for domestic consumption remained underdeveloped. bankruptcies were frequent among poor peasants and a new land concentration process set in; the number of landless farmers started to increase again. This is why poverty in farming areas continues to be a serious social problem, demanding an urgent solution.

The Chinese Revolution of 1911 has a great significance for the evolution of modern history. It is true that the fruits of this revolution were stolen by Yuan Shi-kai and other representatives of the big landowners and the wealthy bourgeoisie, and that the revolution failed in its first round, but the cause initiated by the revolution was not lost; on the contrary, it promoted an upsurge of democratic revolutionary spirit all over the country, and opened up the way for its further development. Chinese revolutionaries learned lessons from their failures, among them that to implant democracy in semi-colonial and semi-feudal China, to overthrow imperialism and feudalism, and to eliminate the power of military chieftains backed by imperialistic interests, it was necessary to mobilize the popular masses and to create an alliance of workers, peasants, small-scale bourgeois, and national-scale bourgeois. Sun Yat-sen, under the influence of the October Revolution and supported by the Chinese Communist Party, adopted the Three Great Policies of 1924: alliance with the USSR, common action with the Communist Party, and "a mass action in support of peasants and workers." Through these policies, Sun Yat-sen gave a new explanation for the Three Principles of the People, formulated a programme for revolutionary democracy, reorganized the Kuomingtang, and joined forces with the Chinese Communist Party for the creation of a united anti-imperialistic and anti-feudal front. These factors promoted the development of the first Civil Revolutionary War. Under the leadership of the Chinese Communist Party, the Chinese people struggled for several decades to realize and even improve on the vision which Sun Yat-sen was unable to realize during his lifetime. Under the direction of the proletariat the Chinese people created a wide united front, based on an alliance of workers and peasants, and after a long armed struggle finally overthrew the three barriers – imperialism, feudalism, and bureaucratic capitalism – thus fulfilling the tasks of the democratic revolution and laying the foundations for the establishment of socialism. Today, through socialism, the Chinese people are implementing the modernization of their country.

Notes

1. *Selected Works of Mao Tse-tung* (Foreign Languages Press, Beijing, 1975), vol. II, pp. 309–310.
2. Institute of Modern Chinese History Studies, Chinese Academy of Social Sciences, *Zhongguo Jindai Shigao* (A Modern History of China) (People's Publishing House, Beijing, 1983), vol. II, p. 146.
3. Jose Luis Ceceña, *Mexico en la orbita imperial* (Editorial de Nuestro Tiempo, Mexico City, 1976), p. 54.

4. See note 2 above, p. 299.
5. Luis Pare, *El proletariad agricola en Mexico* (Editorial de Nuestro Tiempo, Mexico City, 1980), p. 70.
6. *Liening wenxuan* (Selected Works of Lenin) (People's Publishing House, Beijing, 1972), vol. II, p. 459.
7. See note 6 above, p. 448.
8. *Sun Zhong-shan wenxuan* (Selected Works of Sun Yat-sen) (People's Publishing House, Beijing, 1961), vol. 1, p. 587.

REFLECTIONS ON DEMOCRATIC REVOLUTIONS IN MEXICO AND CHINA

Lixin Shao
Institute of Modern Chinese History, Beijing, China

During the last thirty or forty years, Mexico and China have made impressive achievements in social and economic development. Though there still remains much to be done before these two countries are fully developed, the process of modernization is already under way in both.

Mexico had been a colony of feudal Spain for more than two centuries, and after gaining her independence in 1821 she fell again under the economic control of the capitalist powers and became a semi-colonial, semi-feudal country; while China, formerly a decaying feudal state, was also reduced to a semi-colonial, semi-feudal condition after her defeat in the Opium War of 1840–1842. Neither Mexico nor China could have begun their modernization without first casting off the foreign yoke and smashing the internal feudal shackles.

In both countries, the struggle against feudal oppression and foreign aggression has a long history. But in the beginning these struggles were spontaneous and without a definite aim: sometimes they were undertaken to revive a moribund system, and sometimes to realize a utopian vision. Such struggles were doomed to failure. Both in Mexico and China, the task of ending foreign control and internal feudalism was accomplished through democratic revolution, a revolution aimed at creating a modern state and a modern society.

A comparison between the democratic revolutions in Mexico and China will not only shed light on the two countries' modern history, but will also give us a deeper insight into the present condition of certain other developing countries with similar historical backgrounds.

Paper presented at the Conference on the Modernization Process in Mexico (1867–1940): The Social Transformations, co-sponsored by the United Nations University and El Colegio de México, Mexico City, 19–21 March 1985.

1

Both in Mexico and China, the beginning of the democratic revolution was marked by a struggle in which the revolutionaries tried to destroy the old regime and reconstruct the state and the society according to bourgeois principles.

The Mexican Independence War was directed not only against Spanish rule, but also against the feudal system the Spaniards had brought to Mexico. Hidalgo declared that he was fighting for an elected congress, which would govern Mexico in the name of King Ferdinand. In the territories under his control, he abolished the Indian tribute and ordered the restoration to the Indian villages of the lands illegally taken from them. Morelos maintained that Mexico should be a republic governed by the will of the people, and the haciendas should be divided into smallholdings for the peasants. The Independence War was Mexico's introduction to the era of democratic revolution.

The situation in China was a complicated one. As early as the Taiping Revolution in the mid-nineteenth century, a document with a capitalist flavour had already appeared: *The New Reference Book for Administration*, by Hong Ren-gan. But this document came into being almost at the end of the revolution and had little influence on its actual progress. The Taiping Revolution did reveal the possibilities for a combination of a bourgeois democratic revolution and a peasant revolution, but did not go beyond an old-style peasant revolution in itself. Towards the end of the nineteenth century there was the movement known as the Hundred Days' Reform; but this is not generally counted as a revolution, as it failed without a serious struggle. The epoch of bourgeois democratic revolution in China began with the 1911 Revolution.

There is an interval of a whole century between the Mexican Independence War and the Chinese 1911 Revolution, and this interval can easily be discerned in the difference between the ideological inclinations of the leaders of the two movements. The Mexican Independence War broke out at a time when the worldwide bourgeois revolution was at its height, a time marked by the American Revolution, the French Revolution, and Napoleon's hegemony on the European continent. The leaders of the Independence War grew up in an atmosphere of liberalism engendered by the Enlightenment. Like the participants in the American or the French Revolution, they piously believed in the social system they were fighting for. On the other hand, the Chinese 1911 Revolution commenced at a time when capitalism in Western countries had already entered the monopoly stage, when the inherent contradictions of capitalism had become very conspicuous, and the socialist movements had become widespread. Dr. Sun Yat-sen, the leader of the revolutionary democrats in China, was critical of the oppression of the working class by a small number of capitalists in Western countries, and he showed great sympathy for the socialist movements there. His revolutionary theory, though still one of bourgeois democracy, included the idea that China should not take the same road that Western capitalist countries had already taken, but should pursue a new road to liberty, equality, and happiness.

While the revolutionaries of the two countries had differences in their ideologies, the realities they faced were much the same. To illustrate this, we will compare the situations in Mexico and China with those in England, France, and the British North American colony.

In pre-revolution England and France, the capitalist elements had already developed within the feudal systems for a long period, and the bourgeoisie there had become strong enough to make serious political challenges to the ruling class. The British colony in North America had been built on a bourgeois basis from the very beginning, and the bourgeoisie there had already systematically defied the authority of the suzerain Britain before the revolution. In Mexico and China, however, a number of revolutionary intellectuals, taking those successful revolutions as their models, started democratic revolutions while the bourgeoisie were still very weak or even in formation. In countries like England, France, and the United States, the ideology of bourgeois democracy had grown up in the native soil, while in Mexico and China the revolutionary ideology was, to a great degree, transplanted from abroad. For revolutionaries in Mexico and China, there was a discrepancy between their ideals and the realities they faced. It is not surprising, therefore, that England, France, and the United States began their democratic revolutions with a great struggle that severely weakened the old system and enabled the bourgeoisie to seize, or get a share of, state power, while Mexico and China achieved comparatively less in the first stage of their democratic revolutions.

The Mexican Independence War and the Chinese 1911 Revolution suffered a similar fate, but in different ways. At the beginning the Mexican Independence War had many features of a social revolution. Both Hidalgo and Morelos more or less proposed and practised land reform, consciously seeking help from the masses of oppressed Indians and mestizos. But they were not able to wipe out Spanish rule and feudalism at a stroke; the rich Creoles were afraid of the revolutionary masses, and most of them, including some who had sympathy for the cause of independence, sided with the Spaniards in repressing the revolutionaries. The irony of history is that independence was achieved by various forces united under the conservative "Plan of Iguala," with Iturbide, a reactionary, as their leader.

In the Chinese 1911 Revolution the revolutionaries did not attempt to enlist the masses in their struggle, but made efforts to win over secret societies and New Army soldiers, hoping to achieve their goal by military means. As the revolution lacked social content, the success of the Wuchang uprising led many conservatives – former constitutional monarchists, old-type bureaucrats, and army officials – to join the revolution, and within two months 14 of the country's 24 provinces and regions had proclaimed independence from the Manchu court. Sun Yat-sen said at the beginning of 1912 in his inaugural speech as Provisional President of the Provisional Government that no revolution in history had succeeded more quickly than this one. But the revolutionaries in China were no more fortunate than those in Mexico. As they failed to turn the upsurge of revolutionary sentiment in the masses throughout the country into a motive power, they remained helpless, passive, and compromising in their struggle against the reactionaries. Political power was usurped by Yuan Shi-kai, a representative of the comprador and landlord classes.

It is true that Iturbide's empire was short-lived and Yuan Shi-kai's attempt to set up a dynasty led to his failure and disgrace. But their downfall was brought about more by the division of the reactionaries than by the strength of the revolutionaries, and the republics established or re-established thereafter brought neither democracy nor order to these two countries.

Taking into consideration the realities of the two countries, we should not underestimate the achievements of the Mexican Independence War and the Chinese 1911 Revolution. Mexico had cast off the yoke of Spain, and China had overthrown the Manchu dynasty; both countries had, in name at least, established republican governments. Nevertheless, the democratic revolution in both countries was just beginning, and the realities of the situation were harsh. China suffered heavier imperialist oppression after the revolution, while Mexico, soon after she had won her political independence, lost her economic independence, and later more than once fell victim to armed foreign intervention. In both countries, feudalism was still deeply rooted. Sun Yat-sen was disappointed at the outcome of the 1911 Revolution; had Hidalgo and Morelos lived to see the new-born United Mexican States, they also would have been dissatisfied.

2

This section compares the Mexican 1910 Revolution and the Chinese 1911 Revolution in order to assess the relative status of the democratic revolutions in these two countries in the years after 1910.

The two revolutions were similar in several respects. Both were directed against the same kind of despotic government, one that sold national interests to foreign powers and upheld the feudal system at home. The same factors constituted the crisis of the Díaz regime and the Manchu court. In both countries, the situation developed quickly after the revolution had started, leading to the swift downfall of the old regime. One could even find similarities in some details of the two revolutions. Nevertheless, there were fundamental differences between them.

The ways in which the revolutionaries in Mexico and China dealt with the agrarian problem were obviously different. Molina Enríquez, one of the revolutionary thinkers, viewed the land problem as urgent: in his influential book, *The Great National Problems*, he criticized the hacienda system and proposed that all cultivable land should be divided and turned over to those who cultivated it. In contrast, Sun Yat-sen included the "equalization of land ownership" in the programme of the United League (Tong Meng Hui), not in order to solve an urgent problem but to prevent the possible polarization of the rich and the poor, which would be caused, he assumed, by the rise in land prices in some regions as a result of economic growth; not to push the present revolution forward, but to avoid future revolution. The policies Dr. Sun proposed to realize the "equalization of land ownership," such as land assessment, or the levying of tax proportionate to the land price in certain cases, would be unable to quench the thirst of the peasants for land. In a word, the abolition of the feudal land system was not on the revolutionary agenda.

In Mexico, the peasant struggle for land gave great impetus to the 1910 Revolution. All the revolutionary factions tried to win over the peasant masses with the promise of land redistribution. Articles reflecting the peasants' demand for land were included in the 1917 Constitution. In the Chinese 1911 Revolution, the peasant struggles against feudalism remained spontaneous and scattered; they did not develop into a powerful movement as they had in Mexico, and the officials of the provisional government of the republic sent out armies to suppress the peasant uprisings as the Manchu government had done before.

The attitudes of the revolutionaries in the two countries towards imperialism were different too. Molina Enríquez regarded the foreign interests created in Mexico as a grave danger to Mexican sovereignty. He even considered seriously the possibility that foreign intervention might be the result of Mexico's trying to do away with foreign control. During the revolution, President Madero had tried to curtail the privileges of foreign capital in Mexico, and all the revolutionary forces had denounced the United States' intervention in Mexican internal affairs, especially her occupation of Veracruz and her invasion of the Mexican north frontier. As anti-imperialist sentiments ran high during the revolution, even the reactionary forces assumed a patriotic attitude in order to gain support from the masses. The situation in China was exactly the opposite. The revolutionaries did not dare to take a firm stand against the imperialist countries, about which they even had illusions. To court the favour of the great powers, the revolutionaries recognized all the treaties between the Manchu court and foreign nations, all the loans raised, all the indemnities acknowledged, and all the concessions granted to foreign nations or individuals by the Manchu court. It was a genuine tragedy that, in the 1911 Revolution, the revolutionaries and reactionaries vied with each other for support from the great powers, and the powers finally gave their support to the reactionaries.

Why was there such a sharp contrast between the two revolutions on the two issues mentioned above? First, we should not forget that Mexico had begun her democratic revolution a century earlier; she had won independence and built the republic in the 1820s; she had seen, from 1854 to 1860, the Reform and civil war which dealt a heavy blow to the church, one of the pillars of the feudal system; and she had won the final victory in her bitter struggle against armed foreign intervention and the puppet regime from 1861 to 1867. China, on the other hand, had no such long history of democratic revolution. Naturally, the democrats in Mexico were more experienced than those in China in handling and manipulating mass conflict and in dealing with foreign nations. Second, and more important, the bourgeoisie in Mexico and in China had a different relation to landed property. Among the bourgeois revolutionaries in Mexico, though there were a few persons, such as Madero or Carranza, who owned haciendas, most of the intellectuals – mestizo directors, professionals, employees and army men – whom Enríquez regarded as potential "middle class" had no ties with the haciendas at all. Things were quite different in China. Sun Yat-sen once said: "In the past there have been four categories of people in China, namely, the intellectuals, the peasants, the manufacturers and the merchants. Except for the peasants, all the others are small landlords" (Dr. Sun called the landlords in China small landlords because land in China was not as concentrated as in certain other countries). His analysis was not very exact, but it did reflect the fact that there had been a strong connection between the Chinese bourgeoisie and landed property. The position the bourgeoisie took towards the peasants' anti-feudal struggle was, to a great degree, determined by their ties with landed property, and, moreover, the position they took towards the reactionaries at home and the powers from outside was conditioned by whether or not they had the peasants as their allies.

We can see clearly from the above comparison that, in the early 1910s, the democratic revolution in Mexico had entered the stage of maturity, while the democratic revolution in China was still in its infancy.

3

Both Mexico and China completed their democratic revolutions in the 1940s, the former around 1940, the latter in 1949. Mexico has taken the capitalist road since 1940, while China, since the establishment of the People's Republic in 1949, has embraced socialism. How did this come about?

In 1917, the Russian October Revolution succeeded and the Soviet government was born. This epoch-making event had far-reaching effects upon the liberation movements of the oppressed peoples in colonial and semi-colonial countries. Being oppressed by the capitalist powers for many years and further embittered by the hostility of the powers to their recent revolutions, the peoples of both Mexico and China naturally sympathized with the October Revolution and the Soviet government. Thereafter Marxism-Leninism began to spread quickly in both countries and, with the help of the Comintern led by Lenin, proletarian parties were born.

But the circumstances in the two countries were different at this time. In Mexico, the 1910 Revolution had just successfully reached a new stage, and the bourgeois democrats had seized state power, while in China the revolutionaries had suffered successive setbacks after their transient victory in 1911, and were fighting on in despair. In Mexico, the bourgeois democrats had just turned their anti-imperialism, anti-feudalism programme into the 1917 Constitution – the most advanced of all the bourgeois constitutions in the world at the time; while in China the bourgeois democrats had not yet developed a feasible revolution programme, and were still groping in the dark. In Mexico, the labour movement had already become quite strong, but the workers were mainly under the influence of syndicalism and bourgeois reformism; in China, however, the proletariat did not grow into an independent force on the political stage until the May the Fourth Movement in 1919. Therefore, although the democratic revolutions in both Mexico and China were greatly influenced by the Russian October Revolution, the results were quite different.

In Mexico, the proletarian party was unable to guide the labour and peasant movements, and the bourgeois and petit-bourgeois democrats maintained their leading position in the revolution. While the influence of the Russian Revolution and of the Soviet Union could be clearly felt in the language they used and the policies they followed, what they actually did was to put into practice the principles contained in the 1917 Constitution. I am of the opinion, therefore, that the years 1917 to 1940 in Mexico should be regarded as the continuation and completion of the 1910–1917 Revolution.

In China, although some bourgeois democrats, such as Sun Yat-sen, inspired by the Russian Revolution and influenced by the Soviet government, began to adopt more radical policies, the bourgeoisie in general failed to keep pace with this development. On the other hand, the Chinese Communist Party, soon after its establishment, launched vigorous labour movements and mass struggles against imperialism and feudalism, and became the leading force among the Chinese people. Thus the democratic revolution in

China entered a new stage, which Mao Tse-tung, the former Chairman of the Chinese Communist Party, called the new democratic revolution. To Chinese Communists, the new democratic revolution is an indispensable prerequisite for the socialist revolution.

The way in which agrarian reform, a major task of democratic revolution, was carried out in Mexico and in China could be used to explain the different developments in these two countries since the early 1920s.

Sun Yat-sen, the forerunner of the Chinese democratic revolution, developed his ideas on the land problem in his later years. He realized that the participation of the peasants was of paramount importance for the revolution, and he expressed the wish to learn from Soviet Russia, and to adopt the policy of "land to the tillers." His plan was a concrete one. First, the government should use its power to free the peasants from their conventional ideas, to make them realize that they were not doomed to suffer for generation after generation; secondly, it should help the peasants to unite into organizations, from village up to state level, and should arm them with rifles; lastly, the government, in collaboration with organized peasants, should purchase or expropriate the landlords' property and make the peasants masters of the land.

Dr. Sun's plan for land reform was not carried out by the Chinese bourgeoisie, which had comprehensive ties with landed property. During the 1924–1927 Revolution, the bourgeoisie did not teach and organize the peasants, and when the latter started to organize with the help of the Communists, the bourgeoisie were in such a panic that they aligned themselves with the landlord class and tried to put down the peasant movement. The Chinese bourgeoisie, therefore, were not qualified to lead the democratic revolution.

The process of agrarian reform in Mexico, on the whole, coincided with Dr. Sun's plan. From the 1920s on, the government sent numbers of teachers to the countryside to eliminate illiteracy and to fight against the obscurantism nurtured by the priests. After Cárdenas had assumed the presidency, he and other organizers of the ruling party travelled up and down the country, calling for peasant unity. The peasants were first organized into agrarian committees, which were then combined into regional committees. The regional committees were next united into peasant leagues at the state level, and finally these leagues were merged into the National Peasant Confederation. In meeting the petitions for land made by the agrarian committees, the government expropriated large tracts of land from the haciendas for distribution. Furthermore, in order to protect the land reform from sabotage by the White Guards, the government organized the peasants into militias and gave them weapons.

While agrarian reform in Mexico was backed up by the might of the state machinery after the bourgeois democrats had taken power, in China it had to be carried out step by step, through intense class struggle, against a government which at the time believed it could maintain itself by sheer military force, without making social reforms. The consequence was that the land reform, well co-ordinated with the armed struggle and with the consolidation and expansion of the revolution base areas, enabled the Communist Party to take over state power.

As the agrarian reforms in Mexico and China were led by different classes and parties, their results were not the same. Mexico slowed down and even stopped her land distribution after 1940 and the remaining semi-feudal haciendas were gradually changed into plantations managed in a capitalist way; but China, after the establishment of the People's Republic in 1949, continued her land reform, completing it by 1952. While in Mexico there were still a large number of rural people without land, in China the slogan "land to the tillers" became fact.[1] It could be said without prejudice that the agrarian reform in Mexico had its limitations, and that the reform in China was carried out in a thorough manner.

The most important point is that, in an economically backward agricultural country such as Mexico or China, whichever class or party leads the agrarian reform will naturally gain influence over the vast masses of peasants, thus becoming the leader of the revolutionary democrats and in a position to decide the course of the country's further development. In this light, the fact that Mexico and China took different roads of development in later years could be viewed as the natural result of their respective democratic revolutions.

Note

1. This policy was later rendered meaningless with the establishment of the rural People's Communes. The new rural "responsibility contracting system," introduced under the current reforms, is a step back towards this policy.

INDEX